Your Whole Life

YOUR WHOLE LIFE

Beyond Childhood and Adulthood

James Bernard Murphy

PENN

UNIVERSITY OF PENNSYLVANIA PRESS

PHILADELPHIA

A volume in the Haney Foundation Series, established in 1961
with the generous support of Dr. John Louis Haney.

Copyright © 2020 University of Pennsylvania Press

All rights reserved. Except for brief quotations used for purposes of review or scholarly citation, none of this book may be reproduced in any form by any means without written permission from the publisher.

Published by
University of Pennsylvania Press
Philadelphia, Pennsylvania 19104-4112
www.upenn.edu/pennpress

Printed in the United States of America
on acid-free paper

10 9 8 7 6 5 4 3 2 1

A catalogue record for this book is available from the Library of Congress
ISBN 978-0-8122-5223-1

To My Children:
I never would have grown up without you.

But where is it, the beginning of our acts? Our life, when we want to grasp it whole, is like those plants you can never pull out of the soil with all their roots.
  François Mauriac, *Thérèse Desqueyroux*

CONTENTS

Introduction. The Story of Your Life   1

PART I. STORIES OF DEVELOPMENT

Chapter 1. Human Nature from a Developmental Perspective   7
Chapter 2. Development as the Recapitulation of Nature in Aristotle   33
Chapter 3. Development as Preformation in Augustine's *Confessions*   46
Chapter 4. Development as the Recapitulation of History in Rousseau   62
Chapter 5. Development as Juvenilization in the Synoptic Gospels   76

PART II. UNIFYING THE WHOLE

Chapter 6. All of Me: Stages and the Whole of Life   93
Chapter 7. What Am I? Human Beings and Human Persons   116
Chapter 8. Who Am I? A Storybook Life   143

Conclusion. A Practical Guide to Life Writing   177

Notes   187

Index   245

Acknowledgments   255

Introduction

The Story of Your Life

A full understanding of a human person, it is often said, would tell us how she is like every other person, how she is like some other people, and how she is like no other person. This book is focused entirely on how each of us is like every other person—by virtue of our shared human identity.

Today we celebrate many particular racial, ethnic, sexual, ideological, and religious identities; we are suspicious of allegedly universal identities. Yet, in a world of particular identities we need, more than ever, to be reminded of our common human identity. For even though the affirmation of particular identities often promotes healthy self-respect, affirming these identities also creates a great deal of conflict, setting Jew against Arab, white against black, woman against man, Christian against Muslim, straight against gay. If the affirmation of particular identities is to lead to a world of greater tolerance, justice, and harmony, then we must learn also to affirm our common humanity.

To claim a unique and important human identity is widely regarded as an arbitrary preference for our own species. Should not we honor intelligence and altruism in whatever animal they appear? What is so special about human beings? A proper understanding of human nature does not disparage other species. Quite the opposite: we share many of our biological and psychological powers with other animals, especially mammals and primates. What makes human beings unique is that, so far as we know, only human beings possess a biological basis for rational and moral agency; that is, only human beings are by nature persons. Personhood is worthy of reverence in whatever creature it might appear.

Who am I? Many of us attempt to answer this question by looking at our family tree. When asked about his lineage, Napoleon famously retorted:

"I am my ancestors." The view that "I am my ancestors" explains the widespread appeal of evolutionary theories of human nature. Virtually all of the myriad scientific and philosophical studies of human nature during the past century take it for granted that we must focus on our family tree. Since humans have descended from primate ancestors, we assume that we have inherited their traits. In this book, by contrast, I shall be looking not at ancestors but at children—not at the family tree but at the baby pictures.

Who am I? I am the person who developed from a microscopic embryo into an adult human being. This book is about how we develop, not how we evolved—about how we grow up from infancy, not how we descended from other primates. To be sure, evolutionary and developmental processes can be distinguished but not wholly separated. Human development has itself evolved over time and evolution works largely through changes in the timing of development. Nonetheless, developmental biology has its own explanatory principles which are quite distinct from those of evolutionary biology. Developmental biology stems from Aristotle while evolutionary biology stems from Darwin. What this means is that developmental biology is more goal-directed (that is, teleological) than is evolutionary biology. True, local evolutionary adaptation is partly goal-directed, but evolution as a whole has no goal. Development does have a goal, and developmental processes are unintelligible apart from that goal. Developmental biology offers a unique window on human nature. We shall explore four basic stories of human development as elaborated by Aristotle, Jesus of Nazareth, Augustine, and Rousseau.

This book will fundamentally change the way you think about your own life. Instead of assuming that you were once a child but are now an adult, I will show that you have always been a child, adolescent, and adult—all at the same time. What are called stages of life are not temporal phases that we occupy one at a time; they are parts or facets of a whole human life. As children we prepare for adulthood and as adults we attempt to recapture our childhood. We are never stuck within the horizon of any one stage of life; rather, through the powers of imagination and memory, we always live in relation to the whole of our lives. The whole of a life is fundamentally prior to these temporal stages. Just as an organ apart from an organism is merely a clump of tissue, there is no childhood or adulthood apart from the whole of a life. I defend a developmental and holistic view of human life in which we are always growing and always declining, always learning and always forgetting, always living and always dying. A human life is of a piece.

When attempting to explain something as multifaceted as a whole human life, there is an understandable impulse to divide and conquer, that is, to analyze a life into discrete stages. If a whole life is too difficult to grasp, then perhaps we might attempt to understand infancy, then childhood, then adolescence, then adulthood, and finally senescence. This explains why hundreds of books are published each year about particular stages of life. But we cannot possibly grasp a human life by summing up a series of stages, because, as we shall see, the whole of a life is prior to each stage. Only in light of the whole does any stage have meaning. When it comes to a human life, truly we murder to dissect.

What accounts for the unity of a human life over time? I offer a developmental story of human nature based on a nested hierarchy of three powers. First, each person's unique human genome ensures biological identity over time; second, each person's powers of imagination and memory ensure psychological identity over time; third, each person's ability to tell his own life story ensures narrative identity over time. Just as imagination and memory rest on our biological identity, so our autobiographical stories rest on our psychological identity. We are storytelling animals, but our autobiographical powers rest on our psychological and biological powers. Narrative is not the foundation of personal identity but its capstone.

Why does it matter that we live our lives in relation to the whole? Because practical wisdom depends on the ability to bring the perspective of our whole life to bear on each present moment. What appears good to me as a child or as an adult may well differ from what appears good to me in relation to my whole life. Through the power of narrative, we gather up the time of our lives to be fully present in every moment.

In this book, I will be defending the substantial unity of a human person whose life endures through time. Because a human being is an irreducible whole (including biological, psychological, and narrative powers), our lives can have personal coherence over time. The whole temporal expanse of a life is prior to any of its stages, just as a whole human person is prior to any of her organs or powers. We can tell stories about our past, present, and future only because we possess a certain kind of complex unity at any one time. What we are as human beings makes it possible for us to lead the life of a human person.

Philosophers will notice that, although I am often critical of Aristotle, my philosophical perspective is thoroughly Aristotelian. Aristotle is the only great philosopher who was also a biologist, and his biological understanding of development is what makes him the essential guide to human life. I agree with philosopher Peter Hacker: it has been a major misfortune that no great modern philosopher was also a biologist, meaning that there is no worthy modern successor to Aristotle. We are fortunate that Wittgenstein and his students have articulated many of Aristotle's insights about the unity of biological humanity and psychological personhood in a modern idiom.

The focus of my scholarship has always been to elaborate Aristotle's nested hierarchy of development. According to Aristotle, to become a good and excellent person, we need to inherit the right natural endowment, acquire the right habits, and reflectively adjust those habits through right reason. In this nested hierarchy, our habits rest on our biological nature while reason rests on our habits. Aristotle also extended this story to political development, in which we begin with natural resources, develop social customs, and then revise those customs through rational law. In my first book (*The Moral Economy of Labor: Aristotelian Themes in Economic Theory*), I explored the nested hierarchy of the natural, customary, and stipulated division of labor. Specialization in work begins with natural aptitudes; these natural aptitudes lead to various customary divisions of labor; finally, legislators and managers create deliberately stipulated divisions of labor within a society or firm. I then turned to the development of law, from natural law to customary law to positive law in my books *The Philosophy of Positive Law* and *The Philosophy of Customary Law*. By natural reason, human beings grasp, inchoately, rules of conduct; these rules are then fleshed out through particular social customs; finally, reflection on these customs leads to the deliberate stipulation of positive law. In *Your Whole Life*, I explore a nested hierarchy of human development from biological growth, to psychological awareness, to autobiographical narrative.

The study of a human life is intrinsically multidisciplinary. Although this book is framed by basic philosophical questions and arguments, I have drawn illustrative material from biology, psychology, political science, sociology, linguistics, biblical exegesis, anthropology, and literary theory. I have attempted to refer to studies reflecting major currents of scholarship in those fields. The questions we shall consider about the shape of a human life are timeless ones, but the empirical illustrations are undoubtedly time bound. This book is thus perched between timeless questions and transient answers, which is the story of every human life.

PART I

STORIES OF DEVELOPMENT

CHAPTER 1

Human Nature from a Developmental Perspective

What does it mean to be human? Before we attempt to answer that question, perhaps we should first ask: Where do we look if we want to see human nature? Do we look at the spontaneity of children or at the acquired skills of adults? If we believe that our inherent nature is very different from our acquired culture, then we might well study children. We often say that children act more naturally and spontaneously than do adults. Since ancient times, philosophers have hoped to discover children who somehow grew up untainted by any particular set of social customs. If we could only find a purely natural child, would we then have a true picture of what it means to be human? A few "wild children" have been discovered who somehow managed to survive largely outside of any human community. Nothing is more natural to human beings than language, yet the few children known to have grown up outside of any human community not only lacked the ability to use language, they were also unable to learn any language. Purely "natural" children turn out to be very unnatural. Still, there is something right about this "argument from the cradle."[1] In small children, we see natural hunger, thirst, fear, anger, frustration, and joy in all their raw vitality, relatively unmediated by particular social customs and rules. Small children are much less concerned with appearing to conform to social expectations than are most adults. Adults often praise the impulsive honesty of small children who have not yet learned to censor themselves. And many parents look with horror to see their own children corrupted by the particular vices of adult society. In many respects, babies and small children around the globe are more like each other than they are like their own parents. Observing children, especially young children, is one invaluable way to see what it means to be human.

Perhaps we should reject the assumption that human nature and human culture are opposed to each other. What if it is our nature to be nurtured by a particular set of social customs? What is more characteristic of human nature, after all, than acquiring culture? It takes decades of education to actualize our natural capacities for literary language, mathematics, and the creative arts. If we want to see what it means to be human, we should look at Einstein, Beethoven, and St. Francis—or, more precisely, look at them in the midlife prime of their adult lives. Perhaps we are most fully human when we realize our innate human potential for intellectual, artistic, and moral excellence in skilled activities. Beginning with Aristotle, biologists have always defined the nature of any species by studying specimens in their reproductive maturity. The implicit assumption here is that an organism either too young or too old to reproduce is just not a good example of that species. How can we know what an organism is until we can see what it can do? The prime of life is precisely when we are most capable of actualizing the range of human potential—when we are, in short, most fully human. Children are full of unrealized potential, and the elderly have lost many of their human abilities. Only in the apex of adulthood are we fully human. The great glories as well as the great crimes of history are almost always the achievement of those in their prime. Observing adults in the prime of their lives gives us a unique perspective on what it means to be human.

Since ancient times, philosophers have not been able to agree about whether human nature is revealed best in childhood or in adulthood. Both young children and prime-of-life adults reveal something essential about what it means to be human. We ought to resist the urge to choose.[2] A human life is essentially a work in progress. To be human means that there is always a gulf between what we are now and what we might become.[3] Every young organism grows and develops; only human beings retain a robust capacity for growth and development throughout their lives. Being human means never fully growing up. Moreover, only human beings have the capacity to lead their own lives and to guide their own development. Each of us has aspirations in the present which guide our development into the future. "Become what you already are!" captures the paradoxical nature of human development.

Every society possesses a folklore that distinguishes several "ages of man," or stages of human life. William Shakespeare codified much ancient lore in his "seven ages of man": infancy, childhood, adolescence, youth, maturity, old age, and senescence.[4] In addition to these traditions of folk wisdom, comparative embryologists since Aristotle have distinguished several distinct stages of embryonic development. The development of embryos proceeds through an invariant sequence of stages: each stage is the necessary precondition for subsequent stages, and development is marked by discontinuities between stages. During the nineteenth century, biologists began to ask whether all human development also proceeds through such an invariant sequence of stages. Developmental biologists and psychologists, including Sigmund Freud, Stanley Hall, Carl Jung, Jean Piaget, and Erik Erikson, extended stage theories of embryonic development first to childhood and then to the whole of human life.

Does a human life proceed through an invariant sequence of discontinuous stages? Must the oral stage precede the genital stage? Is adolescence a necessary precondition for adulthood? Most empirical studies of human development during the twentieth century have failed to confirm these theories of stages. By the late twentieth century, studies of human lives have taken a more holistic approach to the entire life span, life course, or life cycle. Put simply, the empirical study of human physical, psychological, moral, and spiritual development has decisively undermined the view that there are sharp discontinuities or radical qualitative changes in human development. Human life is of a piece.[5] At every "stage" we are learning and forgetting, growing and deteriorating, gaining and losing. The balance of learning and forgetting, for example, does usually vary from childhood to old age, but the idea that children merely learn while the elderly merely forget is demonstrably false. Because of what is called habit interference, everything we learn makes it harder in some ways to learn something new (think of languages): in short, every gain in development leads to a loss and every loss to some potential gain.[6]

It is puzzling that we associate physical and intellectual decline with old age. After all, every athlete and dancer knows only too well that our strength, agility, and speed begin their irreversible and inexorable decline in our late twenties. Male sexual potency also notoriously begins to decline in the twenties and female fertility in the late thirties. Our sensory acuteness already begins to decline in late adolescence: teenagers see, hear, and taste better than do adults. In short, as soon as we start growing we also begin to decline. "Birth," wrote Samuel Beckett of one of his characters, "was the death of him."

Intellectual decline is also not limited to old age, just as intellectual growth is not limited to youth. To live is to learn, and we never cease learning—or forgetting. Cognitive psychologists distinguish the "fluid" intelligence (that is, our problem-solving heuristics) we use in chess or in math from the "crystallized" intelligence (that is, our total stock of information) we use to understand a work of literature or history. Our fluid intelligence begins to decline in our thirties while our crystallized intelligence does not normally begin to decline until our seventies. Studies of various kinds of creativity show even earlier patterns of decline: creative reasoning about physical causation may begin to decline in late childhood while creative reasoning about the causes of actions may begin to decline in late adolescence.[7] At every age, we are gaining and losing, growing and declining, learning and forgetting.

Psychological studies of maturation also undermine theories of development as an invariant sequence of stages. Yes, there are a few "critical periods" and invariant sequences in human development. One must have receptive language before expressive language. We must crawl before we can walk, and we must experience puberty before we can reproduce. Otherwise, psychological, emotional, social, and intellectual development vary hugely by culture and by individual. It is not precocious but normal for many children to be more mature than many adults. And although we must pass through puberty, we need not pass through adolescence. In the pure theory of stages there can be arrested development but no skipped stages or reversals. Yet children often do skip stages and adult emotional maturation often involves actual and measurable reversals. Human development is real, but it does not proceed through an invariant sequence of qualitatively distinct stages. Instead, the younger anticipate the achievements of the older: almost everything we can do well later, we were doing badly earlier. Human maturation is like a well-crafted story in which the early chapters foreshadow later developments.[8]

But if human development is not well described as a sequence of stages, then why does every human culture divide a normative life into age-graded stages?[9] The answer must be practical rather than theoretical. There are sound moral and legal reasons for treating individuals differently at various ages of life. We do not want small children getting married or serving in the army. Even if development were perfectly continuous, practical reasoning about proper moral and legal responsibilities would still require us to divide a life into partially arbitrary age-graded stages. It is not feasible in practice to treat each individual according to her own unique developmental trajectory. The stages of human life serve invaluable practical purposes for assigning rights and duties, praise and blame—even if they are a poor guide to understanding actual human development. If we are to protect vulnerable children or senescent elders, law and morality must draw bright lines across human growth and decline, whether or not those lines reflect actual stages of development.

Indeed, as we shall see, every human child learns and can recite a life script defining all the important milestones and stages of a normative life in her society. To be a human being in a modern society means knowing at what age we are expected to start and finish school, get married, have children, start a career, and retire. Of course, not every individual life in a particular society follows the normative script, but everyone interprets his life in relation to that shared script. We all know when we are early or late in reaching these normative milestones. Moreover, every age-graded stage of life includes its own standards of conduct. The ages of man or the stages of life are the ubiquitous forensic categories in human life: they guide virtually all of our myriad practices of praise and blame. "Act your age" is the only universal moral imperative in human life.[10] This life script teaches us not only what to expect at each stage of life but also how to treat people in other stages. We have compelling practical reasons, then, for assigning human beings into age-graded stages.

The objective shape, then, of a human life does not fit into a sequence of stages. Just as important, we do not subjectively experience our lives as a rigid series of stages. When a plant or animal is in a particular stage of development, it cannot see beyond the horizon of that stage. Do caterpillars dream of taking flight? Does a cat miss her carefree kittenhood? What makes human beings unique is our capacity to see our lives as a whole.[11] The language of stages is misleading when applied to how we think of our own lives.[12] Unlike kittens, children above the age of about two are aware of their future as adults. Children often wonder about adulthood—its freedoms, powers, and duties. Many of the games of make-believe enjoyed by children involve pretending to be adults. Living in a world designed for grown-ups, children are often reminded in very unpleasant ways that they are not yet adults. Most children are ambivalent about becoming grown-ups but accept its necessity. Are children stuck in childhood? By the power of imagination, children can escape childhood just as they can escape our galaxy. But children can do more than imagine their adult lives; children can focus their energies and conduct on the project of becoming successful adults. Children may dream of living with dinosaurs or space aliens, but they take action to become adults.

Children are not stuck in childhood. They already imagine their futures and attempt to live their lives as a whole. Similarly, adults are clearly not stuck in adulthood. Every adult reflects on his childhood—often with ambivalence. Adults commonly compare the full bloom of their mature achievements with the seedlings of their childhood hopes or fears. Adults even attempt, in ways ranging from the ridiculous to the sublime, to recapture their childhoods. Nothing is more common than for children to act with the gravity and speak with the insight of "adults" or for adults to act and think in ways called "childish."[13] Chronological age bears little relation to emotional, moral, or spiritual maturity.

We are often told that childhood is a time for playing and learning to trust others, that adolescence is a time for learning to separate from parents and establish one's own identity, and that midlife is when we regret our past, realize that our present options are limited, and dread the future. It should be clear, however, that none of these challenges is remotely restricted to a particular stage of life. We should enjoy play throughout our lives; learning to trust others and to establish one's own identity never ceases. From the moment we are born, our future options are being restricted; everything we learn makes it more difficult to learn new things. To be human is to regret the past and dread death. The most famous "midlife" crisis in history occurred when John Stuart Mill turned twenty.[14] At the very most, we might say that some of these challenges are usually more salient at certain times of life.

Many adults see maturity as the capacity to recapture the genius of childhood: indeed, the pinnacles of adult accomplishments are often attributed to rejuvenation. Freudian psychoanalysis is not the only theory of human development that counsels adults to return to their childhood for a second chance to face its anxieties. Children are prone to romanticize adulthood, just as adults frequently romanticize childhood. Whether child or adult, we can deliberately adopt the project of either growing up or of rejuvenation. Human beings are defined by the unique ability to see life as a whole, and the human beings who are best able to do this are the elderly. In this sense, and in others, we are most human when we reflect on the meaning of our whole lives in old age.

If we think of childhood and adulthood in relation to maturity rather than in relation to age, we can see that childhood is intrinsically and inescapably oriented toward adulthood: every child expects to grow up. A child who did not realize that she is growing up would be either severely impaired or already an adult. To be a child is to anticipate adulthood. Similarly, to be an adult is to measure one's distance from one's childhood, to reflect on what one had feared and what one had hoped for as a child. Disillusioned innocence is essential to the meaning of adulthood. Just as a human organ is essentially dependent on a whole human body, so childhood and adulthood are essentially dependent on a whole human life—so long as that whole is at least imagined.[15]

What would it mean to be an adult without a childhood? An adult without a childhood is merely an overgrown child. Consider the biblical account of Adam and Eve. Although they seem to have adult size, they cavort innocently around Eden fully naked, like children. Only after they disobey God and suffer punishment do they become adults—when they realize that they can never return to their childhood paradise. Another parable of the perils of missing childhood is Mary Shelley's *Frankenstein*: the creature of the novel is described as a monster only because he has the size and strength of an adult but the mind of a child. Adam and Eve, just like Frankenstein's creature, learn the hard way that adult virtues are the product of trial and error—of memory and experience—over time. This time of replacing innocence with experience is called "childhood" even if we were already fully grown. There is no other way of becoming an adult.

Does the fact that childhood is essentially oriented toward adulthood mean that childhood is only a time of preparation for adulthood? Is childhood merely a necessary evil to be endured for the sake of adulthood? Not at all. A child who understands her adult destiny has good reasons for putting off those burdens for as long as possible. Why rush the inevitable? Moreover, preparation for adulthood need not mean assuming adult discipline and responsibility. As we shall see, often the best way for children to prepare for adulthood is to prolong their childlike innocence and playfulness. Some human goods and virtues come more easily to children. Adults can learn (or relearn) these virtues from children. Childhood has its own inherent value in addition to preparing us for adulthood. If childhood were only a time of preparation for adulthood, then a child who died before reaching adulthood would have had a wasted life.

Just as there is no sleep without wakefulness, there is no childhood without adulthood or adulthood without childhood. Although there are mountains of books about childhood, about adulthood, and about the other stages of life, we need to understand our lives as a whole, because we live our lives at every stage in view of the whole. My theme will not be childhood, adulthood, or elderhood. My theme is humanhood. A human life is a story that interweaves past, present, and future—a narrative that unifies childhood, youth, and adulthood. Strictly speaking, there is no such thing as a philosophy of childhood or of adulthood, since each of these notions intrinsically requires the other. For the same reason, there is no history of childhood or history of adulthood: there is only a history of the relations between adults and children.[16] A philosophy of childhood without a philosophy of adulthood is like a philosophy of life without a philosophy of death or a philosophy of causes without a philosophy of effects. There is only a philosophy of the complex interrelations between childhood and adulthood within the stories of our lives. Like all good narratives, our life stories will be full of irony: we might well say that as children we aim to become the adults we never shall be, while as adults we aim to recapture the childhood we never had.

To be human is in an important sense to be a child, an adolescent, an adult, and elderly all at the same time. No one ever fully graduates from childhood or adolescence: we carry our childhood and adolescence with us into adulthood. We are like Russian matryoshka dolls who add new outer selves as we grow while retaining our former selves within. The "stages" of life are less like rungs of a ladder and more like layers, parts, or facets of the whole. But even these images fail to capture the interpenetration of the stages of our lives. A human life is a story in which the beginning foreshadows the end and the end recapitulates the beginning.

Our human capacity for uniting our past and our future into the present makes us "time binders." If plants bring chemicals together through photosynthesis and if animals bring space together through perception, then humans bring time together through narratives.[17] Because language stabilizes our memories of the past and our hopes for the future, we are able to tell stories that unify all the stages of life. A fully mature human person, then, experiences life as an ongoing autobiographical narrative.

A human life is like a baseball game. From the outside, a ball game seems to be just a sequence of innings, as a human life seems to be a sequence of stages. But from the inside, a ball game is always played as a whole. In the first inning, the players and coaches adopt a very different strategy than they adopt in later innings. Early in the game, players reserve energy and surprise plays needed in future innings, and coaches reserve pitchers and batters. In later innings, players and coaches know much more about their opponents and have learned from mistakes in earlier innings.

Near the end of a game, teams will often attempt a "rally" to recapture the youthful energy of the first innings. Players and coaches play every inning in relation to the whole of the developing game: the game as a whole is prior and more important than the various innings. Whether we are children, adolescents, adults, or seniors, we should play the game of life always in relation to the whole.

If we always live our lives in relation to the whole, then what difference is there between a child's life and that of an adult? A child has a prospective view of the whole of life—this whole is an imagined whole. An adult has a prospective as well as a retrospective view of life—a whole of memory as well as of imagination. As we grow, we do not move through stages but through a developing conception of the whole of our lives, from an imagined whole to a remembered whole. Or, rather, each stage of life provides us with a unique relation to the whole of life. Is a child's imagined whole more truthful than an adult's remembered whole? Does any particular stage of life offer a privileged vantage? We like to think that old age offers the most comprehensive understanding of the whole, but the memory of the aged is often no more reliable than a child's expectations. From the time children are about three years old, they can tell a story (often fanciful) of where they came from and where they are headed. The content of this narrative develops over time but not the basic human capacity to see life as a whole.

~

Development turns out to be a very puzzling and even paradoxical idea. To make sense of development, we must first discuss two more basic ideas: time and change. Development is a kind of change that takes place over time. The concepts of time and change are inseparable: time is just a way to measure change, and without change, there could be no time. How would one be aware of time passing were it not for something changing? For something to change it must also remain the same. Were something to vaporize into nothing we would not say that it has changed but that it has vanished. In the words of the philosopher Immanuel Kant, "only the permanent changes."[18] What do we call the permanent substrate that underlies change? Ever since Aristotle, we call it a "substance." A substance is an entity that retains its identity despite certain kinds of change over time.[19] The best example of the unity of a substance is a human being, who retains his or her identity as an animal with a rational nature through rather dramatic changes from embryo to senescence.[20] Not all change, of course, is compatible with substantial identity over time: death, for example, marks the end of a living substance.

One way for a substance to retain its identity over time is to never change. According to many philosophers, God retains his identity by never changing. But other substances, such as biological organisms, retain their identities by constantly changing. According to Plato, every tissue in our body is continually dying and being replaced. In this sense, the journey of a human life is like the journey of the legendary ship of Theseus. Over the course of a long voyage, every single plank, sail, and rigging of Theseus's ship was replaced—leaving it to philosophers to debate whether it was still the same ship.[21] During the voyage of a human life, every one of our cells dies and is replaced. Are we the same person at the end? We call this continual renewal of cellular life "metabolic" change. But metabolic change does not itself constitute development.

A human life is a developing whole, and development involves more than mere change. To develop is to change from worse to better or from better to worse. To grow up is to develop; to deteriorate is also to develop. We thus speak of the events of our lives or of history as "good developments" or "bad developments." To develop means to change in relation to some goal or purpose.[22] Metabolic change is also directed toward a goal, namely health. Every organism has an intrinsic disposition to maintain healthy functioning in the face of internal and external disturbances. But we do not normally call these homeostatic changes "development." Development refers to cumulative changes to the actualization (or loss) of an organism's intrinsic powers. Both growing and declining involve development.

What is the goal or purpose of development? Biologists tend to define the goal of development as reproductive maturity. The science of developmental biology has long been the study of the growth of an organism from conception through puberty. After reproduction, it was assumed, the organism had completed its mission and reached its goal. The rest of its life was thought to have little or no biological importance. According to traditional biology, a chicken is nothing more than one egg's way to make another egg.

In the case of a human life, of course, we care about more than reproduction. We do not think of the goal or purpose of a human life only in terms of having children. A good human life means a lifelong quest to realize or achieve some goal: to become a virtuous person, to create a new idea or work of art, or to build a community. We do not retire after having our kids. Even developmental biology is increasingly studying the whole human life course. In the new developmental biology, the goal of life is no longer reproduction; the goal of life is death. According to some recent research, death itself may well be genetically programmed, meaning that we keep developing until we die. Our expiration dates may be set at the moment of conception.

In human beings, then, we can distinguish mere physical maturation from many other kinds of maturation. We often talk about someone's emotional, psychological, social, intellectual, or spiritual maturity. Biological development is measured in relation to biological maturity, just as other kinds of development are measured in relation to other kinds of maturity. What is the relation of these kinds of maturation to chronological age? Only in the case of reproductive maturity is there a close relation between age and maturation. We can predict at birth when someone will be reproductively mature. Notoriously, however, emotional, moral, intellectual, or spiritual maturity have little relation to chronological age. Many small children throw fewer temper tantrums than many adults. Time is not the mother of perfection. Aging is not at all the same as maturing.[23]

Development is paradoxical: a biological substance can change only because it remains the same. The very word "development" in many European languages literally means an unfolding of what is already there. We use the same word to describe the process of manifesting a photographic image: the image already exists on the negative but becomes more fully realized when developed.[24] The construction of a building develops according to an already existing blueprint. An organism, however, is not constructed from without but grows from within. Traditional photographic film did not develop itself but had to be developed by a machine or person. A closer analogy to biological development would be Polaroid-style self-developing film. An organism requires an external environment in which to grow, but that environment is already genetically internalized. Each species is intrinsically adapted to its own normal environment. To develop is to become what we already are.

The philosopher and biologist Aristotle pioneered the idea that development means the actualization of a goal inherent to an organism. An acorn, he says, has the goal of becoming an oak tree and, in the right setting, will strive to do so. How do we know that an organism is striving to realize a goal? Because we can see a plant or animal pursue its inner purpose even in the face of myriad obstacles. Biological development is relentlessly goal directed—although this striving is obviously not intentional.[25] A plant will grow toward the sun in the face of many obstacles, but no one thinks that the plant is deliberately trying to reach the sun. Human development toward reproductive maturity will happen whether we like it or not. Only radical surgery or starvation could prevent a child from reaching puberty. But human development toward psychological, intellectual, moral, or spiritual maturity requires the deliberate, conscious, and intentional pursuit of those goals.[26]

What is permanent, and what changes in human development? We identify what is permanent with the notion of a human nature. At the instant of conception, the gonadal cells of our parents reorganized into a new and unique individual organism with an intrinsic impetus toward growing into an adult rational and moral agent. In normal circumstances, this impetus will achieve that goal; but even when maturation is blocked by internal disease or external injury, we never cease being human beings with an intrinsic impetus toward rational and moral agency. This drive to maturation, that is, our rational nature, does not itself develop; it came into being the instant we emerged as a living organism during conception.

Modern developmental biology emerged from comparative embryology, a science founded by Aristotle. Embryology was the science of development from fertilization until birth, and many of our ideas of lifelong human development—ranging from conception to death—reflect the influence of the science of embryology. Indeed, as we shall see, all of the dominant stories of development in biology and psychology have their origin in embryology. Why embryology? I asked above whether human nature is more evident in infants or in adults. Biologists, again since Aristotle, have argued that the nature of life is most evident in embryos because the embryos of all animals (like the seeds of all plants) resemble each other more than do mature specimens. Indeed, we might say that embryos of different species resemble each other more than they resemble their respective adult forms.

Aristotle and later comparative embryologists noticed that all embryos develop through an invariant sequence of distinct stages. The idea that human development, from infancy to old age, proceeds through an invariant sequence of stages is just an extension of the theory of embryonic development to the rest of human life.[27] In addition to the centrality of the idea of stages, embryology created the presumption that development belongs only to the young. Only very recently have biologists and psychologists started to think of development as a lifelong human project.[28]

Many aspects of our psychological, moral, and intellectual development cannot be directly ascribed to our biological nature. We often describe someone's development as the result of both their internal growth and their external environment, both nature and nurture. The interactions of organism and environment are very complex, making development itself hard to predict.

We often contrast an organism to its environment, but each entity implies the other. There are no organisms without environments, and there are no environments without organisms. Through evolutionary adaptation, every organism has genetically encoded the physical, chemical, and biological parameters of its normal environment. What this means is that a human being has evolved to breathe only the earth's air, drink only the earth's liquids, eat only the earth's foods, and move only in the earth's gravity. Were the earth's chemistry or biology or physics to change rapidly or dramatically enough, we could become extinct. The human organism has internalized its normal, earthly environment. Most other organisms have internalized even more restricted environments, so that if they are moved far from their native habitat they cannot thrive or even live. Like turtles, then, each of us carries our natural home with us.

At the same time, what counts as an environment is determined by the activities of organisms. Every organism transforms external nature into a suitable home: "environment" just means the surroundings of an organism. My backyard contains as many different environments as there are species of organisms. The study of the relations between organisms and their environments is called "ecology"—a word which literally means the science of households. Every organism is genetically adapted to its home, and that home is transformed by its resident organisms. To speak of organisms without environments or environments without organisms makes as much sense as speaking of homes without residents or residents without homes.

Development literally means an unfolding of what is already present. But human development is more than merely an unfolding of our genetic potential. The actualization of our genetic potential requires certain kinds of environments, such as our earthly home. Human development is largely linguistic and cultural, meaning that we need more than merely a suitable physical home but also a place of cultural learning. Development takes place between the organism and its environment. When we focus on the pole of the organism, we describe development in terms of maturation: an organism is internally programmed to mature with only minimal inputs from the environment. Indeed, as I have noted, organisms strive for maturity even in the face of environmental obstacles—not all of which can be surmounted. All inner-directed kinds of development are called "maturation."

When we focus, however, on the pole of the environment, we describe development in terms of learning. All forms of growth that cannot be attributed to maturation are attributed to learning. We often say that we mature into puberty but that we learn language. The idea is that we will grow into puberty no matter what our environment but only in a linguistic environment can we learn to speak, let alone read or write. Linguist Noam Chomsky provocatively claims that language is no more learned than is puberty, because he thinks that the basic grammatical structure of language is genetically encoded. We must not press this contrast of maturation and learning too far. An organism can mature only by learning to cope with its environment just as an organism can learn only within the parameters set by its genome. In other words, puberty requires the right environment while language requires the right genes. No matter how much we talk to our dogs, they will never talk back.

Aristotle famously observed that "all human beings by nature desire to know." It makes little sense to sharply contrast maturation and learning in a species that matures by way of learning. That is why we often describe intellectual, emotional, and moral learning as kinds of maturation. Not all kinds of learning foster maturation, but cumulative learning aimed at achieving personal ideals shares many features with biological maturation. That is why, as we shall see, biological theories of development are so illuminating of intellectual, moral, and spiritual development. The continuity between the processes of maturation and learning gives unity to the ideal of lifelong human development, which has physical, psychological, and moral dimensions.

But the interactions between maturation and learning make it very difficult to theorize development. There is no widely accepted general theory of development in biology today.[29] Studies of development, nonetheless, continue to be inspired and guided by a few basic stories of embryonic development. These stories are now regarded not as genuine theories from which testable hypotheses might be deduced but as paradigms or metaphors of development. Each of them continues to play an important role in understanding development, even though none of them could be called a general theory of development. There have been many special theories of physical, biological, and psychological development over the centuries, but they all stem from a few basic stories or metaphors of embryonic development.[30]

The most basic biological distinction is between direct and indirect developers. Fishes, reptiles, birds, and mammals are direct developers because the embryo grows into maturity without going through a larval stage. Many invertebrates, amphibians, and insects, by contrast, are indirect developers that mature through the drama of metamorphosis. Biologically speaking, there is no doubt that human beings are direct developers, but human development is more than just biological. Physically, children are undoubtedly more like kittens than like caterpillars; but psychologically, children might be more like caterpillars. In other words, are children just smaller adults or fundamentally different kinds of creatures?[31] Some psychologists compare children to caterpillars and adults to butterflies—even though, in other respects, we begin life as playful butterflies but then transmogrify into stolid caterpillars.[32] Here we see that these biological theories are not mutually exclusive when applied to the diverse kinds of human development. In their physical strength, children are just small adults, but in their thinking and imagining, they are very different kinds of creatures. Children's thinking is not merely an inferior version of adult thinking but arguably is different in kind.[33] It is tempting to see adolescence as a kind of chrysalis from which parents hope that a very different kind of person emerges! To the extent that we see continuity between children and adults, we see direct development, and to the extent that we see discontinuity between children and adults, we see indirect development.

The first of these foundational stories of direct development is known as recapitulation, of which there are two main variants. Biological recapitulation holds that in the growth of a human being, we develop through the whole range of "lower" life-forms. Before theories of biological evolution, this meant that human development recapitulates the ladder of nature: we begin life as a plant, then become a reptile, then a mammal, then a primate, and finally, a human being. After the emergence of Darwin's theory of evolution, recapitulation enjoyed a new popularity. After all, Darwin argued that human beings descended from earlier and lower life-forms, extending back to the beginning of life on earth. It was not much of a stretch to argue that the development of the human organism passes through all the stages of the evolution of life. Indeed, modern genetics insists that each of us has inherited DNA from every period of life on earth. So at a genetic level, a human being does recapitulate the entire history of life. Ernest Haeckel popularized this idea of recapitulation in his slogan "ontogeny recapitulates phylogeny": the development of each organism summarizes the entire evolution of life.[34] Every biology student notices that a human embryo looks like a small fish and even has gill arches.[35] And indeed, there is a sense in which humans grow like a plant in the womb, then emerge as kinds of nursing mammals before becoming little primates and then, perhaps, rational persons.

There is also a historical story of recapitulation according to which the development of each individual person summarizes the history of the human race.[36] In this view, popular a century ago, children begin life as wild and primitive hunter-gatherers, then they settle into agricultural routines at elementary school, next they master urban learning and technology in high school, and finally become modern Westerners as adults. The leaders of early twentieth-century child psychology—Sigmund Freud, Stanley Hall, Jean Piaget, and Carl Jung—were all historical recapitulationists.[37] They all frequently compared the untamed antics and imaginative flights of children to what they called "primitive savages." These psychologists described various mental illnesses as a regression to an earlier stage of social and psychological development. Psychosis was compared to infant tantrums and to primitive ecstatic rituals. The races and cultures of the contemporary world were also frequently arrayed in a hierarchy from infantile to adult. Citizens of Western Europe and North America turned out to be the only adults in the world. John Stuart Mill compared the "backward" societies of his world to children who needed the adult supervision conveniently provided by the British Empire. In short, recapitulation is a handy way to organize the messy complexity of evolution, history, and development along a single hierarchy from lower to higher.

A second story of development is known as preformationism. In this story, development is merely a matter of getting larger. Ancient Greek philosophers argued that "nothing can come from nothing," meaning, among other things, there is nothing wholly new. Everything must come from something like it: humans come from humans, plants from plants, rocks from rocks. If you see something emerge that seems new, it must have been there in some way all the time. Everything emerges from something either similar or actually preexisting. One very simple and radical version of preformation is the homunculus or "little man" said to preexist in a human sperm or egg: here human development is nothing more than a matter of the little man growing bigger. It is easy to mock the homunculus theory, which does just defer the question: where did the little man come from? The most extreme form of preformation is preexistence, or the idea that we lived before our current embodiment.

Modern genetics has inspired a revival of preformationist thinking. The view that a fertilized egg at conception contains all the instructions for developing and maintaining a human being is just a genetic variant of preformationism. The human genome is often said to contain a complete little man: everything we ever become is in a sense already there. Because of cloning, we now know that every cell in the human body contains a complete human genome capable of generating another human being. Each of us has a homunculus in every somatic cell of our bodies! Noam Chomsky and many others believe that the universal syntax of human language is already encoded in our genome. A great deal of what we consider cultural learning might indeed already preexist in our genome.

A third story of development is known to embryologists as "epigenesis" but could be called "individualization." Here development is the process whereby the generic becomes the specific and the outline becomes the detailed blueprint. This story emerged in biological science in opposition to preformation, since individualization describes the emergence of new structure and form during the course of development. Preformation posits growth without differentiation while individualization is differentiation with growth. The laws of embryology of Karl Ernst von Baer are the classic expression of this story. According to individualization, the embryo starts as a vertebrate, then becomes a mammal, then a primate, then a human, and then a unique person. A human embryo, says von Baer, does not resemble the adult form of any previous species, as in recapitulation. Rather, a human embryo resembles the embryonic forms of other members of its own genus, family, and kingdom. Development does not summarize the history of the mature morphology of organisms. Instead, the development of every organism begins with the simple, generic form of its kind. Contemporary developmental biology combines aspects of both preformation and epigenesis: "the genetic instructions according to which development proceeds are indeed preformed, but their realization is epigenetic, i.e. turns on influences acting on the embryonic cell from the outside."[38]

A fourth story of development is known as "neoteny." This word comes from the Greek meaning "to stretch out or prolong youthfulness." Neoteny is juvenilization. Neoteny refers to the timing of developmental sequences. By slowing down development and extending each developmental phase, human beings retain many characteristics of the juveniles of their primate ancestors. Human gestation, for example, lasts for around twenty months, only nine of which are spent in the womb. At nine months our heads become too large for the birth canal of a bipedal mammal. Human beings are born more immature than any other placental mammal. Our developmental phase of sexual immaturity, that is, childhood, is roughly twice as long as other primates. As a result of these delays in development, over the course of human evolution, we have become ever more youthful in morphology and behavior when compared to other apes. Today, adult human beings in many ways resemble infant apes more than we resemble adult apes. Our erect posture, our large heads, our hairlessness, our relatively flat face, and our small teeth make us "sexually mature, fetal apes."[39]

All mammals are most capable of learning when they are young. Human beings uniquely preserve a youthful capacity to learn throughout their lives. Again, all young mammals engage in playful contests, but only human mammals continue to play throughout their adult lives. Why would natural selection favor juvenilization as an evolutionary strategy? There are many hypotheses, all of them speculative and controversial. Most biologists believe that prolonging childhood enables humans to master a much more complex repertoire of cultural practices before facing the burdens of reproduction. Since we are by nature cultural animals, we need a long period of time to learn a huge range of linguistic and behavioral codes. Juveniles are less specialized and more adaptive than are adults. Adult primates are highly specialized in morphology and behavior suited for particular environments. By remaining juvenile primates, human beings have the flexibility to adapt to any number of environments.

Such is the complexity of biological development that all of these stories are still invoked by contemporary developmental biologists. At a sufficiently high level of generality, they are all true and illuminating, despite the huge differences between them.[40] For example, recapitulation and neoteny are often described as fundamentally opposed: recapitulation means that humans accelerate their development through the adult stages of all of our ancestors; neoteny means that humans delay their development so that they remain juvenilized primates. In recapitulation, humans pass through the stages of their adult primate ancestors and go beyond them; in neoteny, we never reach the maturity of our adult primate ancestors. Recapitulation means overdevelopment while neoteny means underdevelopment.

But these two stories can be reconciled if they describe different aspects of human development. In some ways, we are overdeveloped primates, while in other ways we are underdeveloped primates. Our underdevelopment might serve to make possible our overdevelopment. Human development has been compared to archery: the farther we pull back the arrow, the farther it flies ahead. Perhaps neoteny is what makes possible recapitulation. By prolonging gestation, infancy, and childhood, human beings are capable of transcending the adult achievements of our ancestors. We retain some juvenile features of our ancestors while transcending them in other ways. We remain playful, flexible, and docile like juvenile apes so that we might become even smarter and more skillful than adult apes. Underdevelopment serves overdevelopment: a classic strategy of indirect success.[41] Who could have thought that the best way to outperform the adults is to remain children? Within the primate family, human beings are the prodigies—the annoyingly precocious kids who in some ways never grow up but in other ways surpass the grown-ups. In short, over the past four million years, humanoid primates have been growing ever younger while steadily outperforming all other adult primates. We are both younger and older than any other primate. These two facts must be related: juvenilization must hold the secret to our overdevelopment.

If purely biological development is so complex as to require a whole set of radically different stories, then imagine the complexity of complete human development—biological, psychological, intellectual, and moral. The highest reaches of human development are often summarized as "spiritual" maturity. Saints and moral heroes are often described as spiritually mature because their ideals enable them to transcend the normal bodily and material incentives for status, wealth, or even survival.[42] As we shall see, the wisest students of human development have implicitly deployed all of these stories in their accounts of growing up. Why do we turn to these biological stories when attempting to describe human life more generally? Because these stories help us to answer the practical questions we ask about how childhood and adulthood relate to each other in a good human life.

For example, three of our stories—recapitulation, preformation, and individualization—imply that adulthood is the goal of human development. In these stories, the adult holds the key to understanding the child.

In recapitulation, a child is at the stage of a lower animal; in preformation, a child is a tiny, incompetent, and vulnerable adult; in individualization, a child is an unfinished adult. In every case, the child is defined by her lack of adult maturity. These stories portray childhood as a predicament to be escaped, and they describe a child as merely a deficient adult. Their implications for parenting and education are clear and full of common sense. First, children should learn from adults because adults have essentially nothing to learn from children. Second, we should minimize the time we spend as children to escape childhood's dangers and deficiencies. These stories of human development underlie the practices of much of human history, in which children went to work and got married as soon as they were physically able to do so. Until very recently, prolonging childhood through many years of schooling was a luxury reserved for the few.

One reason that these stories of human development have persisted for millennia is that they are largely true. Children are in many respects deficient adults, children do need to learn from adults, and childhood is in some respects a dangerous predicament in a world of grown-ups. Neoteny is the only story of human development in which childhood is seen as the key to adulthood. Here development is defined in terms of juvenilization.[43] In neoteny, the goal of adulthood is to recapture the virtues of childhood. Neoteny implies that adults have much to learn from children and that childhood represents a kind of idyll in human life that ought to be prolonged for as long as possible. Why do most of us produce our best art, learn foreign languages, and master new gadgets most easily, and ask our deepest philosophical questions as children? Why are children more able to live in the present moment and become lost in imaginative play? Why are children able to forgive and forget harms so readily? These virtues are not unique to children but are characteristic of childhood. The challenge for adults is to recapture the virtues we once had when the paradise of childhood is lost. The French poet Baudelaire once said: "Genius is childhood recaptured."

Today, neoteny seems to be at work not only in human nature but in human culture as well. In the advanced Western nations, the key social markers of adulthood (such as full-time work, marriage, and children) are now reached at a much later age than fifty years ago.[44] Many observers now claim that both childhood and adulthood are disappearing into a universal culture of adolescence. How are we to assess this ongoing juvenilization of our society? Can adulthood be postponed indefinitely? Should it be?

The five basic stories of development—indirect development, recapitulation, preformation, individualization (epigenesis), and neoteny—are often called metaphors of development because each of these stories rests on a different basic analogy. In biological recapitulation, the development of an individual organism is analogous to the ladder or evolution of species. In historical recapitulation, the development of an individual is analogous to the history of human civilization. In preformationism, a mature organism is analogous to a microscopic embryo. In epigenesis, development is analogous to the specification of a general blueprint. In neoteny, development is analogous to the process of rejuvenation. Each of these analogies is illuminating of various aspects of human development, but each analogy can be pushed too far: "The price of metaphor is eternal vigilance."[45]

I will call these "stories" of development, not only because they rest on analogies and metaphors, but because development intrinsically takes a narrative form. A narrative, as I will explain later, is a device for unifying the past, present, and future. Biological development is the story of cumulative growth in which the present is intelligible only in light of its past and in which the past already partly contains the future. The only way to make sense of development is to tell a story in which the beginning foreshadows the end and the end recapitulates the beginning. All of these stories of development have a goal and the pursuit of that goal gives development a narrative unity.

Some geneticists claim that if we knew enough about the genome and about its environment, then, with supercomputers, we might be able to compute the adult organism, that is, to predict its development purely from initial conditions. Most biologists reject this aspiration as a pipe dream.[46] But until we are able to compute an organism, we are left with stories of its unique developmental path.[47]

All specific scientific theories and hypotheses about human development are derived from, or inspired by, these basic stories. Although they all arose from the science of embryology, these five stories illuminate growth and change in human life far beyond the realm of biology itself. Because they are so basic and general in scope, many philosophers, educators, and other students of human life implicitly or explicitly appeal to one or more of these stories in their accounts of human development. How else would one narrate growth and change? The variety of theories of human growth, education, and development often appear as a blooming, buzzing confusion until we see all these myriad views as just a set of variations on five basic stories. Even the major philosophical and theological accounts of human life are rooted in one or more of these basic stories.

Aristotle sees human development as a recapitulation of the ladder of nature. As we develop, we move up the ladder of life from plant, to animal, to human. When Aristotle says, as an aside, that of course "no child is happy" he goes on to explain that no nonhuman animal is happy, either. He compares an embryo to a plant and a newborn to an animal—only in maturation do we become fully human. We all begin with vegetative souls, but in the prime of life, some of us can aspire to become quasi-divine. According to Aristotle, children are somewhere between plants and adult humans—a sentiment that most parents can appreciate.

Augustine, by contrast, gives classic articulation to preformation as the story of development. Augustine attempts to see his life as God sees it—outside of time. In this light, Augustine sees himself from infancy to adulthood as essentially always the same. Most modern readers of Augustine's *Confessions* are so horrified by his dark depiction of a newborn baby already corrupted by sin that they do not notice the deeper logic of his description. The evil concupiscence of a newborn shows us that all human beings are basically the same. We are all conceived, born, live, and die in sin. For Augustine, a baby is just a miniature sinner—exactly like a depraved adult except relatively harmless. Infancy, like every other stage of human life, is a predicament marked by punishment for original sin. Despite Augustine's dramatic "conversion," we shall see that he claims to have always been a Christian.

Erik Erikson modeled his famous "individualization" theory of the stages of human development on the epigenetic story of embryology. Where preformationism denies the emergence of new forms, individualization describes the emergence of new forms through an invariant sequence of stages. In the development of an embryo, particular tissues and organs emerge in a necessary physiological sequence. For example, no lungs emerge until after the heart emerges. Each stage of embryonic growth is defined by a major new organ or function. Erikson similarly argues that each stage of human development is defined by a unique crisis. He says that successful maturation requires a resolution of each crisis through an invariant sequence of well-defined stages. Just as in embryonic development, Erikson claims that failure within a given stage distorts all subsequent development.

Jean-Jacques Rousseau is famous for his view of the natural goodness of children, often sharply contrasted with Augustine's view of natural depravity. But the contrast is not so sharp when we recall that Rousseau argues that although every person is naturally good, we all become depraved through the social competition, greed, envy, and vanity of advanced societies. Rousseau argues that in the course of our development, every person recapitulates the history of the human race. Primordial man in the state of nature was innocent and good, just as every newborn infant is innocent and good. But over the course of history, mankind became corrupted, and over the course of growing up, we become corrupted by society. Rousseau offers a radical new pedagogy to help us raise children who retain their natural goodness amid the corruptions of our society.

Neoteny has a strange history and is not associated with any major philosopher.[48] The biblical Jesus deserves credit for being the first major sage who ever proposed that adults should emulate children: "Unless you become like little children, you cannot enter the Kingdom of God." In a series of texts, Jesus asserts that childhood offers us the key to understanding adult spiritual life.[49] Neoteny does not become a major theme again until Wordsworth wrote that "the child is father of the man." Neoteny emerged in the technical biological literature in the late nineteenth century and became popularized more recently by biologist Stephen Jay Gould and anthropologist Ashley Montagu. These thinkers argue that the goal of human development is to recapture the spirit of childhood.

Returning to the original question about whether human nature is best observed in a mature adult or in a small child, our philosophers have quite different answers. Aristotle, who defines human nature in terms of our innate tendency to actualize our potential, definitely asserts that we see human nature only when the goal of its development is reached in full maturity. The prime of life, says Aristotle, is when we become fully human and capable of true happiness. Rousseau, by contrast, compares human nature to a statue that has been defaced over time by the erosion of the weather.[50] Due to the myriad forces of corruption in human society, we are most likely to find human nature in the pristine condition of a baby or small child. Because Rousseau compares children to men in primitive societies, he also believes that human nature is more evident in our primordial past than in our corrupt present.[51] As for Augustine, who attempts to see human life as God sees it, outside of time (sub specie aeternitatis), human nature is equally manifest in infancy and in adulthood. We are sinners and saints, damned and saved, at every moment of our earthly lives.

∽

Let me now briefly describe what to expect ahead. In Part I, I shall explore four classic stories of embryonic development as applied to the whole of human life. In the hands of Aristotle, Augustine, Rousseau, and Jesus, each of these basic stories of development will powerfully illuminate some but not all aspects of human development. Moreover, because human development is at the center of the thought of each of these sages, these stories turn out to illuminate many aspects of their thought. Reading Aristotle as a natural recapitulationist, Augustine as a preformationist, Rousseau as a historical recapitulationist, and Jesus as a champion of neoteny will focus our understanding of their thought as a whole. In the end, we shall understand both human development and each of these sages better.

Why are these classic stories of development not presented in historical order? Because, as I have noted, the stories of recapitulation and preformation we find in Aristotle, Augustine, and Rousseau all take adulthood to be the goal of human development. Only the story of neoteny found in the sayings of Jesus takes childhood to be the goal of development. These four classic stories of development are inconsistent with each other, and I make no effort in Part I to harmonize them. I ask the reader to enjoy each story on its own before attempting to think about how they might be mixed or matched. How does each of these stories illuminate my own life? Every one of these classic stories is blinded by its own insights.

In Part II, I offer some strategies for seeing life as a developing whole. I begin in Chapter 6 by returning to our four classic stories. Each of these four stories describes stages of life as well as the shape of a complete human life. Here I compare our four stories by asking of each: How do the stages of life relate to a whole human life? What can we learn from each of these classic stories about the shape of a complete human life? Again, I make no systematic effort to harmonize these accounts, which, I believe, would rob each of them of its unique imaginative power.

After comparing our four classic stories of development, I then discuss the two most important contemporary theories of the stages of development: the epigenetic story of Erik Erikson and the philosophical account of

David Norton. Here we find the most sophisticated attempts ever to understand human development in terms of stages. By exploring these contemporary theories of the stages of life we shall find that the whole of a human life is prior to any of its stages. What aspects of development are illuminated and which are obscured by the notion of stages? Are there goods and virtues unique to childhood or to adulthood?

What is puzzling is that these biological stories of development also illuminate psychological, moral, and spiritual development. What does it say about human beings that our biological development reveals so much about our psychological, moral, and spiritual development? In Chapter 7 I will ask what kind of whole a human life is. Are we essentially biological organisms or psychological persons? A person is usually defined as a rational and moral agent. But some human beings are either too immature or too impaired to exercise their rational or moral agency. Are they still persons? Or merely human beings? Is a human life divided into prepersonal, personal, and postpersonal stages? I will argue that the attempt to divide a human life into such stages fails for the same reason that dividing a life into childhood and adulthood fails. As an individual substance with a rational nature, our biological humanity is irreducibly personal. Only an organism that is already in some sense a person can develop into a person. I conclude that our lives are unified over time because we enjoy substantial biological and psychological unity at every moment of our lives.

In Chapters 7 and 8, I sketch a unified theory of human identity over time on the basis of a nested hierarchy of three powers. First, each person's unique human genome ensures biological identity over time; second, each person's powers of imagination and memory ensure psychological identity over time; third, each person's ability to tell his own life story ensures narrative identity over time. Just as imagination and memory rest on our biological identity, so our autobiographical stories rest on our psychological identity. We are storytelling animals, but our autobiographical powers rest on our psychological and biological powers. As I will argue in Chapter 8, narrative offers the key to the unity of human life because our biological development is already a quasi-narrative, and, surprisingly, our memories and our imaginations also have an intrinsically narrative structure. A human life is a story all the way down.

In the conclusion, "A Practical Guide to Life Writing," I show that the aim of this book is ultimately practical. By bringing childhood and adulthood into dialogue, we should be able not only to understand our lives better but also to lead them more wisely. Writing is the most focused and disciplined method of self-reflection, so I have designed a set of writing exercises that recapitulate the main themes of this book by guiding readers through a variety of ways to tell their own stories.

CHAPTER 2

Development as the Recapitulation of Nature in Aristotle

To discover the meaning of anything, we relate a part to a whole. A word gets its meaning from its sentence. Similarly, the meaning of a human life is found in relation to the whole of which our lives are a part. What is that whole? Each of our major philosophers will identify a different whole within which to understand human life. Individual human development can be understood in the context of the whole of the cosmos, the whole of nature, or the whole of history. The growth of each particular person can be seen as a microcosm of nature or history as a whole, just as nature and history are seen as a macrocosm of the developing individual person.

Aristotle pioneered an elaborate analogy between the hierarchy of the cosmos and the development of an organism, especially of a human being. It is important to understand that Aristotle thought that these analogies were not poetic metaphors. For him, analogies are rooted in reality and reflect shared formal structures. For example, biologists today describe the wings of bats as "analogous" to the wings of birds. What they mean is that bats and birds did not inherit their wings from a shared winged ancestor (by "homology"); rather, bats and birds developed wings independently for competitive advantage in their particular ecological niches. Bats and birds do not share wings by poetic conceit but by the real operation of natural selection. Similarly, Aristotle draws analogies between embryos and plants, and between children and brute animals, because of objective similarities in the operative powers of these organisms.

According to Aristotle, everything in the cosmos, from the elements of matter to divine beings, can be ranked into a single hierarchy according to its degree of actuality. What does it mean to be actual? Aristotle contrasts what is actual with what is potential: actuality is active while potentiality is passive. We actualize our potential when we put our powers into effect. When passive matter becomes organized by formal structures, it is able to act, to do things. Because of its form, a chair is more actual—it can do more things—than the lumber from which it was made. An acorn has the potential to become an oak tree, but an acorn is not actually an oak tree. An oak tree is more actual than an acorn because it can do more things than an acorn, including produce acorns. The greater degree of actuality of an oak tree comes from its higher degree of formal organization. The bare elements of matter (earth, air, fire, water) have the least degree of actuality (or form) while the gods are actualized to the highest degree. As matter becomes increasingly organized by formal properties, it becomes increasingly actual, active, and capable. Artifacts, from chairs to computers, get their formal organization from the minds of their creators. Organisms get their forms from their natures.

Later philosophers have dubbed Aristotle's hierarchy of all things "the ladder of nature" or the "great chain of being."[1] One fascinating aspect of this hierarchy is that every higher entity includes all of the formal actuality of those entities below it. A chair includes all the powers of lumber, just as an oak tree includes all the powers of acorns. Aristotle sees human beings as a kind of compendium of all living creatures: our amazing array of powers include the nutritive powers of plants, the perceptive powers of animals, and the rational powers unique to us. Each of us is a composite of plant, animal, and human. Indeed, according to Aristotle, human beings also possess some divine intellectual powers.

Aristotle defines development as moving from a state of less to more actuality, from lower degree of formal complexity to a higher degree. Recall that development means change in relation to a goal, and for Aristotle, the goal of all development is to move from a lower to a higher degree of actuality. By developing, then, we move up the ladder of nature, from mere elements to plants to animals to humans to gods. Indeed, Aristotle famously claims that the supreme goal of human life is to "divinize ourselves."[2]

Aristotle understands development as a recapitulation of the ladder of nature. He argues that human beings begin as plants before becoming animals who ultimately aspire to be gods. For Aristotle, a child is not a miniature adult; a child is more like a different species. A child is potentially human but actually more like a lower animal. Aristotle says very little about the elderly, beyond disparaging their loss of adult powers. Given his theory of recapitulation, one would expect him to say that the elderly regress back into children as they decline from the prime of life. Aristotle's view of development as recapitulation strongly shapes his understanding of the relationship between adults and children.

What is the goal of organic growth? Like all biologists, Aristotle sees development as realizing the fundamental powers of an organism, especially reproductive abilities. Every organism has its own set of species-specific powers and capabilities, but every organism also shares a power common to all living things—the power to reproduce. Aristotle believes that all individual living organisms die but that every species of organism is eternal. Reproduction is the only way for mortal individuals to participate in divine immortality[3]—except for human beings, who can also participate in divinity through intellectual activity. Aristotle does not, however, define biological actualization simply as maximizing reproductive efficiency, as do some neo-Darwinians. For him, a chicken is not merely an egg's way to make another egg. Organisms have a diverse set of essential powers to actualize.

Aristotle describes the stage when we actualize our most important powers as our prime—the acme (Greek *akmē*) of life. As children and as youths we are growing toward our prime, and when we are old, we are declining from our prime. If contemporary American culture idolizes youth, Aristotle idolizes the midlife prime, when we are fully mature and at the top of our game as parents, as citizens, and as philosophers. Aristotle strongly disparages both childhood and old age: we are only fully human in our midlife prime. Aristotle says that we see human nature fully realized only in the prime of life. He does not associate what is natural with what is primitive, childish, or original: "For what each thing is when fully developed, we call its nature, whether we are speaking of a man, a horse, or a family."[4] Indeed, if we were somehow able to choose to live in only one stage of life, who would not choose the prime? For Aristotle, there are no important powers or virtues available exclusively to either the young or the old: everything good in life is to be found in the prime. Aristotle's word for the actualization of our essential human powers in the prime of life is "happiness," by which he means flourishing. Just as plants flourish in their prime, so we flourish in ours.

When is the prime of life? Like modern biologists, Aristotle partly links the prime of life to reproduction. Men and women should marry in the reproductive prime of life which, Aristotle says, begins at about eighteen years for women and thirty-seven years for men.[5] Aristotle goes on to say that we are mentally in our prime at around age fifty.[6] Unfortunately, our bodies and our minds do not share the same prime: "The body is in its prime from thirty to thirty-five; the mind about forty-nine."[7] Our lives, then, lack a single summit but have the shape of a mountain with a broad mesa across the top. There are even different primes for different roles in political life. Aristotle argues that in distributing offices of the state, we should follow the lead of nature, which gives strength to the young and wisdom to the older men. It is both expedient and just, he says, to make the young men soldiers, the middle-aged men councilors, and the old men priests.[8] In this view, the middle-aged prime of life cannot claim a monopoly on civic virtue, since young men are better suited by nature for combat and elderly men to priestly serenity. Nonetheless, Aristotle would no doubt argue that the middle-aged citizens have a natural superiority because they could become soldiers or priests if necessary, while the young or elderly men simply would not be able to exercise the other offices. Moreover, strength—the superiority that Aristotle concedes here to youth—is not a true virtue while the practical wisdom that he associates with older men is.

Today, many psychologists attempt to base their theories on the science of biology. Aristotle's biology, by contrast, rests on his psychology. After all, biology is the science of living things and what makes something alive, by his account, is the "soul." His word for "soul" (*psychē*) is the basis of our word "psychology" but means broadly anything that causes a material body to be alive. Everything living is animated by its soul—yet, there are different gradations of soul. The lowest level of soul Aristotle calls "nutritive" because it enables an organism to absorb food; the next level of soul he calls "perceptive" because it enables an organism to sense its environment; the highest level of soul he calls "rational" because it enables an organism to reflect and to reason.[9] These gradations of soul form a nested hierarchy such that the perceptive soul includes and transcends the nutritive soul while the rational soul includes and transcends the perceptive soul. In other words, we cannot perceive unless we can first eat, and we cannot reason unless we can first eat and perceive.[10]

With his gradations of soul in place, Aristotle can now rank all living things. Plants have the nutritive soul, animals have the perceptive soul, and humans (and divine beings) the rational soul.[11] In short, animals include but transcend plants just as humans include but transcend animals. This linear hierarchy of organisms is called the "ladder of nature." Aristotle certainly did not believe that higher species of life descended or evolved from lower species. His ladder of nature is fixed and eternal. But in the development of an individual organism we do see movement from lower to higher. For Aristotle, the development of each organism summarizes or recapitulates the whole ladder of nature below it. Ernst Haeckel's nineteenth-century biogenetic law, "ontogeny recapitulates phylogeny," applies to Aristotle—so long as we understand phylogeny not as the evolution of species over time but as a fixed ladder of nature.[12]

In his embryology, Aristotle emphasizes this developmental principle: no embryo, he says, is simultaneously plant, animal, and human.[13] Rather, all animal embryos start as plants, just as all human embryos start as plants before becoming animals.[14] Aristotle frequently compares how an embryo feeds from its umbilicus to how a plant feeds from its tap root. The embryo is planted in the uterus and grows from its roots.[15] At a certain point, perhaps at birth, the embryo acquires a perceptive soul.[16]

Aristotle is aware that an animal embryo is not merely a plant, even at its earliest stages of development. He articulates the biological principle that like comes from like—plants from plants, animals from animals, and humans from humans. Every organism generated by human parents is fully human.[17] Human parents cannot generate a plant. In what sense, then, is an animal embryo a plant? Here Aristotle refers to a basic metaphysical distinction between potentiality and actuality. A human embryo is always potentially a rational creature but does not become actually rational until it is first actually nutritive and then actually perceptive. In other words, we do not become actually human until we are first actually plants and then actually animals.[18] In one sense we are always human creatures, but in another sense we develop from plant to animal and then from animal to human.[19]

Soul is the first actualization of a living body, meaning that without soul a body is not alive.[20] We cannot actualize our human rational powers until after we actualize our nutritive and perceptive powers. For Aristotle, body and soul can be separated in thought but not in reality: they develop in tandem. A human embryo does not have the form of a rational creature but the form of a plant. Aristotle rejects what would later be called the theory of preformation: human embryos are not little rational creatures who simply need to grow up.[21] Rather, embryos that are potentially human must develop through actual plant and animal stages. Nor is this account of human development as the recapitulation of the ladder of nature limited to Aristotle or even to ancient philosophers. G. W. F. Hegel, the nineteenth-century German philosopher, also describes the human embryo as a plant and a newborn baby as an animal.[22]

There is agreement among scholars that Aristotle rejects any kind of preformation, but scholars disagree about whether his theory of development is closer to recapitulation or to epigenesis (individualization). In eighteenth-century biology there was a battle between preformationism and epigenesis. According to preformationism, an embryo was already a little man; according to epigenesis, development proceeded from undifferentiated matter into specific forms. Again, these labels are anachronistic but with proper qualifications, they can be illuminating. Sometimes Aristotle describes development as if it proceeds from the generic to the specific powers. He says in one place that an animal develops into a horse or into a man, as if we begin with a generic soul that develops into a specific soul.[23] To see why this cannot be true, consider that Aristotle is quite clear that there is no such thing as a generic soul. He compares the concept of soul to the concept of figure: there is no generic figure, there are only triangles, quadrangles, and the like. Similarly, there is no generic soul, only nutritive, perceptive, and rational souls.[24] Human development, then, is not a process of specification whereby a generic soul becomes a human soul. Human development is a recapitulation through the sequence of the specific plant, animal, and human souls.

According to epigenesis, an organism develops from relative simplicity to greater complexity. This is certainly true of Aristotle's theory of development. The ladder of nature is a graded progression from simpler to more complex life-forms. As human beings recapitulate the ladder of nature from simple plants to complex rational animals, we also inevitably move from the simple to the more complex. Aristotle's recapitulationism is very difficult to distinguish from individualization, but to decide between them we need only refer to his doctrine that there is no generic soul. Stephen Jay Gould argues that Aristotle's recapitulationist analogies serve his developmental epigenesis.[25] But Aristotle's recapitulationism merely creates the appearance of epigenesis, given his hierarchy of species from simple to complex.

Aristotle's moral psychology is oriented toward answering the question: how do we become excellent and happy human beings? The answer is that we must recapitulate the ladder of nature, traversing through the stages of plant, animal, human and even reaching for the divine. Because the human rational soul includes and transcends the plant and animal soul, human reason can train, discipline, and harmonize our animal souls in accordance with our human and divine ideals. How does reason train and discipline our animal appetites and desires? Human reason trains animal desires by means of habits. Aristotle says that to become good and wise requires three things: a good inherited natural constitution, the formation of good habits, and the right rational ideals.[26] Infants are born with natural powers; children develop those natural powers into habits; adults rationally direct their habitual powers into virtues.[27] In such a nested hierarchy, there is no loss in development: each stage includes and transcends the stages below it. Aristotle sees this same hierarchy in the ladder of nature: animals live by natural instinct, sometimes partially modified by training and habits, while human beings alone have reason.[28] Just as in the ladder of nature, habit bridges animals and humans, so in human development, habit bridges infancy and maturity. Habit perfects nature just as reason perfects habit.

While discussing the centrality of happiness in human life, Aristotle casually offers this observation: "of course, no child is happy."[29] In other places, Aristotle also takes it for granted that "no one in his right mind would want to return to childhood."[30] Aristotle is certainly aware that adults often describe children as being happy. How does he explain this common practice? He says that we call children happy when they are behaving as good little ladies and gentlemen. Children are only happy when they anticipate adult maturity.[31] I might observe parenthetically that we also praise brute animals when they mimic adult human beings—as when parrots talk, horses bow, or dogs shake hands. So we are consistent in our practices of praising!

Some of Aristotle's leading commentators have accused him of being a coldhearted bachelor who has contempt for childhood.[32] Yet it will be more illuminating to look to Aristotle's psychology, biology, and metaphysics rather than to his biography if we are to understand his provocative claims about children and the relationship of childhood to a complete human life. To understand why "no child is happy," we need to understand what Aristotle means by a child.

Children are best understood on the ladder of nature and in relationship to plants and animals. Being a plant is a lot like being asleep, and children spend a lot of time sleeping.[33] One step above plants are brute animals. Aristotle says that children cannot be happy for the same reason that an ox or horse or any other animal cannot be happy: children lack the capacity for reason and rational desire, which are the prerequisites for virtuous actions.[34] Moreover, no animal can participate in the rational activity of contemplation.[35] Aristotle insists that animals, like children, are capable of voluntary action but not rational choice.[36] Instead of pursuing happiness through rational choices, children and brute animals pursue pleasure.[37] Consequently, Aristotle says that we place no value on the esteem we receive from children and animals, and this fact in turn explains why we feel no shame before animals and small children.[38] Just as the ladder of nature ascends from the physical to the spiritual, the development of each individual ascends from the bodily and irrational soul to the rational soul.[39]

In Aristotle's hierarchy of moral traits we also see his recapitulation theory at work. He compares the most heinous human beings to beasts: a bestial person, he says, is below the level of either virtue or vice. We would call such a person "criminally insane." Indeed, he says that a human being without any sense of justice is the worst of all animals.[40] A merely vicious human being is more like a child. Aristotle treats moral development as a progression from animal to child to adult. The same tawdry pleasures, he says, appeal equally to boys and to foolish or bad adult men. Moral failure for Aristotle stems from arrested development: bestial and vicious adults are stuck at the level of brutes and children.[41]

That children often act like plants or animals does not mean that children simply are plants or animals. Every child is a potential adult or an adult in training. According to Aristotelian teleology, a child relates to an adult as would a part to the whole or as would the incomplete to the complete.[42] Aristotle illustrates how children relate to adults in his discussion of how natural virtue relates to true virtue. Children possess natural virtues, which are the seeds of true adult virtue. We often see in children an innate impulse to goodness, which lacks rational understanding of that good. Similarly, we also see spontaneous impulses to cruelty in children which also lack rational understanding. These childish impulses to good or bad fall short of true virtue or vice precisely because they are not subject to deliberate rational understanding and control. Whether these natural seeds actually develop into true virtue or vices will depend on the habits cultivated in children as they mature.[43] Aristotle observes the natural courage of child soldiers, which, he argues, is not admirable because it resembles the unthinking courage of brute animals. By contrast, the full virtue of courage involves an accurate perception of the dangers being faced.[44] Children have the seeds—but only the seeds—of true virtue.

If human development recapitulates the ladder of nature, then there is no good reason to want to return to childhood, since that would mean returning to a lower form of life. Aristotle says that just as no one wants to be a grazing animal, so we also have no good reason to return to childhood.[45] Because the higher stages include and transcend the lower stages, there is no loss in moving from animal to human or from child to adult. Since the human soul includes the animal and plant souls, the human person realizes all the excellences of plants and animals—plus the rational excellences. Similarly, the adult realizes all the excellences of a child—plus the rational excellences. In this development from incomplete to complete, there is no loss and no reason to prefer the lower to the higher.

To the extent that Aristotle defines human happiness and flourishing in terms of our physical, moral, and intellectual excellences, he is bound to devalue persons who are incapable of such attainments. Because Aristotle defines human capabilities according to the standard of mature, well-educated men who can master the full range of human excellence from combat to philosophy, he demotes slaves, women, and children to subordinate positions within the family and within the polis. According to this conception of the prime of life, children are so radically incomplete that Aristotle defines them as mere extensions of their parents. He says that it is not possible to act unjustly toward one's child any more than one might act unjustly toward oneself.[46] Given that we cannot in principle act unjustly to children, it is not surprising that Aristotle goes on to endorse mandatory infanticide for eugenics and mandatory abortion for population control.[47] Of course, these views were common in the ancient world, as was the life and death power of a father over his children.

Aristotle denies that young children love their parents: "parents love their children as soon as these are born, but children love their parents only after time has elapsed and they have acquired understanding or perception."[48] Aristotle implicitly acknowledges the asymmetry of parent-child love in other places. He endorses the principle that all benefactors love the benefited more than the benefited love their benefactors. Parents, he says, love their children more than their children love them; mothers love their children even more than do fathers.[49] Even artisans love their creations, he says, more than their creations would love them if they came to life. Poets, says Aristotle, dote on their poems as if they were their children.[50] These asymmetries flow from Aristotle's principle of virtue as an activity: the love expressed by benefactors is more active than the love expressed by the benefited. Accordingly, we love our children more than we love our parents because we work harder for our children, and mothers, who are the most active in caring for children, love children the most.[51] We should expect Pygmalion to love Galatea more than he is loved by her and Frankenstein to love his creature more than he is loved in return. However, Aristotle uses the same term (*philia*) to describe a mother's love for her child and a child's love for her mother. He claims that these loves differ only in degree.

Aristotle sees happiness as fundamentally rooted in the virtuous enjoyment of the primary goods of human life, especially citizenship and friendship. A central good of human life is citizenship; Aristotle famously defines human beings as political animals. Consistent with his focus on the exercise of capacities, Aristotle defines citizenship as the activity of ruling and being ruled, that is, the ability to exercise political offices, ranging from soldier to statesmen. This is why children and the elderly cannot be called citizens, except in a qualified sense.[52]

Another central human capability is that of forming true or character friendships: "anyone who is happy, then, must have excellent friends."[53] Here again, children and the elderly fail: since character friendships require the possession of a stable moral character and the rational choice of a worthy friend, children are excluded from true friendship. Inferior kinds of friendship, Aristotle says, "occur in children, brutes, and bad men."[54] Aristotle does admit that young adults are capable of friendships of pleasure but not of true friendships.[55] In fact, Aristotle argues that a good mature adult ought to strive to be his own best friend, which no brute animal or child can do.[56] Aristotle observes that friendship can serve to partially compensate for the defects of youth and old age: "It helps the young, too, to keep from error; it aids older people by ministering to their needs and supplementing the activities that are failing from weakness; those in the prime of life it stimulates to noble actions."[57] Since the function of true friendship of character is precisely to foster noble actions, we see here that only those in the prime of life enjoy the full meaning of friendship. As for the elderly, Aristotle says that they tend to be sour and ill-tempered, making it difficult for them to form any kind of friendships.[58]

The primacy of the prime of life is evident in Aristotle's denigration of play, the good most salient in childhood. In Greek, the words "child," "to play," and "education" all have the same root.⁵⁹ Aristotle says that adult life consists of three kinds of activities: occupation, which involves work that is necessary for sustaining mere life; play, which involves the relaxation necessary for sustaining occupation; and leisure, which involves the free activities that constitute living well. For Aristotle, play is subordinate to occupation, since play is the "recreation" of the energies required for work. He even compares play to medicine we must take to sustain our occupations.⁶⁰ Occupation and play are then subordinate to leisure, which is the time devoted to activities enjoyed purely for their own intrinsic value, especially politics and philosophy.⁶¹

From these principles of adult activities, Aristotle derives his principles for childhood education. Since "the first principle of all action is leisure," freeborn, male children must be protected from all purely vocational kinds of education and from any paid employment.⁶² These kinds of training, he says, stunt the body and mind. Still, children must be taught reading and writing, since these skills prepare them for both occupation and leisure. Aristotle also emphasizes the study of music, which prepares them for both leisure (by shaping their moral character) and for relaxation.⁶³ But Aristotle denies that we ought to educate the young in the arts of play: "Now obviously youths are not to be instructed with a view to their amusement, for learning is no amusement but is accompanied with pain." Aristotle even denies that boys should be introduced to the joys of intellectual activity: "Neither is intellectual enjoyment suitable to boys of that age, for it is the end, and that which is imperfect cannot attain the end."⁶⁴

Plato, on the other hand, frequently praises play not only for children but for adults as well. In the *Laws*, Plato argues that occupation is for the sake of leisure, and leisure is for the sake of play: "What, then, will be the right way to live? A man should spend his whole life at play—sacrificing, singing, and dancing—so that he can win the favor of the gods." The Athenian goes on to say that human beings are puppets in a divine play.⁶⁵ Through play, human beings participate in the cosmic play of the gods.

Since play is often associated with children, an association reflected in the Greek words, is Plato's endorsement of play an endorsement of childhood as a model for adults? Plato himself clearly associates play not so much with children as with the gods. The examples the Athenian gives of play in the crucial passage of the *Laws* (sacrificing, singing, and dancing) all refer to religious rituals, not to children's games.⁶⁶ Moreover, he says that human beings are like puppets in a divine theater: we are literally the playthings of the gods. By playing we imitate the gods more than we imitate children. Plato indeed tells us that God, not man, is the measure of all things, and that a good person imitates God.[67] What do we learn about human life if we adopt a divine perspective? We learn that the "serious" activities of adults look as ridiculous to the gods as the "serious" activities of children look to adults. The gods are as superior to human beings as adults are to children. This cosmic perspective ought to temper adult condescension to children.[68]

Aristotle's ethics and politics often pick up where Plato's *Laws* leaves off, and in the *Politics*, Aristotle follows Plato by agreeing that occupation is for the sake of leisure. But when it comes to what to do with our leisure, Aristotle breaks decisively from his teacher: "what ought we to do with our leisure? Clearly, we ought not to be playing, for then play would be the end of life." Leisure for Aristotle is a serious matter that ought to be devoted to philosophy and politics. Plato's cosmos is fundamentally ironic: from the standpoint of the gods, what human beings regard as serious activities are actually deeply hilarious, while what we regard as merely silly and playful turn out to be our most important and serious pursuits. There are faint traces of this Platonic irony in Aristotle's thought, but in general, Aristotle endorses the priority of the serious over the playful.[69]

In the *Nicomachean Ethics*, Aristotle repeatedly contrasts the virtue of the serious middle-aged man with the trivial amusements of the childish man of play. Aristotle quotes Anacharsis here with approval: "one should play for the sake of being serious."[70] Although Aristotle does recommend allowing children to play until they are six years old, after that childhood means preparation for adult life.[71] Whereas Plato's god is a god of play, Aristotle's god is a god of contemplation.[72] In short, Plato associates play with what is divine and Aristotle with what is childish.[73]

Aristotle follows Plato by arguing that adults should attempt to imitate the gods. Since happiness is a function of the transformation of potency into act, the gods enjoy full happiness, since they are pure actuality. He argues that happiness extends as far as does contemplative activity, which is the activity most characteristic of the gods. Divine beings are the most perfectly happy; human beings enjoy imperfect happiness; and "animals have no share in happiness." Aristotle even claims that no being can be happy that "does not have some share of a divine element in its nature."[74]

In the course of human development, we traverse the whole ladder of nature from plants to the gods. But the apex of human development is reached by the middle-aged person in what Aristotle calls the prime of life. Only a person in his prime who is able to actualize his full potential for moral and intellectual virtue and who has sufficient good fortune may be blessed with happiness. According to Aristotle, happiness stems from activities of the soul in accordance with virtue. We are happiest when we are at the top of our game in the prime of life. When we are young, we are only potentially happy, and when we are old, we have lost our happiness.[75] The most blessed and most fully complete life would be one in which childhood preparation and elderly decline were minimized so that the prime approximated the whole temporal extent of life. Aristotle's god, who is most perfectly happy, has no childhood and no old age: god is always in his prime.

CHAPTER 3

Development as Preformation in Augustine's *Confessions*

The theory of preformation seems incompatible with the whole notion of development. If something was already there from the beginning, then where do we find development? The biology of preformation is not limited to the theory of the *homunculus*, in which a little man hiding in the sperm or ovum simply grows larger. As we noted, many geneticists argue that the contemporary theory of the genome is a kind of preformationism. Nor is preformation limited to our genome: many other aspects of our life show the same continuity. In size and strength, an embryo or infant really is just a little adult. And our temperaments—even our particular loves and fears—often remain constant throughout our lives.

Augustine attempts to view human life from God's point of view (sub specie aeternitatis), that is, outside of time. This means that many aspects of our lives are preordained—whether in divine foreknowledge, in predestination, in the moment of creation, in Adam's fall, or even in our own preexistence. Augustine's thought about human life is full of seeming paradoxes: we have a free will to choose any course of action even though God knows in advance exactly what we will choose; nothing is more important than our choice whether to obey God even though our salvation was predestined before the world began.[1] One wonders why Augustine bothers to tell God the story of his early life in his *Confessions*, given that he insists that God knew how the story would end even before it began.

Augustine's *Confessions* is a book rich with paradox. While relating his life's journey, Augustine manages to be both excruciatingly intimate and highly conventional. He reveals his own lust, vanity, and arrogance within the familiar biblical narrative of being lost and then found, of sinning and of repenting, of turning away from and turning toward God. His story is uniquely his own and the story of every human soul.[2] The famous conversion scene under a fig tree in a garden—where Augustine suddenly picks up a Bible and reads a verse at random to discover his future—is certainly dramatic, if highly conventional. His tearful confession of his own sins strikes us as both self-abasing and self-aggrandizing: he persuades us that his humility is unsurpassed. What seems to be the story of Augustine's lifelong search for God turns out to be the story of God's search for him.[3]

At first reading, we are struck by the stark contrast between his life before and after his conversion to Catholic Christianity. He summarizes his emotional journey in the opening prayer to God: "our hearts are restless until they rest in you." We expect him to travel from disquiet to quietude, from misery to joy, from bondage into freedom. At a deeper level, however, *Confessions* is the story of the continuity of human life. Although he promises us a journey from restlessness to rest, Augustine remains agitated throughout, and even after his "conversion" we see Augustine berating himself for his continual sinning.[4] Augustine discovers that there is no rest to be found during his earthly sojourn.[5] He interrogates himself to the third degree from the time he was a nursing infant through the writing of his *Confessions*.[6] As we shall see, he was born a sinner and he dies a sinner, he was born a Christian and he dies a Christian, he was born seeking God and he dies seeking God. He was always wounding himself, and God was always healing him.[7]

What about his dramatic conversion? It turns out he experienced many conversions throughout his life.[8] Scholars describe him at various stages of life as being an ordinary pagan, a Manichaean, an Academic Skeptic, and a Neoplatonist. Yet his biographer suspects that throughout all of these stages, Augustine continued to practice his childhood Christian faith.[9] No doubt there were some genuine changes in his life: while always in need of help, he learned the hard way that he could not help himself. While always soul-sick, he learned how to find a doctor. But, looking back on his life, Augustine realized that he was entrusted to God's maternal care from the beginning. Although he sometimes felt himself far from God, he came to see that God was never far from him. The more Augustine changes, the more he remains the same. If we scrutinize our own life's journey, from infancy to midlife adulthood, with such energy and honesty, will our lives also seem preordained?

Among other things, Augustine's *Confessions* tells the story of his own life up to early middle age. Although Augustine is not the first author ever to tell the story of his own life, Augustine is a pioneer in the new genre of autobiography. Why is it ludicrous to imagine Aristotle writing an autobiography?[10] According to his own theory, Aristotle did not become Aristotle until he actualized his potential in his midlife. The chasm between his childhood animalism and his mature rationality is just too wide to be bridged by a narrative. Aristotle the boy and Aristotle the man do not have enough in common to be protagonists of the same story. If the past is a different country, then the boy Aristotle is a different species. Were we to ghostwrite Aristotle's autobiography for him, we would highlight the boy's adventures collecting bugs.

Autobiography depends on the capacity of a person to see his life as a whole, to see the seeds grow into the flower, to see the man in the boy and the boy in the man. Augustine taught us to see our lives as a whole, to see that everything we ever come to love or to fear is foreshadowed in our childhood loves and fears. Augustine blazed a new path to maturity, that is, to self-understanding—a path that circles back through childhood. That we now take this indirect route for granted shows how much we live in the world Augustine created.

Although Augustine attempts to see his own life as a whole, most readers do not see his *Confessions* as forming an integral whole. Books 1 through 9 are clearly autobiographical and relate selected events of Augustine's life in roughly chronological order. But Book 10 is devoted to a long discussion of the nature of memory, Book 11 to the nature of time, and Books 12 and 13 to an exegesis of the account of creation in the Bible. Even among scholars there is no agreement about how the final books relate to the autobiographical books. Augustine is often accused of being a bad writer,[11] and some translations of the *Confessions* simply omit the final three books.[12]

Yet these final books, with their account of God's eternity, the creation of the world, and the nature of time and of memory, provide us with the keys for understanding Augustine's autobiography. Augustine's philosophical commentary on the account of creation in Genesis in the *Confessions* led him, years later, to develop his theory of preformation through the "seminal reasons." Augustine's search for God by means of memory in the *Confessions* draws on the Platonic theory of preexistence known as "anamnesis." Augustine's learned about both of these kinds of preformationist theories from the books of the Platonists that he mentions reading in the

Confessions. Scholars agree that while in Milan, Augustine read the Latin translations of the works of the Greek Platonists Plotinus and Porphyry,[13] who indeed discuss both creation by means of seminal reasons (*logoi spermatikoi*) and knowledge as recollection of a past life (*anamnesis*). Let us briefly consider these preformationist theories to see how they illuminate Augustine's understanding of the shape of his own life. However improbable it may seem, encountering these Platonic theories of memory and of creation returned Augustine to himself.[14]

Augustine did not believe that he had special or privileged access to the truth about himself. He often expresses frustration at his inability to understand his own motives.[15] He famously said that man is a deep abyss—a mystery to himself.[16] Although it is often said that Augustine sought the truth about God by looking within himself, it is equally true that he sought the truth about himself by looking to God, especially God as revealed in Scripture and in philosophical speculation. Because he believes that God is closer to us than we are to ourselves, Augustine seeks to discover himself in God.[17]

Augustine frequently asks what it means to be created in God's image and likeness.[18] What does Scripture tell us about God? According to Augustine, Scripture, at least when interpreted philosophically, tells us that God is eternal. This does not merely mean that God has always lived or that he will never die; rather, God is outside of time entirely. God sees past, present, and future simultaneously.[19] According to Augustine, God created everything in the universe simultaneously and instantaneously. Space and time did not emerge until the universe came into being. The universe was not created in time but together with time.[20] The question of what God was doing *before* the creation makes no sense: the relation of time to eternity is not a temporal relation. The Bible describes six days of creation merely to make vivid to our simple minds what took place instantaneously and outside of time.[21]

When Augustine returned later in life to the exposition of the story of creation in Genesis, he adopted the ancient Greek theory of preformation to explain how instantaneous creation is compatible with development over time. In his *Literal Interpretation of Genesis*, Augustine sets forth a theory of "seminal reasons," which are the seeds of all development in the natural world. To understand this theory, let us briefly examine its origins in Greek philosophy. Parmenides, an early Greek philosopher, argued that change was paradoxical and illusory, since something which changes both remains the same and does not remain the same. Only what does not change, he said, is real, despite all appearances to the contrary. Parmenides's logically rigorous arguments against the reality of change forced his successors to attempt to account for change and development with greater sophistication. Anaxagoras, for example, responded to this challenge with his theory of primordial seeds. He agrees with Parmenides that nothing wholly new could ever arise or perish: "How could hair come from what is not hair or flesh from what is not flesh?" Everything must, then, arise from seeds which contain all the elements of the developed entity. Seeds are microcosms of the cosmic macrocosm.[22] This account of primordial seeds seeks to combine changelessness (everything already exists within the seed) with the reality of change (seeds do grow).

The Stoic philosophers later combined Anaxagoras's seeds with Aristotle's notion of reason to give us "seminal reasons." Aristotle argued that every organism contained an immanent principle or rationale of its own development—what he called its purpose (*logos* or *telos*) and what we might call its genome. Some Stoics argued that these seminal reasons originated in God's mind and led to the generation of every specific natural kind; other Stoics simply identified God with the seminal reasons.[23] Seminal reasons are latent causes of the generation of all things in accordance with the passage of time, again combining divine changelessness with the reality of corporeal change.[24] The reasons were divine and unchanging while the seeds contained the power of growth and change.

Augustine adapted the theory of seminal reasons from the Stoics and from Plotinus.[25] Unlike the Stoics, Augustine strongly distinguished the immaterial reasons in God's mind, which are the templates for all created entities, from the instantiation of those divine reasons in the matter of the seeds. The *causal* reasons in God's mind play a purely formal role in creation; the *seminal* reasons play a formal and material role in creation, just like all seeds. The instant of creation is when the divine reasons become the physical seeds of every created organism. These seeds are material but not visible; they are invisible potencies planted by God in the act of creation.[26] Here Augustine contrasts creation with development: all the seeds are created instantaneously, but they appear in history over the course of time, according to God's providential care.[27] As Augustine says: "just as the seed contains invisibly everything which later appears in the tree, so the earth possessed everything which was to appear in the course of time."[28]

Augustine knew from Scripture that all living organisms did not appear at the same moment on earth: plants preceded animals, and animals preceded man. Unlike modern literal interpretations of Genesis, Augustine is not committed to the idea that dinosaurs and humans lived together. His theory of seminal reasons enables God to create everything in the heavens and the earth simultaneously and instantaneously while also permitting the range of organisms to appear over the course of eons of natural history. The biblical six days of creation are interpreted to refer to the distinct epochs of indeterminate length over which the various organisms appeared on earth. This account, therefore, combines instantaneous creation with ongoing divine administration of the universe.[29]

Development, according to Augustine, is limited to organic life: the inorganic and the spiritual universe appeared fully formed at the instant of creation. What this means is that the physical earth, the heavenly bodies, the angels, and the soul of Adam were created instantaneously and simultaneously, in their finished form, at the moment of creation.[30] All the seminal reasons containing the potencies for every living organism also came into being at the instant of creation.[31] Every human body was created as a preformed seed at the moment of creation.[32] After all, says Augustine, we do not call parents the creators of men or farmers the creators of corn. Parents and farmers merely plant the seeds created by God.[33] The sequence in which each human body appears on earth and is joined by a rational soul is determined by God's administration of the natural order.[34] Augustine leaves open the question of whether Adam's soul alone was created in finished form in the beginning or whether every human soul was created in finished form in the beginning.[35] If Adam's soul alone was created in the beginning, then subsequent human souls could either be derived from Adam's soul or could be independently created with the generation of each human body.[36]

Augustine's theory of seminal reasons commits him to at least one form of the soul's preexistence.[37] Augustine never wavers from his view that Adam's soul was created before Adam's body. Recall that Adam's soul is created in finished form at the moment of creation, but Adam's body is preformed in a seminal reason, to be actualized later.[38] So Augustine is clearly committed to the preexistence of Adam's soul. Whether Augustine was ever committed to the preexistence of human souls generally is what I will now briefly consider.

Augustine's *Confessions* is the story of how Augustine searches for and discovers God both in Scripture and by means of his memory.[39] How could memory lead us to discover God? Perhaps we remember a vision of God from an earlier existence. According to Plato, our souls are immortal and preexisted long before entering our bodies at birth. During this preexistence, our souls saw and learned everything before forgetting what they had learned during the trauma of our birth.[40] What we call learning is actually remembering what we once knew. Indeed, some of the ways we ordinarily describe learning sometimes makes it sound like anamnesis. For example, we sometimes say that we recognize the truth or the correct answer, just as we recognize a person whom we once saw. It is difficult to understand how we could know that we found the truth or an answer unless we knew already what we were looking for. For example, one cannot look up a word in the dictionary without already knowing how it is spelled; and in solving math problems, how do we know when to stop unless we already knew the right answer. Socrates argues that in general we cannot search for anything, the truth included, unless we already know what it is. Many philosophers today agree that all learning, especially the learning of our native language, depends on knowledge we innately possess and, in a sense, recall.

Augustine often describes learning as a form of recollection, leading many scholars to assert that he once held this Platonic doctrine, which he learned from Plotinus.[41] In one early work, written before the *Confessions*, Augustine writes about our souls entering our bodies and then forgetting what they knew in their previous existence.[42] The *Confessions* are rich with the language of anamnesis—vision, memory, search, and recollection. Augustine describes his search for the one true God in terms of remembrance, as if he once knew but then forgot his God. Augustine follows Socrates closely by asking: How could I know that I have found the true God—rather than some false god—unless I recognize Him? In Augustine's version of Platonic preexistence, each person's soul originally existed with God and with knowledge of divine happiness, which we lost when we fell into our earthly bodies.[43] In this view, we begin our existence as souls or souls with purely "spiritual" bodies in the vision of divine splendor, but then we fall into our earthly bodies from which we must attempt the ascent back to our heavenly home.[44]

Certainly, there are many echoes of this idea of preexistence in the *Confessions*. Augustine acknowledges that he has a body, but he identifies with his soul alone.[45] Augustine even rehearses Plato's argument that we cannot find something unless we already remember what it is. "How then shall I find you, if I do not remember you?"[46] In one place, Augustine seems to describe this preexistent vision of God: "You took me up that I might see that what I saw existed, and that I, the seer, did not yet exist."[47] Similarly, Augustine points out that we all seek happiness. Yet how could we look for happiness if we did not already know what it is? But when did we experience the perfect bliss that we now crave? "I ask simply if happiness is a thing remembered—for how could we love it if we did not recognize it? . . . For happiness is not seen by the eye, like a physical object."[48] Scholars now generally agree that Augustine relies on a theory of Platonic preexistence, at least in his early works, including *Confessions*.[49]

Augustine grounds human life in a metaphysics of preformation and even preexistence. He insists that we cannot understand our temporal journey except against the backdrop of our timeless soul. Our heavenly home exists outside of time, but our created world and our very selves are dispersed and dissolved into past, present, and future.[50] We never fully see the whole of our lives, only a succession of parts over time.[51] In this false and merely visible world, things rise and fall, grow and decline, are born and die.[52] We cannot understand the whole because we never see the whole: we are mired in the temporal parts. We are tormented by our desires for temporal things that soon pass away. If only we could see the whole, we would not become so attached to mere parts. If only we could see our lives—past, present, and future—as a whole, as God sees us. Then we would not make so many mistakes that stem from seeing our lives only in parts.[53] Young people, especially, are prone to see the end of an episode in life as the end of life itself. How many suicides stem from this failure to see or even imagine the whole of our lives?

To see our lives as a whole, we attempt to see ourselves as God sees us. What is human life like sub specie aeternitatis? Because we are made in the image of God, we do have some capacity to see our lives as a whole. We can participate, to a limited extent, in God's eternal perspective: "You see not temporally, work not temporally, rest not temporally, but you make us see in time, and see time itself, and see the release from time."[54] God invites us to share at least partly in his timelessness. God's eternity is an eternal now: past and future are contained in the present.[55] How do we share in God's eternal present? When Augustine investigates our subjective experience of time, he notes that our minds can stretch to bring past and future together into a present moment.[56] What is the past, he says, except present memory? And what is the future, except our present anticipation? Our minds stretch forward to anticipate the future and backward to recall the past. Subjective time is simply the capacity of our minds to stretch backward through memory and forward through anticipation, thus bringing past and future into a moving present moment.[57]

Augustine illustrates this eternal present with the example of reciting (that is, singing) a memorized psalm. Before starting, he anticipates the future lines; and as he recites, he remembers what he has already read, so that the whole psalm, though recited over time, exists simultaneously in the stretched duration of the present. He says that his mind reaches in opposite directions by anticipating the future lines and remembering the past ones. As he recites, anticipation shrinks and memory grows until anticipation ends and the completed psalm is deposited into memory.[58] Augustine explicitly notes that the shape of a human life looks just like this: at every moment, we anticipate the future and remember the past. As we age, anticipation wanes and memory waxes. Augustine seeks to give his life the narrative unity of a psalm.[59] Psalms usually move from distress to comfort, from danger into safety, and from doubt into faith. Yet Augustine's own life does not seem to share this narrative arc.[60] We do not know the whole of our lives as well as we know a psalm. What gives Augustine's life its unity is the recurring tone of his prayer. Like the psalmist, Augustine finds the truth of his life in the plaintive tone of his honest appeal to God.[61]

Through our ability to stretch our minds from the past into the future, we share, however imperfectly, in the timeless present of God. Given God's ability to see his life as a whole, Augustine even asks why he arranges his life's story in temporal sequence.[62] Time is simply not as real as the eternal now. The truth of Augustine's life is in his ever-renewed, present-moment devotion to God, not in his memories or expectations. It is for the reader's benefit, not God's, that Augustine relates the story of his life in chronological order.

～

In the aftermath of the Romantic idealization of childhood innocence, readers of Augustine's *Confessions* are usually shocked by his descriptions of the sinful depravity of even newborn babies. Augustine tells us that he cannot remember his own infancy, but he tries to reconstruct his own experience as an infant from his observations as an adult of other infants—including, probably, his own son.[63] What does Augustine see when he observes infants? He claims that he saw one infant consumed with envy at the sight of his nursing sibling.[64] Although nature provides infants with everything they need in the form of a nursing mother, Augustine notices that infants are not satisfied with having their natural needs met. Infants demand that their wants be met, as well. Here, the contrast with brute animals is clear: puppies and kittens are satisfied by having their needs met, human babies already have unlimited wants.

How do infants, who by definition cannot speak,[65] make their wants known to the adults around them? Augustine interprets the crying of babies as an aggressive attempt to coerce adults to meet not just their needs but also their wants. When adults do not meet all of their wants, babies take revenge by crying: "I threw a tantrum because adults did not obey a child, free people were not my slaves. So I inflicted on them my revenge of wailing."[66] Augustine cannot help but notice the irrationality of this behavior: babies demand even things that are harmful to them, and they tantrum if adults withhold what is harmful.[67] Instead of living in harmony with an external world that is meeting its natural needs, the human baby confronts that world with unreasonable and unlimited wants and then takes revenge when those wants are not fully granted.[68]

In this crying baby, Augustine sees the permanent pattern of human life. Unlike other animals, the human animal is out of sync with her natural setting. We are not satisfied by having our needs met because we can imagine wants without limit; we can also imagine not having our basic needs met, creating anxiety. No matter how securing and nourishing our actual world is, it will never conform to our imagined world. For this reason, the world appears to us as potentially or actually hostile. With human wants unlimited by natural needs, this anxious grasping at objects is what Augustine called "concupiscence." Here we find not just the seed but the full pattern of the adult frenzied pursuit of sex, power, and possessions.[69] The objects pursued change over the course of our lives, but not the underlying anxiety and frustration in a world hostile to our imagined wants. If only we could accept our place in the natural order, as do puppies and kittens, and trust God and our parents to care for us. Here we see the intimate relationship of disordered wants to pride. Our refusal to accept our place in the natural ecology of needs leads us to an aggressive desire to dominate others. Augustine "recalls" throwing tantrums when adults would not submit to being ruled by infants or when free people would not become his slaves. Many of our needs can be met only with the cooperation of others, so in our anxious and disordered pursuit of our wants, we seek to manipulate and control those around us. Augustine recalls his days as a schoolboy when he lied to his teachers and parents in order to indulge his trivial desires.[70] Pride in refusing to accept our proper place leads to disordered desires, which in turn cause us to manipulate and control other people.

Augustine strongly emphasizes the primordial and permanent character of human sin. Not only are we born to sin, we are conceived in sin.[71] Human life is not a journey from childhood innocence into adult sin—we were always sinners. The fact that, according to Augustine, human beings after Adam were never in a state of innocence shows why Augustine does not consider each human life to recapitulate the history of the human race. Adam enjoyed a state of innocence denied to all his progeny.[72] Augustine emphasizes the sinful wretchedness of infancy, not because infancy is especially sinful, but to underscore the sinful wretchedness of the human condition.[73]

Augustine is aware that many people consider small children to be morally innocent. Yes, he tells us, small children are innocent, but only in the most literal sense of the word "innocent," which means "not harming" (*innocens*). Small children want to harm and try to harm themselves and others, but they are incapable of doing so because of their physical weakness: "The harmlessness of babes is in their body's effect, not their mind's intent."[74] He says that a baby's tantrums are regarded as trifles because the baby is so tiny; we would not tolerate a tantrum in a grown-up, who is dangerous. We grow out of our tantrums in the sense that we learn to control our own limbs, but we do not grow out of the frustrations and anger that lead to tantrums.[75] From the time he was still in his mother's womb until the moment he writes his *Confessions*, Augustine describes—and indeed, berates—himself for being a sinner.[76]

Still, human nature is complex. We were created good but, with Adam, we fell into corruption. The permanent truth of our good created nature is that we depend on the grace of God every moment of our lives for sustenance. Our radical dependence on God is nowhere more evident than in our infancy. When Augustine sees a baby nursing, he credits God with the milk and the natural instincts that bring mother and baby together: "my God, my rescue at every stage."[77] A baby also perfectly exemplifies the beauty and intelligent design of the human body, including our wholesome natural instincts.[78] With both a good created nature and a corrupt fallen nature, every infant is a complete paradigm of the human condition: "Infancy, indeed, starts this life not with smiles but with tears; and this is, in a way, an unconscious prophecy of the troubles on which it is entering."[79] At the same time, when we are "born again" in the spirit of Christ, we must return to our infancy, this time trusting God to satisfy all our true needs. Augustine repeatedly compares the state of grace to that of a baby blissfully nursing: if only we could recover the trust we never truly had in God's bounteous sustenance.[80] Augustine returns to infancy in his own "conversion" experience.

As Augustine relates his growth from speechless infancy to verbal childhood, he wonders what these stages really mean. He asks whether *I*, that is, his deepest sense of himself, actually went from infancy to childhood. Or was it merely his body that developed? How could his infancy leave him? Where did it go?[81] What part of us changes as we grow up, and what part remains the same? Augustine notes that he did develop in the sense that he learned to speak. And elsewhere he asserts that an infant or child lacks the full development of his physical body. When infants or children die, he assures us, they will rise again with fully developed, adult bodies.[82] What this means is that human beings in heaven are neither adults nor children even though everyone will have a fully developed body.

Augustine's childhood and schooling exemplify his permanent status as simultaneously sinner and saved. He memorably describes himself as "so little in size but so large in sin."[83] The terror of being beaten, whipped, slapped, rebuked, and otherwise tormented by his teachers and parents dominates Augustine's memories of his early school years.[84] Augustine displays very poignant sympathy for himself as a boy, dreading yet another painful and humiliating beating. He says that we should not make light of a schoolboy fearing his punishment any more than we would make light of an adult facing the rack, tearing hooks, and the other instruments of torture.[85] He compares his school punishments to the trials of the martyrs![86] Augustine observes that all those beatings only strengthened his resolve to defy his teachers; he observes as well that no amount of physical torment could succeed in forcing him to learn Greek, while he enjoyed learning Latin without any need for intimidation.[87] He also notes that his teachers were just as terrified of social ostracism as were his fellow students: in his school, there were no grown-ups.[88] He compares his childish competitions for winning trifles to the so-called adult competitions for gold, estates, and slaves. The stakes change, but the vanity, pride, and greed remain the same. So much for the innocence of children—or of adults.[89] Yet, Augustine notes that Jesus himself praised the humility of little children by saying: "Unless you become like one of these little ones, you cannot enter the Kingdom of Heaven." Why would Jesus command adults to emulate the humility of children, when Augustine knows that he was already puffed up with vanity as a child? Augustine concludes that Jesus must have been referring only to the small stature of children. The humility of children, then, is purely physical, not ethical or spiritual.[90] Children and adults differ mainly in size.[91]

Later in life, Augustine would sometimes disparage childhood in stark language reminiscent of Aristotle: "in fact is there anyone who, faced with the choice between death and a second childhood, would not shrink in dread from that latter prospect and elect to die."[92] Aristotle and Augustine, however, have very different reasons for disparaging childhood. Aristotle says that we would not return to childhood for the same reason that we would not wish to become a grazing animal: Who wants to surrender his human rational faculties? Augustine's stated preference for death over a second childhood comes in the context of looking back on the beatings he received in school.[93] Even in old age, Augustine looks back in horror at his scholastic torments. Although he conceded that those beatings were not for him morally or even academically improving, Augustine thought they were improving for others, so he never denounced the practice of corporal punishment at home or in school. What is worse, his own doctrine of original sin became the most common justification for corporal punishment from the Middle Ages to the late nineteenth century. Given Jesus's praise of children and his tender care for them, one might have expected Christians to reject harsh corporal punishment of children. But the doctrine of original sin provided a convenient justification for treating even little children as hardened criminals. Few people have suffered more from corporal punishment than Augustine, so it is sadly ironic that his thought became the most influential justification for it.[94]

It is often said that Augustine was raised as a Roman pagan and became a Christian only as an adult. Although Augustine's mother was always a Christian, his education was the sole responsibility of his father, who was not then a Christian. Augustine claims, however, that he was a Catholic Christian catechumen from the moment of his birth: "I was signed already with his cross, seasoned with his salt, when I left the womb of my mother." During a childhood illness, Augustine says he prayed fervently to God and begged his mother to be baptized. He says that everyone in his household had Christian faith except for his father.⁹⁵ Whatever Augustine's spiritual wanderings later in life, he was already indelibly marked and set aside for Christ from his birth. If there is such a thing as the baptism of desire, then Augustine was already baptized as a small child. Moreover, in the fourth century, it was common for a person to consider himself a Catholic Christian long before baptism.⁹⁶ Did Augustine "become" a Christian as an adult or simply grow into his Christian faith gradually over time? In so many ways, then, Augustine the man is already there in Augustine the boy.

Augustine's account of his own life can be embarrassingly intimate yet at the same time so full of familiar biblical conventions that scholars wonder whether he massaged the details of his own life to fit biblical narratives or whether he massaged his interpretations of the Bible to mirror his personal narrative. The parallel between the biblical story of the forbidden fruit leading to the sin of Adam and the story Augustine tells of his teenage theft of a neighbor's pears is especially striking. At age sixteen, Augustine essentially reenacted Adam's original sin by stealing pears from a neighbor's orchard. Augustine's reflection on this incident helped to persuade him of the limits of Platonism, since a Platonist would interpret this theft as reflecting the triumph of physical appetite over rational virtue. In this view, Augustine knew that it was wrong to steal the fruit, but his appetite overcame his rational scruples. But Augustine came to reject this Platonic interpretation: he recalls clearly that he never even ate the pears he stole. So, if he never ate the pears, why on earth would he steal them?

To discover the answer to this puzzle, he studied the biblical story. When the serpent seduces Eve, he does not appeal to her appetite but to her pride: "if you eat, you shall become like God."⁹⁷ Eve was tempted, not by her bodily appetite for fruit but by her spiritual vanity. Augustine concluded that, according to the Bible, sin originates, not in bodily appetite but in spiritual pride.⁹⁸ When reflecting on his own theft, Augustine also sees nothing but spiritual perversity and the desire to be God: "I dined on the crime itself, which is what I wanted to savor. If I tasted any of the pears, it was the crime that had flavor for me." By doing what was forbidden and escaping punishment, Augustine felt a godlike omnipotence: "by the love of my own robbery, was I imitating you—in, admittedly, some grotesque and twisted way?"⁹⁹ Just like Eve, the adolescent Augustine wants to be divine, not merely human. Deeper than any merely bodily desire is the spiritual perversity of pride, of thinking that we are better than other people and that ordinary moral or legal rules do not apply to us. Augustine insists that he would not have committed this theft were it not for the encouragement of his friends. Again, his pride, or more precisely, his vanity, leads him to fear shame before his friends rather than shame before God.[100]

At every stage of his life, Augustine tells us that he was torn between two wills, one physical and one spiritual, and that the conflict was shattering his soul.[101] Augustine is very hard on himself as a teenager: "I burned to be engorged with vile things. . . . Is there any crime I might *not* have committed, who could love a crime without motive?" Yet, at the same time, he sees himself as always belonging ultimately to Christ: "By your mercy, my innocent heart had devoutly drunk in that name [Christ] with my mother's milk, and stored it deep within."[102] As he grows into intellectual maturity, Augustine notes the paradox that he was closer to God as a small child. All of his immense learning has only drawn him deeper into false understandings of God. He reflects that he would have been better off as an uneducated child who never strayed from mother church.[103] At least small children know that they are not self-sufficient, that they depend on adults and ultimately on God for their sustenance. Augustine the adult believed that he was "captain of his soul," but his adult independence led to his own moral and spiritual ruin. Augustine asks: "And what is any man whosoever if he is but a man?" Unless we can recapture our childlike dependence on God, we adults are lost.[104] Adulthood, says Augustine, is overrated. His only son, Adeodatus, died in the love of God at age sixteen; Augustine tell us that he does not regret his son's early death.[105] Each of us can find his savior at any age. Compared to eternity, what significance is there to the human life span?

As an adult, Augustine continually looks back into his past—sometimes to measure his distance from his childhood and sometimes to attempt to recapture aspects of his childhood. Recall that when he was gravely ill as a boy, he pleaded for baptism; but when also perilously ill as a young man, Augustine did not look to baptism. In this case, he was wiser as a boy.[106] To see one's life as a whole is to look ahead in one's youth and to look back in one's maturity. When he decides to become an adult catechumen in the Catholic Church at Milan, he notes that he was resuming the status he had assumed as an infant.[107] At age thirty, as he studies Christian doctrine and scriptures with Ambrose, he rejoices in returning to the church of his childhood, when "the name of Christ had marked me as a child."[108] Looking back on this wayward youth, Augustine notes his unchanging faith in

Christ; yes, his youthful faith was fuzzy and hazy but tenacious.[109] In addition to looking back on his childhood, Augustine—in the throes of being born again in the Milan garden—returns to his infancy by losing control of his limbs.[110] Augustine's progress toward spiritual maturity is possible only by a return to childlike helplessness. Ever since, we have all recognized the impossibility of truly growing up without revisiting and recapturing aspects of childhood.

Scholars debate the question of precisely when Augustine "returned" to the Catholic Church.[111] But according to Augustine, he never left the Church. Where outsiders see a dramatic "conversion" in the Milan garden or a series of conversions, Augustine emphasizes the continuity of his relationship to God.[112] After all, the fact that Augustine might have strayed from God does not mean that God ever strayed from Augustine: "To you, earliest and latest beauty, I was slow in love."[113] Augustine's journey in life was indeed a conversion—but only in the original meaning of that word, namely, the act of returning.[114] Augustine saw our lives essentially as a journey away from and then back to God.[115] His favorite images of human life were the parable of the prodigal son and the wanderings of Ulysses—both stories, like Augustine's own, of homecoming. Our beginning is also our end.

CHAPTER 4

Development as the Recapitulation of History in Rousseau

Whereas the ancients looked to nature to find the meaning of human life, moderns tend to look to history. The pivot between ancient and modern views of human life is the Bible, which presents itself as a divinely guided history of the human race, from the creation of the cosmos in Genesis to the end of the world in Revelation. Since ancient times, readers of the Bible have seen their own lives recapitulate the first chapters of Genesis. Just as Adam and Eve were created good and innocent, but then fell into disobedience, sin, and shame, so each human person is born (at least relatively) good and innocent but then inexorably falls into sin. We saw that Augustine interprets his own life in relation to the history of the human race in the Bible. In the story of Adam's fall, Augustine sees his own sin and disobedience; in the story of Jesus, Augustine sees his own hope for redemption. Yet Augustine denies that Adam's progeny ever experienced a state of moral innocence—unlike Adam, we are already conceived in sin. For this reason, Augustine's account of human development is not truly a recapitulation of biblical history. Having found so much meaning in the sacred history of the Bible, Augustine then sought to discover the meaning of secular history. His book *The City of God* is an attempt to discern divine purpose in the history of the Roman Empire. Many medieval and modern philosophers, ranging from Joachim of Fiore and Giambattista Vico to Hegel and Marx, have also attempted to find the meaning of human life in a theory of history. Although the idea that a human life recapitulates the history of our species may strike us as fantastical, recall that Sigmund Freud, Stanley Hall, Carl Jung, and Jean Piaget all compared human development to historical evolution—and children to "savages."

Jean-Jacques Rousseau's investigation of human nature is structured around a set of analogies between the history of the human race and the development of each individual person. Although Rousseau never refers explicitly to a "noble savage," he does argue that simpler and more rustic societies did have virtues that have been generally lost in European urban civilization. When a modern European person develops from innocent goodness in childhood to sophisticated corruption in adulthood, he is recapitulating the history of the human race. In the case of Aristotle, we are certain that he developed his theory of the ladder of nature independently of his theory of individual human development. No one thinks that Aristotle's ladder of nature is a recapitulation of human development.[1] In the case of Rousseau, the priority of theories is not so clear. Rousseau's account of human history is clearly shaped by his account of human development, just as his account of human development is shaped by his account of human history. Whatever the true priority, Rousseau and his commentators frequently draw analogies and comparisons between his histories and his developmental narratives.[2] Although I shall draw on all of Rousseau's published works, the focus of this chapter will be a careful comparison of Rousseau's account of human history in the *Discourse on the Origins of Inequality* (*Second Discourse*) with his account of individual human development in *Emile*.

Rousseau is famous for the rhetorically dramatic openings of his major treatises, which encapsulate the whole argument in a memorable aphorism. For example, the opening of *Emile*: "Everything is good as it leaves the hands of the Author of things; everything degenerates in the hands of man."[3] This dictum applies equally well to the history of the human race and to the development of each individual person in modern society. Perhaps even more familiar is the opening of Rousseau's *Social Contract*: "Man is/was born free, and everywhere he is in chains."[4] To say that "man *was* born free and everywhere he is in chains" refers to human history, in which our primeval natural freedom has been irretrievably lost during the rise of civilization. To say that "man *is* born free and everywhere he is in chains" refers to the development of every modern person, who is born to freedom but loses it to the corrupt customs of domination and servility in all civilized societies. Finally, Rousseau offers us his "great principle" that "nature made man happy and good, but that society depraves him and makes him miserable."[5] Here again individual development recapitulates human history.

Rousseau's enemies often accused him of arguing that Europeans should abandon civilization and return to a primitive or rustic society. But Rousseau insisted throughout his life that we could no more return to prehistoric society than an adult could return to the naivety of childhood.[6] Individual human development and historical evolution are both irreversible for the same reason: knowledge destroys innocence forever.[7] As Rousseau put it: "Human nature does not go backward, and it is never possible to return to the times of innocence"—a dictum that applies to development as much as to history.[8] You cannot go home again. Indeed, in Genesis an angel with a flaming sword blocks our return to Paradise. Rousseau defines human nature in terms of our capacity for learning, which he calls our "perfectibility." Of course, for Rousseau, perfectibility is more likely to be morally corrupting than morally uplifting. For better or worse, the law of perfectibility explains why we cannot ever return to naive simplicity. The education of each person recapitulates the perfectibility of the human species over time. We teach children the lessons acquired by all of human history, in abbreviated form. Rousseau's education of his imaginary pupil, Emile, adopts the maxim of education through recapitulation: "Teach the oldest things to the youngest people." Emile's development encapsulates the history of the human race.

Rousseau's natural history of man begins with his critique of seventeenth-century "state of nature" theory. In these thought experiments, philosophers such as Thomas Hobbes and John Locke attempt to imagine the human condition outside of any political community, in order to understand why human beings would construct a body politic. Although Hobbes and Locke sometimes imply that the "state of nature" is historically prior to the rise of polities, they also insist that the international society of states is also a state of nature, since there is no world government. A state of nature exists whenever human beings relate to each other outside of political authority. State of nature theorizing is a way to understand human nature and begins with Socrates's story of the ring of Gyges. In this myth, Gyges discovers a ring that makes him invisible—and to be invisible is to exist outside of any political community or authority. What does Gyges do in the state of nature? He murders the king and seduces the queen.

Socrates's interlocutors interpret this story as a thought experiment about the deep proclivity to injustice in human nature: when we are under surveillance and political control, we repress our true nature, but once we are invisible and outside of politics, we express our true nature. Rousseau objects to this inference. He claims that Gyges's conduct reflects not human nature but social corruption. Rousseau would argue that Gyges was already full of socially induced pride and envy before he found the ring. In fact, Rousseau tells us that if he personally had been in possession of Gyges's magic ring, he would use it only to bring happiness to every human being.[9]

Rousseau sometimes describes his forays into man's original condition as "hypothetical," revealing its debt to seventeenth-century state of nature theories. But Rousseau's speculative history is more than merely a thought experiment about human nature. Rousseau really believes that we can understand ourselves only through the study of what he revealingly calls "the first embryo of the species."[10] Given the lack of much direct evidence of human prehistory, Rousseau looked to contemporary travel reports of "primitive and savage" societies around the globe. Here, Rousseau assumes, without argument, that the backward peoples of his own day must resemble our remote ancestors. What most sharply distinguishes Rousseau's state of nature from that of Hobbes is that Rousseau claims that prehistoric man radically differs from contemporary man.[11] Indeed, men in Hobbes's state of nature embody the competitive and possessive individualism of Hobbes's own day.[12] According to Rousseau, Hobbes's account of the "war of all against all" describes the societies of contemporary Europe, not the state of nature.[13]

Rousseau's experimental investigation of human nature went beyond state of nature theorizing. Although Rousseau is often described as someone who naively asserts the "natural goodness of human nature," he was quite realistic about the profound wickedness and corruption of virtually all human beings in existing social circumstances. Not only are human beings generally quite bad, but we seem to be getting worse, suggesting that our badness cannot be natural. According to Rousseau, pure natural goodness can be attributed only to primordial man in the state of nature—a state, says Rousseau, that is now irretrievably lost. A qualified kind of natural goodness is theoretically possible in a few circumstances, however improbable these are in practice. Our vices all stem from our inability to live with other human beings while remaining ourselves. In society, we are tragically torn between our authentic self and our social self. We serve others for selfish reasons, and we manipulate others for selfless reasons. Social man oscillates unstably between extreme egoism and extreme altruism: "he is the man who, when dealing with others, thinks only of himself, and, on the other hand, in his understanding of himself, thinks only of others."[14] Once we exit the state of nature, says Rousseau, we cannot live happily either with other human beings or without them.[15]

Rousseau's proposals for recapturing a measure of the happiness which is our birthright are rather extreme but quite logical. Either we submerge our individuality completely into a collective general will or we withdraw entirely from social life.[16] The collective solution requires the cultivation of civic virtue with the rigor of Spartan discipline.[17] The individualist solution requires a philosopher to withdraw from society into solitude so that he might find his true natural self within[18] or for him to be raised and educated apart from corrupting social influence, under the guidance of a philosopher.[19] All of these theoretical solutions are highly improbable in practice, and it is not clear how much hope Rousseau had in his own remedies.[20] Emile's growth from physical relations to moral relations to civic relations closely parallels the evolution of the human race from the state of nature through household economy and into civic virtue. Rousseau says about his story of Emile's development: "This ought to be the history of my species."[21] Emile's story is the history of humanity.

Rousseau strikes a pose of Socratic ignorance when discussing primordial man and when discussing children. He claims that we know nothing about human nature and that we know nothing about childhood.[22] Reading these together, we can see that one reason that childhood is unknown is that childhood gives us a clear picture of human nature.[23] Our nature has been largely effaced by the course of human history and by our own upbringing. Both history and development serve to estrange us from our own deepest selves. Curiously, Rousseau sounds utterly confident in his capacity as an old man to discover his own human nature in his autobiographies. Somehow, his own social prejudices, faults, follies, and vanities did not obscure his natural goodness.[24]

Rousseau insists that primeval man resembles other primates more than he resembles modern man. What accounts for Rousseau's confidence that our remote ancestors were almost wholly unlike us? Alone among his contemporaries, Rousseau adopts a conception of "deep time" in his natural history of man.[25] Whereas biblical history spans a mere six thousand years, Rousseau claims that human history actually spans hundreds of thousands, if not millions, of years.[26] This immensely greater scale of time permits profound transformations of human beings, even at an imperceptible rate of change.[27] If human history were limited to the scale of biblical history, then it is no wonder that the prehistoric man in Hobbes's and Locke's state of nature appears so similar to us. But if human history spans millions of years, then primordial man might well be startlingly different from us.

Rousseau argues that primordial man differs from us as much as an infant differs from an adult. Hobbes's man in the state of nature is unmistakably an adult: competitive, possessive, and violent; Rousseau's man in the state of nature is more like an infant: without reason, without speech, and timid.[28] Rousseau even calls the first man in the state of nature an overgrown newborn: "This man-child would be a perfect imbecile, an automaton, an immobile and almost insensible statue."[29]

Rousseau frequently describes natural man as an animal—but an animal with a difference.[30] Early man might originally act in ways indistinguishable from other animals. Yet unlike brute animals, says Rousseau, man alone has a "faculty of self-perfection" both as an individual and as a species. After a few months, an animal is all that it will ever be; after a year, a species is the same as after a thousand years.[31] To use the language of Aristotle, natural man is actually a brute primate but potentially a rational man. This is how Aristotle describes an infant: a creature who actualizes his animal soul but who possesses a rational soul. Rousseau points out that infants recapitulate our natural history by first walking on all fours and then on two feet.[32] Rousseau tells us that our perfectibility is evident in our long infancy and childhood—human beings are immature longer than any other species.[33] Our long childhood enables us to perfect ourselves. The way Rousseau describes newborn infants applies equally well to primeval natural man: "We are born weak, we need strength; we are born totally unprovided [with instincts], we need aid; we are born stupid, we need judgment."[34] Rousseau directly compares natural man to children when he comments on how slowly we evolve: "the species was already old, and man remained ever a child."[35] Natural man was also innocent like small children.[36]

Traditionally, human beings were defined as social animals or linguistic animals. But Rousseau insists that natural man lived in isolation because he lacked both language and reason.[37] Social life is dysfunctional for man, says Rousseau, because we were not evolved for society. Only after many centuries of evolution did language appear in early human beings. In both infants and in primeval man, language first emerges as a way to express our passions: man's first language, both as a species and as infants, is "the cry of nature."[38] Rousseau even tells us that to study the origin of human language we need only observe infants.[39] The way Rousseau characterizes primordial human language clearly comes from observing children, as when he describes early man using onomatopoetic words and one-word sentences.[40] Rousseau tells us that Emile "will use speech with all the simplicity present in its first founding."[41]

Instead of being tormented by jealousy, envy, spite, and other social passions—or haunted by the past or anxious for the future—man in the state of nature feels only delight in the sheer fact of his present existence. Primeval man enjoys the goodness of his own present vitality and condition.[42] In discussing Emile's development, Rousseau argues that, at birth, Emile lacks the pleasant sentiment of his own existence. As Emile moves his limbs and perceives the world around him, he begins to delight in the goodness of his own life.[43] How do natural man and baby Emile escape the social anxieties of civilized adults? Like all other animals, we are born with a healthy kind of love of self that Rousseau calls *amour de soi*. This love is what motivates us to protect our lives and promote our own well-being. Because we love ourselves, we delight in the sentiment of our own existence, just as we delight in the existence of anything we love. As human beings enter society, however, we develop a different kind of self-love, which Rousseau calls *amour propre*—a love of ourselves in relation to other people. Rousseau distinguishes two kinds of *amour propre*, namely, vanity and pride. With this pathological kind of self-love, we lose any direct relationship to our own self; instead, we love ourselves only in the eyes of others. We come to value our reputation more than our actual self. When Rousseau describes both natural man and small children as innocent, he means precisely that they love themselves directly and absolutely, without any invidious comparisons to other people.[44] Rousseau sees the beginning of pride in spoiled infants who use crying to manipulate adults. To prevent the premature emergence of pride, Rousseau offers this maxim for child-rearing: give a child everything that it needs and nothing that it wants.[45]

Man in the state of nature, says Rousseau, was a vegetarian.[46] Rousseau believes that this diet reflects his peaceful nature: carnivorous animals, he says, are violent and cruel.[47] Interestingly, Rousseau does not mention that Adam and Eve in Paradise were also vegetarian (Gen. 1:29). Rousseau argues that the best proof that primordial man was vegetarian is the fact that children prefer fruits and vegetables to meat.[48] Rousseau even quotes Plutarch's tirade against meat eating to prove that hunting, killing, butchering, and eating animals makes human beings cruel and violent. Rousseau then insists that we not "denature" children by feeding them meat—not to protect their health, but to protect their character.[49] In this case, as in many others, it is difficult to know whether Rousseau's account of human history is shaping his account of human development or vice versa.

According to Rousseau, many adults misinterpret the violent displays of anger of small children or of savages as evidence of natural human wickedness. Recall that Aristotle compares the tantrums of small children to the intemperance of bad adults. Adult vices, says Aristotle, often reflect arrested development, for bad adults remain children. We saw that Augustine argued that an infant is innocent only in the physical sense that an infant cannot harm due to sheer weakness. In Augustine's view, the only difference between a wicked infant and a wicked adult is power and strength. Thomas Hobbes also compares a bad adult to an overgrown child. However, Hobbes says that children lack both the strength and the willful malice of wicked adults, so that a bad man resembles but is not morally the same as an overgrown child.

Rousseau picks up this theme by first accusing Hobbes of saying that an "evil man is a robust child."[50] Rousseau then wonders if natural man is also a robust child.[51] Rousseau develops Hobbes's thought experiment by imagining an overgrown child who would beat his mother or strangle his brother when inconvenienced by them.[52] Few things are more terrifying than the combination of the ferocity of a child's tantrum with the strength of an adult man. Just as Hobbes exculpates the child from accusations of wickedness, so Rousseau exculpates natural man and contemporary savages from the same accusation. Natural man, says Rousseau, is neither morally good nor morally wicked. He is innocent of all morality. Virtues and vices are a function of social life, and primordial man is essentially presocial.[53] If children were raised like Emile, outside of society, then this defense of natural man would also apply to Emile, who is innocent of both moral goodness and badness because he lives outside of society. In this sense, natural man is an overgrown child—if that child is Emile.

It is puzzling that Rousseau also offers a very different argument about the relation of childhood to evil. Both Augustine and Hobbes argue that the greater size and power of adults makes their aggression more wicked than that of children. But Rousseau claims that it is not power but weakness that leads to evil. Here Rousseau concedes that the child is wicked but only because of his small stature. Rousseau interprets the tantrum of a child as expressing his frustration at not having the power to obtain what he desires. Once he is grown, says Rousseau, he will not throw these tantrums because he will have the power to get what he needs.[54] Although Rousseau describes this aggressive child as "wicked," he cannot mean morally evil. Rousseau repeatedly says that before the age of reason, there is no morality in our actions. From the point of view of adult society, the actions of small children can be called good or bad; but small children, like natural man, are innocent of moral good or evil.[55] Rousseau attacks Hobbes, but his real target is Augustine, who argued that infant tantrums reflect original sin. According to Rousseau, natural man and small children both behave in ways that are incompatible with modern social life, but this dysfunction is due to evolution, not to original sin or malice. Our basic human nature evolved in a nonsocial context, says Rousseau, so we should not expect men to function smoothly in the artificial setting of modern societies. Rousseau here seems to anticipate the argument of many modern Darwinians, who attribute dysfunctional human behavior today to the incongruity of modern society with the setting of human evolution. Natural selection designed us, so to speak, for a social and physical environment that has little in common with modern urban societies. According to Rousseau, we should expect to see a lot of dysfunction.

The aggressive and destructive behavior of children and savages stems from their attempt to dominate the world rather than to submit to necessity. What Rousseau calls "education by things" means the proper relation between human desires and our physical needs. In a state of natural goodness, our desires do not exceed our physical needs.[56] Unfortunately, human vitality overflows its bounds so that a child or a savage invests physical objects with an independent will. Surrounded by a world animated by wills, the child attempts to command everything around him and becomes furious if the world does not obey.[57] All savages, like all children, are animists. They see personality and will in all natural forces and organisms. Both children and savages attempt to placate or command the world of things. Once a child learns that he is subject, not to the caprice of men, but to the necessity of nature, he will become rational and accepting of his fate.[58]

Natural man, whether a savage or a child, is a Stoic—he is indifferent to his own pain and discomfort. Nature treats man as Sparta treated its citizens—only the most robust survive.[59] According to Rousseau, our healthy and Stoic endurance of physical pain is corrupted by social relations. For example, when a child is alone, he endures his minor injuries from falls without crying; but when a child is with an adult, he looks to the adult to interpret his own pain. If the adult panics, so will the child, but if the adult remains Stoic, so will the child.[60] Natural man and savages face death without struggle or complaint; Emile will also face his own death with Stoic resignation.[61]

Natural man relates directly to the physical world, unmediated by the distortions of social passions; natural man makes use of nature to meet his real physical needs, not to gratify his vanity by impressing others. Behind the scenes, Rousseau carefully choreographs Emile's education so that Emile seems to be instructed directly by nature, free from social prejudice. Since books mediate our relationship to nature and, indeed, often become a substitute for nature, the only book Rousseau permits Emile to read is, of course, *Robinson Crusoe*. Here Emile imaginatively identifies with man in the state of nature, who relates directly to the physical world, unconcerned with social status. *Robinson Crusoe* teaches Emile how to become independent and self-sufficient.[62]

In late childhood, Emile knows the physical relations of man to things, but he knows nothing of the moral relations of man to man.[63] Yet Rousseau knows that Emile, unlike Robinson Crusoe or man in the state of nature, is destined for society.[64] Emile originally lived in the social isolation that marks primordial man: Emile is not raised by his parents because in the state of nature there are no families. Rousseau claims that Emile has no more attachment to his sister than to his watch; and the age difference between mentor and pupil means that Emile is not even attached to Rousseau.[65] Although there are no families in the primordial state of nature, families do eventually emerge due to the accidents of history. Indeed, Rousseau tells us that families are natural, even if not primordial.[66] Because Emile's development must recapitulate human history, Emile must be educated for a future family, despite not being raised in a family. His education will take him out of the pure state of nature and into social, and ultimately into civic, life.

How will Emile preserve his natural goodness amid the rivalries and vanities of social life? His challenge is to remain natural within an artificial world. His early childhood education taught him to be self-sufficient and to make his own judgments. Since he never had peers, he was never tempted to make invidious comparisons or to feel rivalry. As Emile moves from the state of nature into society, his physical education must now give way to a moral education. As Rousseau says, natural man in the state of nature is quite different from natural man in the state of society. "Emile is not a savage to be relegated to the desert. He is a savage made to inhabit cities."[67] Emile must learn to be in society without being of society—to live with other people without living like them.⁶⁸ Paradoxically, says Rousseau, the best way to prepare a child for life in society is to raise him in on a desert isle or on the moon.⁶⁹

If our absolutely first sentiment is the delight in our own existence, then our first social sentiment is pity. The healthy self-love that characterizes both natural man and children is often mistaken for selfishness or even cruelty. Certainly, our *amour de soi* can cause us to neglect the good of others as we actively promote our own well-being. But healthy self-love involves no desire for superiority, let alone a desire to injure another person. Even healthy self-love would make all human social relations impossibly competitive were it not for the natural sentiment of pity. Rousseau says the "ferocity" of our desire for self-preservation is tempered by our pity, which he describes as our innate repugnance to see a fellow human being suffer.

Ironically, the sentiment of pity already involves the beginnings of vanity, since pity requires us, says Rousseau, to compare our situation to that of another person. Pity makes social life possible but also contains the seeds of social corruption. Eventually, our social vanity and pride will undermine our natural pity, which is "obscure and lively in Savage man, developed but weak in Civilized man." Nonetheless, Rousseau tells us that in the state of nature, pity "takes the place of laws, morals, and virtue" because pity constrains our healthy self-assertion.⁷⁰ In the education of Emile, Rousseau does not wait for natural pity to emerge on its own. He cultivates Emile's natural pity by arranging for Emile to visit and to assist people who are poor or ill.⁷¹ When primordial man or Emile have their self-love restrained properly by pity, then they will adopt the same quasi-moral maxim: to promote one's own good with the least possible harm to others. In the childhood of the human race and in the childhood of each person, there is only one rule of morality.⁷²

According to Rousseau, happiness is a function of the ratio of our desires to our strength. In childhood, our natural desires exceed our meager physical strength; in adulthood, our unnatural and vain desires greatly exceed our physical strength. A natural child is much happier than a vain and envious adult. A creature whose powers were equal to his desires would be perfectly happy.⁷³ Just before puberty, human life experiences a golden age in which our powers equal or even exceed our desires.⁷⁴ When Emile is fourteen years old, he is very self-sufficient because anything that he wants to do, he has the strength and skill to do. He has not yet entered adolescence, when his fantastical desires will greatly exceed his competence.

As a species, we enter the exact same golden age at the beginning of our social lives, in what Rousseau calls "nascent society." In these simple communities there are stable families in permanent dwellings who exchange surplus goods with each other but who lack a rigid division of labor or social hierarchy. In nascent society, we find a golden mean between the indolence of savages and the frenetic industry of civilization.[75] Rousseau calls this happiest of epochs "the veritable youth of the world" since it corresponds exactly to Emile's late childhood. But whereas natural desires are limited by each person's needs, social desires are competitive and unlimited. Once men's desires began to exceed their individual strength, they began to resort to domination, servility, and social hierarchy.[76] As Emile enters his own nascent society, Rousseau observes that "all men are still equal in his eyes."[77]

Since families are natural to man once he leaves the state of nature, Emile's moral education centers on the training of his passions toward a worthy wife. In the state of nature, a man simply takes a woman when he reaches the age of puberty, solving the problem of sexual anarchy. In society, youths must negotiate the treacherous gap between physical puberty and civil puberty, that is, the age of marriage.[78] Rousseau devotes a great deal of ingenuity when steering Emile through these turbulent adolescent years so that his sexual passions remained focused on his future wife. Natural society includes basic economic production and exchange; Emile learns a trade so that he can be economically self-sufficient within a rustic society.

Even nascent society presents dangers of moral corruption. When people gather to enjoy musical performances, rivalry and envy already begin to appear.[79] Emile can no longer rely simply on his natural goodness; he must develop the discipline of virtue. To be naturally good is to do what is right spontaneously—so harmonious is our desire with our nature. Virtue, for Rousseau, is the strength required to do our moral and legal duty in the face of our social passions to the contrary.[80] Natural goodness requires no effort, but virtue requires self-control.[81] Natural goodness makes us good for ourselves; we are good for others only when we become virtuous.[82] Virtue shields natural goodness from the dangerous storms of the social passions. According to Rousseau, urban settings are especially conducive to the cultivation of vanity, rivalry, and envy because of the ubiquity of social comparisons.[83] Rousseau blames cities for the corruption of the human race and steers Emile away from them.[84]

In Rousseau's account of the history of our species, nascent societies were not durable in the face of growing inequality, rivalry, and the lust for domination. The rich began to enslave their neighbors in the quest for ever greater distinction. As soon as one society formed a body politic and raised an army to protect itself, every society was forced to enter political life.[85] Although political society often claimed to protect the weak, in practice, government only strengthened the rich and destroyed natural freedom and equality forever.[86] As political communities came into conflict with each other, a person was even more likely to be killed by a foreigner than by other men in the state of nature.[87]

Emile's moral education culminates in his founding a family and a stable household. Because the world that Emile inherits is divided into different political societies, Emile must transition from his moral education to his civic education. Rousseau begins Emile's civic education by having him travel around Europe to study and observe a variety of different constitutional regimes so that Emile can make an informed choice about where to settle and perform his civic duties.[88] Rousseau then teaches Emile the principles of political justice. Emile, who as a boy lived only for himself, must now merge his individual will into the collective will of all his fellow citizens. Only by surrendering all of his desires to a rational and collective whole does Emile avoid the fatal divisions between his private interests and his public duties. He forfeits his natural freedom in return for the civic freedom of citizens.[89] Even vanity and pride are ennobled by civic virtue —we become proud, not of ourselves, but of our country.[90]

Emile's education in physical relations to other beings, in moral relations to other men, and in civic relations to his fellow citizens closely parallels the evolution of the human race from the primordial state of nature, through nascent society, and into political life.[91] Yet scholars have pointed to a fundamental discrepancy between these two accounts since the history of the human race in the *Second Discourse* ends in misery while *Emile* ends in bliss.[92] Rousseau's historical epic is tragic while his bildungsroman is comic. Perhaps this contrast is not surprising since Rousseau wrote *Emile* to offer hope for pedagogical escape from the tragedy of human history. If only we could preserve our natural goodness amid the corruption of modern social life!

Rousseau's two accounts are not as opposed as they might seem. What if Rousseau's account of human history in the *Second Discourse* is not wholly pessimistic? Even though Rousseau argues in the *Second Discourse* that man has irretrievably lost his natural freedom and equality, he concludes the essay by arguing that modern despotism and moral inequality rest, not on nature, but on the accidents of history. Unlike nature, history can change rapidly. Moreover, Rousseau's praise for the civic virtue of the Romans hints at a way to create civic freedom and equality, even if we have lost natural freedom and equality.[93] So Rousseau offers some grounds for optimism for the future of the human race.

At the same time, perhaps Emile's story is not as blissful as it seems. Rousseau's philosophical romance concludes with Emile and Sophie joyfully having just married and expecting a baby. Do they live happily ever after? In an unfinished sequel to *Emile*, Rousseau's portrait of the future of his pupils turns surprisingly dark. As soon as Rousseau leaves young Emile and Sophie, their lives become a bad melodrama. A daughter dies and they fatefully move to Paris. Sophie becomes pregnant by another man and Emile abandons his family—only to be then captured and enslaved by Barbary pirates![94] Yet, throughout these misfortunes Emile retains his Stoic serenity, leading some readers to see his education vindicated, while other readers see the failure of Rousseau's pedagogical project.[95] Like the human race, Emile and Sophie were raised innocently in the country, but then settled in a big city—with all the fateful consequences we would expect from reading Rousseau.

CHAPTER 5

Development as Juvenilization in the Synoptic Gospels

In all of the stories of development we have seen so far, childhood is merely a way station on the journey to adulthood. The goal of development is to become an adult, which is why a child is so often characterized as immature, infantile, incomplete, irrational, and underdeveloped. The death of a child is thought to be especially tragic because the goal has not been reached, the project remains unfinished, and the life cut short. We even disparage any delays on the treadmill to adulthood as "retardation" or "arrested development." By contrast, children who fast-forward into adulthood are praised as precocious, as good little ladies and gentlemen. Since the goal is adulthood, the sooner the better.

The theory of development as juvenilization provides an important corrective to these more familiar ways of thinking about development.[1] What if childhood actually holds the key to adulthood? What if human nature is marked above all by juvenility?[2] According to the theory of biological recapitulation, the development of every human being ought to summarize the history of our ancestors. After passing through plant and mammal stages, children should resemble our adult primate ancestors before reaching human maturity. But instead of human children resembling adult primates, adult humans turn out to resemble infant primates. Indeed, our large brains, our flat faces, our upright posture, and our relative hairlessness all resemble fetal apes.[3] Moreover, during the course of hominid evolution, humans are growing younger and younger. Modern humans resemble fetal apes while our human ancestors resembled adult apes.[4] Compared to other primates, human evolution has taken us from adulthood to infancy. This means that human adults also resemble human embryos much more than other adult primates resemble their own embryos. Compared to all other primates, humans never really grow up: we get larger, but we do not change shape nearly as much.[5]

The nineteenth-century comparative anatomists and embryologists who described this human juvenilization attributed it to our prolonged childhood. Developmental biologists had long known that infancy and childhood are much longer in humans than in other mammals or even other primates. One reason why we retain the juvenile features of our primate ancestors is that our development is delayed and arrested at an early stage.[6] The key insight here is that if we compare changing patterns of development in different species, we can explain a good deal of evolutionary change. The way that evolution modifies the morphology, physiology, or behavior of an organism is typically by modifying the pattern of its development. In short, the evolutionary emergence of new species over time is largely the result of changes in the patterns of development within an organism. Development itself evolves, which leads to the emergence of new species.[7] In comparing patterns of development, biologists look at the timing of growth—its beginning and end—as well as the rate of growth for a particular organ or trait. These patterns of growth not only vary widely across species but also within organisms. For example, a neonate's brain grows much faster relative to the body, but later in childhood the body grows faster relative to the brain. Every organism is a mosaic of organs and traits, each with its own developmental "clock."[8] These changes in patterns of growth lead to dramatic changes in adult organisms.[9]

The term "neoteny" has been used by biologists and others to describe two very different aspects of juvenilization. The human retention of the infantile or fetal traits of ancestral primates is often called "paedomorphosis." Three kinds of developmental processes can produce this retention of juvenile features, one of which is called neoteny, or the slowing down of development before sexual maturation.[10] Neoteny is the developmental retardation that can produce paedomorphosis. According to biologist Stephen Jay Gould, what matters is not any list of juvenile features in human adults but the overall pattern of developmental retardation in humans. Gould argues that human beings are "essentially" neotenous.[11]

The prolongation of human infancy and childhood is well known. Human gestation, measured by growth rates, lasts for about twenty-one months.[12] What this means is that human babies have the growth rates of primate fetuses: "Human babies are born as embryos, and embryos they remain for about the first nine months of life."[13] The reason that human babies are born halfway through gestation is because, any later, their large heads would exceed the dimensions of the birth canal. Human babies are born uniquely immature and dependent.[14] This extreme prolongation of infancy and childhood is deeply paradoxical in relation to standard accounts of evolution by natural selection. After all, helpless infants and small children are extremely vulnerable to accidents, illnesses, harsh climates, shortages of food, and predators.[15] Every year in which we are so small and dependent reduces our odds of survival. So why would humans evolve in such a way as to greatly prolong this period of extreme vulnerability?[16]

Not only does our prolonged childhood mean greater vulnerability, it also means delayed reproduction. If the point of natural selection is to maximize reproductive success, then it is deeply puzzling why human beings delay sexual maturation by prolonging childhood. Is it not safer for our survival as a species to reproduce as soon as possible? Biologists hypothesize that prolonged infancy and childhood must provide very large compensatory advantages in human survival. Most scholars believe that our prolonged childhoods permit the extensive learning that characterizes our species. Lacking a fixed repertoire of instincts, human beings must master a great deal of knowledge about their world and about their societies. Why do we need to learn so much as children? In all animals, maturation is strongly correlated with loss of mental and physical plasticity.[17] By prolonging childhood, we prolong the period in which we learn most readily. Compared to other mammals, human beings remain lifelong learners. Our prolonged childhood also permits us to enjoy a much longer period of play. Biologists, anthropologists, and psychologists are just recently discovering the many functions of play in human survival and well-being. Some scholars now argue that we do not play because we are young; rather, we are young so that we can play.[18] Finally, our prolonged dependence on our caregivers creates very strong emotional bonds within the human family.[19] The survival advantages of greater learning, play, and family attachments must be very great to compensate for the risks of prolonged dependence and delayed reproduction.

We know that human adults retain many anatomical features of infant primates. The most important human anatomical feature is our face, which is uniquely expressive. Face-to-face communication is the inescapable basis of human social life. The evolution of the human face is strongly neotenous, which is why we look like infant apes.[20] Do we also retain infant behavioral traits as adults?[21] Anthropologist Ashley Montagu argues that human paedomorphosis extends well beyond our posture and includes a whole set of behavioral traits that we associate with children, such as curiosity, joyfulness, optimism, creativity, and wonder.[22] As other primates mature, they specialize both morphologically and behaviorally to fit particular ecological niches. Only human beings specialize in generality and retain the flexibility to adapt to a huge range of environments. The pioneering ethologist Konrad Lorenz argues that what is uniquely human is to always remain in a state of development—that is, to never grow up.[23] Humans alone remain adaptive, flexible, playful, and creative throughout our lives.

Studies of domesticated animals suggest that neoteny always includes behavioral, as well as anatomical juvenilization. Domesticated animals both resemble and act like the juveniles of their wild ancestors.[24] Adult dogs, for example, with their floppy ears, piebald fur, and wagging tails resemble wolf puppies more than they resemble adult wolves. Dogs routinely solicit attention, play, grovel, whine, bark, and wag their tails like wolf puppies but not like mature wolves. Today's dogs are big wolf puppies just as today's humans are big fetal apes.[25] Domestication seems inherently to produce neoteny. Russian biologists led by Dmitry Belyaev conducted a forty-year experiment domesticating the silver fox (*Vulpes vulpes*). They selectively bred these foxes on the basis of tameability alone. Yet to their great surprise, the domesticated foxes also had piebald fur, curly hair, curled tails, and floppy ears. Juvenile behavioral traits, such as tameability and playfulness, are genetically linked to juvenile anatomical traits.[26]

Can domestication partly explain human neoteny? Human evolution parallels the juvenilization produced by the domestication of other animals. As we saw, Jean-Jacques Rousseau was the first philosopher to argue that human beings are the only self-domesticated species. Rousseau, of course, lamented the loss of our primitive vigor and freedom during the process of self-domestication. Many anthropologists claim that women may well have taken the lead in the domestication of other animals. Perhaps, as Voltaire once quipped, man is the last animal domesticated by woman.[27]

Geneticist J. B. S. Haldane argues that we can expect future human beings to mature much more slowly and to be better learners and more playful than human adults today.[28] He predicted that human evolution in the future "will probably involve a still greater prolongation of childhood and retardation of maturity."[29] Perhaps we are seeing this prolongation of childhood in the social customs of industrialized societies today. I have already noted that the markers of adulthood, such as completing schooling, holding a job, getting married, and having children, are now achieved at a much later age today than fifty years ago.[30] Whether or not our biological maturity will become increasingly delayed, our sociological maturity is increasingly delayed.[31] Psychologist Erik Erikson noted the relation of biological to social neoteny: "It is human to have a long childhood; it is civilized to have an even longer childhood."[32] Is social neoteny replacing biological neoteny? Will prolonging childhood lead to more creative and productive adults?

We might indeed anatomically resemble our juvenile primate ancestors and relatives, but we do not behave at the level of juvenile primates. Our physical development might be arrested compared to other primates, but we surpass all other primates in cognitive, linguistic, and social behavior. Human children surpass the linguistic achievements of apes by age three. Human cognitive development shares many features with that of other primates at very early stages, but we quickly develop intellectual and cultural capacities far beyond any other primate. In these cognitive, linguistic, and behavioral traits, it seems that we are overdeveloped, not underdeveloped, compared to our primate relatives. But Montagu argues: "What neoteny tells us is not that we remain arrested at the level of the fetus or child, but that we continue to develop the generalized traits that are seen in fetuses and children, rather than become restricted by adult specializations that constrain other primates."[33] We are both underdeveloped and overdeveloped. We are both younger and older than other primates.

Biologists Michael McKinney and Kenneth J. McNamara argue that theories of neoteny are misleading because human development, compared to that of other primates, is characterized not only by the prolongation of infancy and childhood but also by the prolongation of every stage of development. This extension of every stage of growth explains why humans live longer than any other primate. By prolonging each stage of development, human maturation is characterized by overdevelopment in the course of a life. Theories of neoteny argue that childhood is prolonged by the delay of the rate of maturation compared to other primates.[34] Yet perhaps human rates of development are not delayed, but the time spent in each phase of development is simply extended.[35] This sequential overdevelopment would explain why human beings surpass all other primates in cognitive and linguistic behavior.[36] Other biologists, however, claim that we grow older than other primates because we grow more slowly, and we live longer because we stay younger.[37]

The role of neoteny in human development continues to be debated in increasingly subtle ways. Some biologists are attempting to reconcile human juvenilization with our supreme adult achievements. Compared to our ancestors and primate relatives, human beings are precocious kids who manage to outperform the adults. Juvenility somehow makes possible greater maturation; retardation somehow makes possible overdevelopment.[38] Erikson says that "long childhood makes a technical and mental virtuoso out of man."[39] We are back to an ancient image of human development: the more we pull back the arrow, the farther it flies forward.

Whatever its biological basis, the idea of rejuvenation—of recapturing the virtues of childhood—has always been a prominent theme of human culture. Rejuvenation is a selective return to childhood. Most adults, even most scientists, cease asking "blue sky" questions as they mature, but Newton and Einstein famously claimed that their insights stemmed from retaining a childlike and naive wonder about the natural world.[40] Nor is rejuvenation limited to individuals. The creative effervescence of whole cultural epochs is often described as a "renaissance." Cultural rejuvenation involves the unlikely combination of the creative genius of the young combined with the historical wisdom of the old—exemplified, perhaps in the American founding.[41]

One can only marvel at how often we attribute the supreme achievements of adults to a recapturing of childhood, despite the traditional denigration of children as deficient adults. The biblical Jesus was the first prophet of neoteny: "Except ye be converted and become as little children, ye shall not enter the kingdom of heaven" (Matt. 18:3).[42] In all three synoptic Gospels, Jesus rebukes his disciples for not welcoming the small children; Jesus then tells his disciples that unless they each become like a small child, they cannot enter the kingdom of God. The disciples are startled by this outrage to their adult status and honor. Since when are children in any way superior to adults? Scholars tell us that in the ancient world, whether Greek or Jewish, for an adult to be compared to a child was highly insulting.[43] If, according to a fundamental principle of biblical hermeneutics, the teachings of Jesus that are most likely to be authentic are those that create a scandal for their audience, then what Jesus says about children is highly likely to be authentic.

Adults in the ancient world, no matter how low their social status, at least had the satisfaction of feeling superior to children. The disciples of Jesus did not have many groups below them, apart from slaves and children. They might have been especially offended by Jesus's suggestion that they ought to look up to children. Of course, Jesus's teaching and ministry were largely focused on honoring members of marginal and subordinated groups, such as women, Samaritans, lepers, the poor, and the despised. His longest recorded conversation is with a Samaritan woman (John 4). In this sense, Jesus's startling attention to children is consistent with his ministry as a whole. After all, Jesus also repeatedly admonishes his followers to think of themselves as servants and slaves.

What exactly is it about small children, according to Jesus, that adults ought to emulate? Biblical scholars are divided on this question. One school of thought emphasizes the objective or external characteristics of children, such as their neediness, their low social status, their helplessness, and their vulnerability. Another school of thought emphasizes the more subjective spirit of children, such as their lack of self-consciousness about their own honor, their naive trust in adults, their moral innocence, and even their playfulness. This distinction between the objective and subjective dimensions of childhood is illuminating. Jesus's dramatic actions and words concerning children draw our attention to both dimensions of childhood. More emphatically than any other figure of the ancient world, Jesus enjoins adults to emulate children.

Since Mark's Gospel is generally regarded as a source for the other synoptic Gospels, we start with his account. In chapter 9 (33–37), Jesus asks his disciples what they were arguing about. They do not answer Jesus because they are embarrassed that they were arguing about who will be greatest in the kingdom of God. Jesus then says to them: "Whoever wants to be first must be last of all and servant of all." Then Jesus placed a small child (*paidion*) in their midst and took him in his arms. He said to them: "Whoever welcomes one such child in my name welcomes me, and whoever welcomes me welcomes not me but the one who sent me." The lesson here seems to be about pride and humility. Jesus rebukes the pride of his disciples by contrasting their self-importance with the humility symbolized by a small child and by Jesus's embrace of that child.

In Robert Gundry's authoritative commentary on Mark, he develops an objective interpretation of this story. According to Gundry, the small child in Mark 9 is not an object of imitation but of reception. Jesus places the child in the midst of his disciples not to invite them to imitate some putative virtue of the child but simply to show them how to become a "servant of all." Jesus warns his disciples that the kingdom belongs to the "last of all" and the "servant of all." In Gundry's telling, the child is objectively the "last of all" in social rank. By embracing the child, Jesus himself becomes the "servant of all," extending hospitality to even the lowest ranked members of society. It is not the child who is imitated but Jesus himself, who objectively makes himself even lower than a little child by his humble service to that child. According to Gundry, the lesson is one of humble service, of making oneself a servant of the servants: "It is the servant, not the child, who occupies last position; and it takes a servant to receive a child."[44]

Gundry's account has the advantage of sticking closely to the text and avoiding speculation about whether children possess or exhibit the virtue of humility in some special way. The disadvantage of his account is that now the story is not really about children at all. The child has become merely a symbol of low social status. The story is simply one about Jesus's own humility. On Gundry's reading, Jesus could have conveyed precisely the same lesson by welcoming or embracing any person of very low social standing, whether a leper, a foreigner, a prostitute, or a publican. Since Jesus does embrace all these marginal persons, Gundry's account of this story fits with the general pattern of Jesus's ministry—but at the cost of not telling us anything special about children.

I agree with Gundry that this story presents a twofold object lesson in humility. But if we combine objective and subjective aspects of childhood into our account, I think this story teaches a much deeper lesson about humility. First, the child is a potent symbol of humility. Jesus dramatically places a child in their midst, right after saying: "whoever wants to be first must be last of all and servant of all." Here the disciples' jockeying for being "first of all" is contrasted with the presence of a child, who is by all objective criteria "the last of all." Is Jesus aiming simply to replace competition for being "first" with competition for being "last"? Is he suggesting that those who want to be greatest in the kingdom ought to try to be the least in this world? This would simply create an inverted but equally invidious competition for status. By setting a child in their midst, Jesus is implying that his disciples should be in some way like this child, not merely being the least in the eyes of the world. Rather, his disciples should become like a small child by somehow adopting the subjective attitude of a child, who is not even aware of social hierarchy. There is a paradox about the direct effort to be humble; it is inherently prideful to aim to be supremely humble. The deepest humility is not about seeking abjection but about becoming unselfconscious about one's rank at all.[45] The people who are most naturally unselfconscious about their rank are small children. By placing a child in their midst, Jesus invites his disciples to emulate a child's indifference to status.

Second, Gundry is right that Jesus also illustrates humility by his action of taking the child into his arms. By welcoming a child into his arms, the locus of humility has shifted from the child to Jesus himself. Since a child is objectively least in society, to welcome a child is likely to be a subjectively humble act. We do not normally enhance our social standing by publicly embracing children or slaves. Consider the contrasting case: since a king is objectively first, to welcome a king is likely to be subjectively prideful, since we bask in his reflected glory. Jesus teaches that to be humble is to warmly embrace those whom society ranks lowest. Paradoxically, to welcome the least is also to welcome the greatest, for by welcoming a small child, we thereby welcome not only Jesus but God his father. Anyone would receive and warmly embrace a king or divine creator, since such an act enhances our own standing. But few are willing to receive and warmly to embrace lepers or beggars or small children. Ironically, such is the only way to embrace and welcome God. Here again, we learn from children.

Jesus's disciples clearly did not grasp the meaning of his lesson, both by precept and by example, that one ought to welcome small children, for in the next chapter of Mark's account (10:13–16), we find people bringing their small children to Jesus to receive a blessing from him. Yet the disciples rebuke them and try to prevent the children from approaching Jesus. Given the disparaging attitudes toward children in ancient society, it is understandable that the disciples would instinctively seek to protect Jesus's ministry from what they regard as trivial distractions. Perhaps because of his earlier attempt to instruct his disciples on the importance of children, Jesus here angrily rebukes the rebukers: "Let the little children (*ta paidia*) come to me; do not stop them; for it is to such as these that the kingdom of God belongs" (Mark 10:14). The disciples had just been discussing their own putative ranks within the coming kingdom, but now Jesus tells them that the kingdom belongs not to them but to little children! Again, Jesus's championing of children scandalizes his disciples. Jesus goes on to ask his disciples not simply to receive and embrace small children but in some way to emulate them: "Truly I tell you, whoever does not receive the kingdom of God as a little child will never enter it." Although these parents brought their children to Jesus simply for a blessing, Jesus goes well beyond their expectations by hugging the children as well as blessing them.

What does it mean to receive the kingdom of God as a little child? Gundry offers his objective theory: "Receiving God's kingdom as a child means submitting to God's rule. What else can a weak and helpless child do?" Gundry is right that the act of referring to the subjective attitudes of children often suffers from "factual questionableness and overpsychologizing modernity."[46] But are we to believe that emulating how little children receive the kingdom is limited to being powerless to reject it? Judith M. Gundry has developed Robert Gundry's objective account of this story. On her account, it is simply the objective neediness of children, their littleness and helplessness that constitute the basis of their receiving the kingdom in the form of receiving a blessing from Jesus. She stresses that the children did not come to Jesus on their own but are brought by their parents to him. Yet, the parents are not held up as models: "Rather, the children, who do nothing, not even believe, and on the contrary resist, *are* models."[47]

The Gundrys are right. If children relate to the kingdom only by their objective need and weakness, then we would expect Jesus to bless a group of indifferent or even resistant children, revealing the power of God's kingdom to reach anyone. But is that what is going on here? Yes, the little children are brought within the vicinity of Jesus by their adult caretakers. Does this imply that these children are indifferent or resistant to Jesus? All it seems to imply is that they are small children and cannot travel on their own. We are told that the disciples admonished "them" to stay away; scholars say that the word "them" could refer to the children, their parents, or both. It is at least consistent with the story that the children are actively approaching Jesus on their own, only to be deterred by the disciples. Jesus, in rebuking his disciples, says: "Let the little children come to me; do not stop them" (10:14). Note that Jesus did not say "let the parents or families come to me." By saying "let the children come to me; do not stop them," Jesus strongly suggests that the children actively want to come to him. Were these children indifferent or resistant, it would be odd for Jesus to say "let them come to me; do not stop them." Instead, Jesus's words clearly imply that the children themselves are seeking him out. Moreover, as any parent knows, it is very difficult to take up children in your arms, hug them, and bless them if the children are indifferent, not to mention resistant. Not only Jesus's words, but his deeds as well, strongly imply willing, cooperative, indeed loving children.

The Gundry picture of passive or resistant children overwhelmed by the active power of God simply does not fit the words or deeds of Jesus. If the children "do nothing," then why does Jesus say "let them come to me" or "do not stop them"? Judith Gundry also says that the children "do not believe." If by "believe," she means an explicit confession of faith, then that would be surprising in small children. But if "believe" means a primordial kind of trust, then these children, who seem to be actively approaching Jesus, do indeed seem to believe in him.[48] Most shockingly, Judith Gundry claims that at least some of the children "resist" Jesus, but there is no scriptural basis for this accusation. Instead, the innumerable paintings of this gospel scene fit the words of Jesus much more naturally, showing children running or walking to Jesus on their own, climbing into his lap, looking him actively in the face, listening to him, and hugging him. In these pictures, the children are fully active in seeking out Jesus's blessing.

Once we acknowledge that these children seem to be actively seeking out Jesus, then we can understand why he tells his disciples to receive the kingdom as do these little children. Note that these children actively approach Jesus even in the face of rebuke by Jesus's own disciples; Jesus does not seek them out, let alone overpower them. These children reveal a naive trust in Jesus and a desire for his loving embrace. To receive the kingdom like these little ones means to run to Jesus full of trust in his loving protection. The goodness of these children naturally attracts them to the goodness of Jesus.

Notice that in the Gundrys' objective interpretation of Jesus's teachings in these stories, children never truly appear. In the first scene, Jesus embraces a child merely as a symbol of a person with low social status, thereby making Jesus "the servant of all." In the second scene, Jesus welcomes the children, who merely symbolize human neediness, weakness, indifference, and resistance. These traits are subsequently overpowered by divine love and mercy. If we are open to considering children not merely as objectively needy or of low status but also as persons with their own distinctive capacities, then we can better understand why Jesus would be willing to create such a scandal by asking adults to emulate them. Children have capacities for humility and for trust that merit the respect of adults.

Matthew's account of Jesus and the one small child seems to draw on Mark's account but with one revealing addition. After again placing a child in their midst, Jesus says to the disciples: "Truly I tell you, unless you change and become like children, you will never enter the kingdom of heaven. Whoever becomes humble like this child is the greatest in the kingdom of heaven" (Matt. 18:2–4). Here Matthew goes beyond Mark. Mark's Jesus merely shows his disciples a child in the context of discussing humility—thereby letting them draw the connection. Matthew's Jesus makes the lesson explicit: you must emulate the humility of a child. But what is the humility of a child? According to Robert Gundry: "This definition does not imply that children humble themselves, but that their small stature symbolizes humility."[49] On this objective view, the only lesson in humility that children can teach us is to be short. We saw above that Augustine pioneered this interpretation. He tells us that children are humble only in the sense of being small and that their humility is purely physical, not ethical or spiritual.[50] But humility is not so much about "humbling ourselves" as about being unselfconscious about rank or status. In the case of the story of Jesus welcoming the children, Matthew's account (19:13–15) is more lapidary than Mark's and lacks the explicit lesson about humility drawn by Mark—a lesson already stated in Matthew 18:4.

Luke (9:46–48) relates the same story of the disciples arguing over who is greater. In response, Jesus places a little child (*paidion*) by his side and tells them that "the least among all of you is the greatest" (v. 48). In his authoritative commentary, Joseph A. Fitzmyer argues that the child here represents merely an objective symbol of humility: "The little child taken by Jesus to himself is the sign of Christian greatness, precisely as the least significant and weakest member of human society." By contrast, we find the subjective virtue of humility only in Jesus himself, who is "prepared to accept and esteem even the smallest of human society."[51] In this objective interpretation, the child becomes merely a symbol of low human status.

Fitzmyer explicitly contrasts Luke 9:46–48 with Luke 18:15–17, which recounts the story about Jesus welcoming the little children: "Truly, I tell you, whoever does not receive the kingdom of God as a little child will never enter it." According to Fitzmyer, in the first story (9:46–48), the little child is merely a symbol of objective lowliness while in the second story (18:15–17), Jesus calls our attention to the subjective spirit of childhood: "Without saying so explicitly, Jesus extolls the openness and sheer receptivity of these tiny human beings. Their freshness, their lack of guilt or suspicion, their loving warmth, and their lack of a claim to achievement are what is being held up to adults accosted by the message of the kingdom."[52] Here Fitzmyer rightly draws our attention to some of the relevant subjective attitudes of children, but his list is not well controlled by the text. As I have observed, what Jesus praises in children is their unselfconscious humility and their open trust in him. I see no textual basis for supposing that Jesus praises children for "their lack of guilt." Moreover, the children who come to Jesus display more than a mere receptivity to the kingdom—they actively seek it.

This contrast between a focus on objective and subjective aspects of childhood reveals a deeper theological contrast. Although scientific and critical biblical scholarship aims at interpretive validity unconstrained by particular religious affiliations, the leading biblical scholars inevitably understand Jesus's cryptic words about children according to their own theological traditions. Robert and Judith Gundry, following Augustine, insist that children relate to the kingdom of God only as passive recipients of divine grace through Jesus. According to the Gundrys, children are indifferent or even resistant to Jesus, but he overpowers them by his mercy. Adults should emulate children by acknowledging that we are essentially just as needy, helpless, and unworthy of divine grace as these little children. By contrast, Fitzmyer attributes the laudable subjective attitudes of humility and trust to children that might well be emulated by adults. In his view, children actively seek Jesus's blessings, and Jesus, in turn, praises the virtues of these children.

Through these contrasts of biblical interpretations, we can clearly see fundamental theological commitments at work. The Gundrys accept an Augustinian-Calvinist theology of total human depravity and unmerited divine grace. Although children do nothing to earn divine blessing, Jesus grants it anyway. According to their view, even when children are resistant to Jesus, he blesses them all the same because they are in objective need of his grace. The Gundrys focus on the objective needs of children because, in Calvin's view, children have no natural desire for divine goodness.[53] By contrast, Fitzmyer acknowledges the virtuous subjective attitudes of children which make them suitable disciples of Jesus. Children by nature are drawn to Jesus, and he rewards their goodness with his blessing. For the Gundrys, when Jesus blesses the children, divine grace has replaced a depraved human nature; for Fitzmyer, following Thomas Aquinas, when Jesus blesses the children, his grace perfects the natural goodness he finds in children. Through the division of biblical commentators into those who focus on the objective status of children and those who focus on the subjective attitudes, we see a fundamental theological divide between the Calvinist and the Thomist view of children. Either Jesus makes children good by his blessing, or he perfects the goodness he finds in them.

Jesus's insistence that adults ought to emulate children scandalized his disciples. Nothing could be regarded as more insulting in the ancient world. Despite the fact that these stories of Jesus welcoming and praising children are included in all three synoptic Gospels, their message was largely ignored by Christian theologians for many centuries.[54] Jesus seems to have scandalized even his remote disciples, down through the ages. Only in the wake of Rousseau and the Romantic revolution have Christian theologians begun to reflect in depth on Jesus's praise of children.[55]

Augustine launched a long tradition of medieval theorizing about childhood when he asked the question: What would infancy and childhood look like were we still in Eden? Recall that Augustine interpreted the infirmity, the ignorance, and the tantrums of childhood as punishment for original sin. In a state of earthly paradise, Augustine imagines that human beings might just skip childhood. He understands that infants cannot be born fully grown, but he speculates that they might just miraculously grow up instantly or, at least, mature very rapidly, like other animals. Augustine is aware that human infants are more helpless than are other young animals. What purpose could there be for the helpless ignorance of childhood apart from punishment for sin?

Similarly, Augustine wonders why Jesus would agree to suffer the wretchedness of human childhood. Why could he not have become incarnate as an adult? Augustine speculates that Jesus expressed his profound solidarity with the human race by agreeing to suffer the full horror of infancy and childhood.[56] According to the story of neoteny, by contrast, human achievements require our uniquely prolonged infancy and childhood. Augustine, like Aristotle, sees childhood only as a necessary evil: ideally, we would skip it or fast-forward through it since our goal is the perfection of adulthood.

Rousseau's thought provides the crucial bridge between the teaching of Jesus and biological theories of juvenilization. Although Rousseau never explicitly enjoins adults to imitate children, he does enjoin adults to respect the intrinsic gifts of childhood by not rushing children into adulthood. Rousseau argues that children are born good and innocent before they are depraved by society. Yet in describing his own childhood, Rousseau is puzzled by his own wickedness. He says that his father was a model parent who neither spoiled young Jean-Jacques nor allowed him to run wild with his peers.[57] Whereas all other children are corrupted by society, Rousseau exonerates society for his own corruption and blames himself. The natural goodness of children did not seem to apply to Jean-Jacques. Moreover, Rousseau's view of children is hardly sentimental. As we saw, he compares a child to man in the state of nature, who is amoral and asocial.[58] A child, says Rousseau, destroys and kills whatever is within his reach, without understanding the meaning of morality. We are lucky that children are so weak.[59] Normally, he says, children are spoiled by their parents and become both slaves and tyrants.[60]

Like Augustine, Rousseau believes that the truth about human life is seen only against the horizon of our death. Even the value of childhood is manifest only in light of child mortality. Rousseau observes that most children will not reach adulthood. In light of this reality, he asks why we subject children to relentless discipline in preparation for an adulthood that most of them will never experience.[61] Given how short is human life, seize the moment: "Love childhood; promote its games, its pleasures, its amiable instincts." Do not adults long fondly for the joy and peace of childhood?[62] Ironically, at a time when most children never reached adulthood, childhood was mainly devoted to preparation for adulthood. Today, in societies in which virtually all children reach adulthood, we encourage children to play and enjoy the present moment. Rousseau warns us not to see a child as merely an adult-in-waiting. A child has its own passions and, as we would say now, "developmental needs." Do not treat a child like a little adult; a child is more like another species of human being. "Childhood has its ways of seeing, thinking, and feeling which are proper to it."[63]

Rousseau not only insists on the importance of the distinctions between adults and children, he also wants to make sure that we do not rush children into adulthood. To foster precocious children leads to a bad childhood and a worse adulthood.[64] Instead of rushing children toward adulthood, seek out all possible delays in their maturation: "Let childhood ripen in children."[65] Rousseau's insistence on prolonging childhood for as long as possible is consistent with the biology of neoteny, for it emphasizes the permanent importance of a prolonged childhood. As it happens, there is now some empirical evidence that a child's long-term capacity for learning can be harmed by rushing his instruction.[66] Rousseau may be right: the best way to prepare a child for adulthood is to protect him from it for as long as possible.

PART II

UNIFYING THE WHOLE

CHAPTER 6

All of Me

Stages and the Whole of Life

To describe the physical development of animals, embryologists have proposed several basic stories—recapitulation, preformation, epigenesis, and neoteny. In one form or another, all of these stories still shape biological theorizing. Integral human development, which has physical, psychological, moral, and spiritual dimensions, is incomparably more complex, so it is not surprising that all of these stories are deployed. At a high enough level of generalization, they are not mutually exclusive, so we benefit from the insights each of them affords. In some ways, we recapitulate the ladder of nature as we progress from merely growing like plants, to moving like animals, to thinking like humans; in other ways, we recapitulate the history of the human race as we first learn to speak, and then to read and write, and then to solve differential equations. We often seem preformed when we notice how little each of us has changed in our basic temperament since early childhood. Finally, when we become parents, we often find ourselves returning to childhood and trying to recapture its virtues.

In each of these stories of development, there is a tension between the various stages of growth and the notion of life as a whole. As I have noted, all of these stories of development originated in scientific embryology before they were extended to the whole of human life. Embryos develop through an invariant sequence of discrete stages; at any particular stage, the embryo is truly stuck in that stage until it "graduates" to the next stage. But for most of human life, we are not stuck in any particular stage. Our present "stage" of development includes in a sense prior stages and future stages. The present, as Augustine observed, is stretched into the past and into the future. Let us explore the complex relationship between stages and the whole of our lives for each of our developmental stories.

Students of human development often describe our growth in terms of stages because human life is characterized by both continuity and discontinuity. Perfect continuity in development would imply imperceptibly gradual change that we would notice only in retrospect—like the proverbial frog in the pot of water, we only realize that we have grown up when it is too late. Perfect discontinuity in development would mean becoming a completely different person at each new stage with no memory of prior stages. Our development is somewhere in between. We do notice periods of rapid change—especially in puberty and then in old age—but we normally retain our sense of identity throughout these changes. Human development involves aspects both continuous and discontinuous.[1] By contrast, the theory of stages presupposes fundamental discontinuity.

What do our major philosophers and sages tell us about the relationship of the stages of life to the whole of a human life? There is something deeply poignant or even tragic in Aristotle's conception of a happy human life. Childhood has no intrinsic value but is only a preparation for the virtues of adulthood; old age also has no intrinsic value but is only a time for the loss of the virtues of our adult prime. In one place, Aristotle famously catalogues at length what he takes to be the characteristic virtues and vices of young men and of old men.[2] The young, he says, are excessively passionate and overdo everything while the old are excessively timid and underdo everything. Neither the young nor the old possess true virtues as a mean between extremes. Aristotle does, however, praise the young for their generosity, nobility, and courage; by contrast, he never praises the old for anything. Their "wisdom" is only cynicism; their "self-control" is only lack of vigor; their "pity" is only weakness.[3] The young have potential virtues; the old have only vices. Indeed, Aristotle lists "old age" among the great evils of life, along with death, injury, and disease.[4] Aristotle does not blame children for their lack of true virtues, but he does blame the elderly for their vices; he compliments children when they show the promise of future virtue, but he does not compliment the aged for their past virtues.[5]

When he comes to the prime of life, Aristotle paints a picture of pure virtue. He says that the prime of life is the golden mean that incorporates all that is good about youth and old age, with none of the defects.[6] The prime of life is not only the most virtuous and happy stage, but it also includes all the virtues and activities that constitute happiness. According to this account, there is no loss when we leave childhood and no gain when we enter old age.

If the prime of life includes all of the virtues of youth and old age, why does Aristotle sometimes say that happiness belongs only to a complete life? Recall that happiness for Aristotle is the actualization of our potential for moral and intellectual virtue. With this notion of happiness as human flourishing, it seems that happiness must be restricted to the prime of life. What does Aristotle mean by a complete life? If happiness belongs only to a complete life, then perhaps no child is happy for the same reason that no adult is happy? Does happiness belong only to the entire temporal extension of life? In some places, Aristotle seems to argue that no one is happy while still alive: "Solon's advice holds good, never to call a man happy when living, but only when his life is ended. For nothing incomplete is happy, not being whole."[7] In this vein, Aristotle also says, "we cannot ascribe happiness to an existence of a single day, or to a child, or to each of the ages of life . . . for nothing incomplete is happy, not being whole."[8]

Aristotle's essential claim is that happiness cannot be ascribed to momentary experiences but only to significant phases of life: "For one swallow does not make a summer, nor does one day; and so too one day, or a short time, does not make a man blessed and happy."[9] I think we should take seriously Aristotle's analogy here between the seasons and the stages of life. Aristotle's choice of summer to illustrate happiness is not accidental, since summer represents the prime of life. Spring is the season of growth, summer of mature bloom, fall of decay, and winter of death. Summer is the most complete season in nature, because summer is when life reaches full bloom. We saw that Aristotle describes an adult as complete compared to an incomplete child. Similarly, a life is complete in its prime because all the important capacities are fully actualized. By a complete life Aristotle does not primarily mean temporally complete but rather complete in its exercise of virtue. Since we can exercise all our virtues only in our prime, this stage of life alone is complete. Consequently, happiness is properly ascribed to the summer of life but not to any one day of that summer. And since the exercise of complete virtue requires a full season of activity, it need not extend to an entire lifetime.[10]

Clearly, then, a flourishing prime of life is necessary for a truly happy life. But is it sufficient? Aristotle is reluctant to describe a life as supremely happy (*makarios*) until it is over, since even a happy prime of life might be undermined by the ravages of old age.[11] It is difficult to imagine, then, how a life could be supremely happy unless one is fortunate enough (like Aristotle himself) to die before losing any prime of life capacities.[12] Childhood is a necessary evil while old age is an evil sometimes avoidable.

Aristotle rightly gives primacy to the prime of life. If we somehow faced the choice of living in only one stage of life, it would make sense to choose the prime. Starting a new family in our prime is an adventure that most of us do not want to miss. If the prime of life were truly the sum of all virtues, then we would wish to be born in full maturity and to die before losing any of our mature powers. But most of us want to enjoy the unique virtues, challenges, and blessings of each stage of life. Childhood and old age, for example, are the periods of life most often liberated from the responsibilities of the prime of life. Who wants to spend his entire life devoted to serious and weighty pursuits? Aristotle's prime of life exercises more than mere primacy: it exercises tyranny over the other stages of life.

In Aristotle's view, we call children happy only when they exhibit intimations of adulthood. I think it more accurate to say that we call children happy precisely when they are least adultlike. For example, as midlife adults, we tend to be all too aware of the scarcity of time. Our anxiety over economizing our time colors all of our activities. When we call children happy, we are often praising their capacity to act as if there were all the time in the world. Both languor and play rest on an escape from the tyranny of chronological time, and children have a special capacity for this escape. We also call children happy because of their moral innocence. They are not burdened with the knowledge of the full extent of human evil that casts a pall over adult life. Most adults believe that they have lost something precious by growing up. Although we might agree with Aristotle that "no one would choose to live with a child's thought for his whole life,"[13] we might desire a temporary return to childhood, which would baffle Aristotle.

Aristotle pioneered the "deficit" view of childhood. For him, children, like the elderly and the disabled, are merely diminished adults. Yet even in his description of these deficits, we can see the distorting effects of his midlife orientation. Aristotle never mentions the deficits most damaging to the life prospects of children—namely, their small size and physical weaknesses, which leave them vulnerable to accidents and to abuse by adults. The tyranny of the prime of life is clearly manifest in Aristotle's complete neglect of the point of view of children, who are often painfully cognizant of the dangers of being little in a world of grown-ups. Aristotle observes that mature adults do not want to return to childhood, but he never notices that virtually all children want to grow up. Surely this fact is deeply revealing of the profound deficits of childhood.

Clearly not all aspects of childhood can be seen as mere deficits. Gareth Matthews points out that most of us will learn second languages faster, produce better art, and ask deeper metaphysical questions as children than we will as adults.[14] Aristotle, despite his extraordinary powers of observation, never once comments on these universal and distinctive gifts of childhood. In short, in the process of maturation, we both lose as well as gain important capabilities. Consider the relative capabilities of children and adults in mastering new technological gadgets. Childhood and old age are not properly appraised according to the standards of adult mastery alone.

Where Aristotle sees sharp discontinuities in human development, Augustine taught us to see our lives as a whole by crafting a narrative to reveal the essential unity of the child, youth, and adult. What are we to make of Augustine's view that children are essentially just like adults, except smaller in size and, perhaps, in understanding? His claim that our bodies and our souls are separable, and that we are essentially our souls, helps to make his preformationism more plausible. For example, we often distinguish a person's physical age from her mental or spiritual age. We all know of children with the preternatural serenity of wise adults and of adults who tantrum like toddlers. A person's intellectual, emotional, and spiritual growth can bear little or no relationship to their bodily development. Although Thomas Aquinas usually follows Aristotle in rejecting a dualism of body and soul, in some places Aquinas allows that divine grace can perfect the soul of a child.[15] For example, Aquinas says that a person of any physical age can receive the sacrament of confirmation. Just as an old man can be spiritually born again, so a child can attain the spiritual perfection of an adult.[16]

Rousseau says that as we mature, we leave the goodness and innocence of childhood, just as the human species left the goodness and innocence of the state of nature. Rousseau understands that human beings cannot return to a natural state any more than an adult can return to childhood. Knowledge destroys innocence forever. Moreover, Rousseau is ambivalent about natural goodness and innocence, just as he is ambivalent about social virtues and culture. Rousseau sees the process of individual maturation and historical progress as involving ultimately incommensurable losses and gains. Rousseau has a lifelong debate with Jean-Jacques about whether he has gained more or lost more in growing up.

Rousseau was not the first to wrestle with the conflicts between innocence and experience. Ancient Jewish and Christian commentators on the Bible frequently interpreted the story of Adam and Eve as an allegory of human maturation. Each of us begins life in a paradise of innocence, dependence, and goodness; as children, we are even unashamed of our nudity.[17] But once we learn that rules can be broken and that trust can be violated, we lose our innocence forever. Some Christian commentators, such as Augustine, reject this analogy. They claim that even children are already expelled from Paradise. But other commentators argue that Adam and Eve were literally children—that is, sexually immature. Still others argue that sexual intercourse existed and was even more pleasurable in Paradise. As for knowledge, some ancient commentators argued that Adam possessed vast knowledge, others insisted that he was deeply ignorant.[18] Some claimed that Adam and Eve worked as gardeners in Paradise; others insisted that work arose only after the expulsion as punishment. Some insisted that Adam and Eve were happy in Paradise, others claimed true happiness is impossible without mature knowledge and experience of both good and evil.[19]

One can easily see the pattern in these arguments about Adam and Eve. If one regards sex, knowledge, work, or happiness as good and natural to man, then one claims that they characterize Paradise. But if one focuses on the moral complexity of sex, knowledge, work, and happiness, then one claims that they arose only when Paradise was lost. Debates about Paradise are also debates about childhood. To praise Paradise is to yearn for a return to the simplicity and naivety of childhood. To disparage Paradise is to accept the necessity of growing up into knowledge, shame, and work. The Christian humanist Lactantius insists that Paradise was never perfectly innocent or good. Merely by having a body, Adam's good soul already has an enemy. He argues that virtue must be tested and proven by conflict with vice: "Paradise would not have been Paradise without the serpent."[20] Lactantius sees the expulsion from Paradise as both a fall and a rise, just like growing up. These exegetical and philosophical debates about the state of innocence in Paradise are all echoed in Rousseau's ambivalences about the state of nature and about childhood itself.

Speaking of his own life, Rousseau certainly expresses no desire to return to his childhood—except in memory. In his autobiographical writings, Rousseau consistently attempts to see his life as a whole in relation to divine and human judgment.[21] At every stage of his life, Rousseau characterizes himself as weak but never cruel—good at heart without being virtuous.[22] Rousseau insists that throughout his whole life he remained himself.[23] Near the end, he hoped not to recapture the goodness of childhood but to make progress toward adult virtue.[24] As an old man, Rousseau did return to childhood in one respect. He rediscovered the simple but profound delight in his own existence.[25] He sees old age as a time to look back, and he notes the irony that we come to understand how to live only when it is too late.[26] Rousseau rejects the adage that wisdom emerges naturally with age: "youth is the time to study wisdom; old age is the time to put it into practice."[27] Rousseau describes Emile's development as a recapitulation of the human journey from natural innocence to social corruption, but Rousseau describes himself in old age as an "elderly child" because he claims to have remained essentially unchanged throughout his life.[28]

What does it mean to define human nature as *homo juvenalis*? It means that we are physically less specialized than other adult primates so that we can adapt to a much wider range of environments. Normally, evolutionary adaptation works by greater differentiation or by increasing specialization to fit particular ecological niches. But such a strategy risks rigidity and overspecialization, especially in the face of rapid environmental change. The history of life—and in particular, the history of extinction—reveals many such evolutionary dead ends caused by rigid overspecialization. According to Gould, here is where neoteny "can now come to the rescue and provide an escape from specialization." By greatly slowing development, animals can shed their highly specialized adult forms and return to the plasticity of youth, preparing for new evolutionary pathways.[29] In the life history of many animal species, recapturing childhood by means of neoteny has meant survival instead of extinction.

But are childhood plasticity and playfulness compatible with adult discipline, perseverance, and mastery? We often praise the curiosity of children, but their curiosity usually lacks focus and staying power. The curiosity of children is too promiscuous to lead to deep understanding. Is it possible to combine the playful curiosity of children with adult discipline and perseverance? More generally, can we retain the virtues of childhood while acquiring the virtues of adults? As philosopher Richard B. Miller puts it, can we mature without growing old?[30]

Jesus commanded his disciples to emulate the humility of small children (Matt. 18:3, Mark 10:15; Luke 18:17). Small children are humble not merely because they are little but also because they are innocent of all awareness of social status and honor. But Jesus also instructed his disciples "to be wise as serpents and innocent as doves" (Matt. 10:16; Luke 10:3; cf. Acts 20:29). In other words, Jesus wants his disciples to become childlike without being childish. Paul explains what it means not to be childish: "When I was a child, I spoke like a child, I thought like a child, I reasoned like a child; when I became an adult, I put away childish things" (1 Cor. 13:11). Paul offers a couple of strategies for combining the wisdom of serpents with the innocence of doves. First, Paul tells us that we should strive to be "infants in evil but adults in thinking"—that is, to be innocent of evil but experienced in the ways of the world (1 Cor. 14:20). If we do what is good instinctively like a child, then we should strive also to be clever like an adult. Second, Paul tells us to be "wise in good while guileless in evil"—that is, to be experienced in choosing the good while naive about evil (Rom. 16:19). Can we really combine a childlike naivety about evil with the prudential wisdom of an adult? Perhaps we might become "infants in evil" by becoming "holy fools" who knowingly accept the risks of trusting strangers on the sound theory that trusting others usually brings out the best in them. No one becomes trustworthy unless we first trust them. A holy fool is childlike without being childish; she is morally innocent without being intellectually naive.

Champions of juvenilization rarely discuss the great difficulties that adults face who hope to recapture the creativity of children. In the first place, old habits interfere with new kinds of learning; and, second, the responsibilities of adult life interfere with the playful freedom of childhood. The psychology of learning reveals just how difficult it is to remain cognitively flexible while developing the skills necessary to master a discipline. The paradox of learning is simply that everything we know serves both to facilitate and to interfere with new learning. For example, my knowledge of one language both facilitates and interferes with learning a new language. Learning to drive a car in the United States makes it more difficult, not less, to learn to drive in England. This phenomenon is known as "habit interference" and many psychologists believe that most of our mistakes, irrationalities, and forgetfulness stem from the interference of old habits. The U.S. Air Force discovered the tragic significance of habit interference when pilots attempted to fly new planes with slightly different arrays of controls.

Habit interference helps to explain why adults lose the cognitive flexibility of children. Every habit we acquire makes it more difficult to learn new procedures, which is why we ask our children to program the new computer. The skillful competence of adults may simply not be fully compatible with the cognitive flexibility of children. We pay an inevitable price in plasticity for the rewards of mastery. But a century of experimental studies of learning do offer some suggestions for how to reduce habit interference. Habits formed by rote memorization and by mechanical practice, such as our habits of speaking, driving, and typing, are the most likely to interfere with future learning. The most difficult part of learning to speak a new language is forgetting your old one.[31]

We cannot wholly eliminate the rigidities of older mechanical habits, but we can minimize their interference with new learning by developing dispositions of critical self-awareness. By the power of critical reflection, we can learn how to disrupt our older routines so that we can adapt them to new challenges. A disposition to critical self-awareness is also a kind of habit, for it is a habit of monitoring and assessing our more specific habits. If we are aware that our old technological habits are dysfunctional with new gadgets, then we will step back, read instructions, consult with experts, and learn anew. These habits of reflective and critical awareness do not eliminate the resistance of older mechanical habits, but they can foster greater flexibility and adaptiveness. We recapture the plasticity of childhood by becoming reflective practitioners, by learning to revise our specific performance habits in light of the general purposes of a task.

The acquisition of general dispositions for reflective and critical self-awareness, in conjunction with the skillful mastery of particular disciplines, is known as the liberal arts. In the liberal arts, we learn not only particular languages and modes of argumentation but also the general principles of grammar, rhetoric, and logic. Specific habits acquired in the context of a disposition to reflect on general principles will remain more supple and adaptive than habits acquired by rote practice. Liberal learning recaptures childhood by retaining a playful and imaginative perspective on our own knowledge and skills. Aware of the rigidities and narrowing of horizons that come with maturation, we return to the basic questions of our profession that captivated us in our youth.

The second profound obstacle to juvenilization is the pressure of the responsibilities of adult life. Childhood varies in length across and even within societies, but whether longer or shorter, childhood is essentially the time of life in which we are free from many of the burdens of adult life. Children do not need to make a living, save for retirement, or raise a family.

Childhood is a time of dependence on adults—a kind of sinecure in which one is protected from the cares of responsibility—so that one can freely explore, learn, and play. This freedom from care in childhood fosters open-ended imagination and blue-sky questions. Psychologist Alison Gopnik says that childhood is the time for the basic research that leads to productive applications in adulthood.[32] Children are known for asking the most profound metaphysical questions because they do not yet know how silly and useless they are. Adult imagination and activity are deeply constrained by the felt imperatives of being useful or helpful now. Children have the freedom to take the long view and to worry about the heat death of the universe. Gopnik compares children and adults to caterpillars and butterflies, so she does not offer suggestions for how adults might recapture the imaginative freedom of childhood. But one can infer from her analysis that if adults wish to free up their imaginations, they must somehow escape the felt imperatives to be productive, helpful, or useful. Adults must learn to indulge in the silly, the impractical, the useless, and the utopian—to the extent that this is consistent with their responsibilities!

~

Sometimes a life is compared to the phases of a day and sometimes to the seasons of a year. These analogies work well in the sense that during the morning we prepare for evening and during the spring we prepare for winter. We see and we live a day or a year as a whole, just as we see and we live our lives, however imperfectly, as a whole. But our ability to take our lives as a whole is lost in Carl Jung's interpretation of the stages of life: "we cannot live the afternoon of life according to the program of life's morning; for what was great in the morning will be little at evening, and what in the morning was true will at evening have become a lie."[33] Jung's observations here about the stages or phases of life are both illuminating and obscuring. As we saw with the virtues of childhood, what is great and true in the morning can be even greater and truer in the evening. The spell of the stages-of-life metaphor dispels all critical awareness of its limitations.

Erik Erikson, following Freud, is confident that modern science will finally solve the puzzles of human development and maturation. He claims that we have learned more about development in the twentieth century than in all of prior human history.[34] It is not surprising that Erikson explicitly applies the embryological theory of epigenesis to the whole of human life.³⁵ He says that the development of personality has its own invariant sequence of stages just as the embryonic development of any organism.³⁶

Historian Philippe Ariès claimed that childhood was created by modern society. By contrast, Erikson claims that society is created by childhood—that is, social institutions accommodate the biological and psychological needs of the developing child.³⁷ Just as environmental trauma can distort the normal growth of an embryo, so social pathologies can distort normal human development. Erikson's theory of psychological maturation acknowledges the distinction between descriptive maturity and normative maturity. He argues that many people and even many cultures reach only a limited kind of maturity because their psychological development is arrested at an early stage. To become fully mature we must resolve the dilemma posed by each stage of life. There is no skipping of stages, but progress through a stage may be retarded or accelerated—which will affect all subsequent stages.³⁸ Erikson's discussions of the crises or turning points that define each stage of development are deeply insightful about the challenges we all face in the course of our lives. But his stages still tend to obscure the fundamental wholeness of human life.

Although Erikson's basic conception of the stages of life stems from embryology, the way he describes these stages relies on scholastic metaphors. He defines each stage by its "tasks" and by what is "learned." We cannot graduate from a given stage until we have "mastered" its distinctive tasks. Just as we cannot learn algebra until we have first mastered arithmetic, we cannot learn "ego identity" until we have first mastered "trust."³⁹ Before we can enter a new stage, we must graduate from the old one. A person cannot become a good parent until he first becomes a worker and potential provider.⁴⁰ Each stage is a prerequisite of the next stage, and only the person who has mastered the first seven stages can hope to face death without fear. His chart of the stages reveals what "must have been developed" and what its "preparatory stages must have been."⁴¹ One wonders if life maturation has the same logical structure as formal schooling. Don't precocious children skip some stages of maturation? Don't many adults return to childhood, either in therapy or by parenting, in order to make further progress? Are we really stuck in one grade before passing the exam and stepping up to the next grade?

Erikson claims that each stage of development is defined by a unique challenge. Yet surely trust, autonomy, guilt, confidence, identity, intimacy, generativity, and integrity are not problems we sequentially solve but the very substance of lifelong maturation. In Erikson's final stage of life, for example, we look back on our whole life in relation to the horizon of our death. Yet, sages throughout the ages have insisted that we should always live in relation to our own death; indeed, we need a memento mori more urgently when we are young than when we are old.

Erikson himself came to appreciate some of the limits of his notion of an invariant sequence of stages. Although he describes his stages as "epigenetic" because they lead to increasing psychological differentiation, he also says that every stage exists "preformed" in human infants.[42] By combining both preformationism and epigenesis, Erikson can accommodate both the continuity of a life and discontinuity of stages. Here Erikson acknowledges that we always live in relation to the whole of life. In his own old age, Erikson came to describe human development as a kind of spiral in which we keep cycling back to earlier stages. In old age, the infant's trust becomes acknowledged interdependence, and in late middle age, the toddler's control over her body becomes acceptance of loss of control. Adolescent passion becomes mature tenderness, and the child's play stage becomes an adult sense of humor. In short, old age recapitulates all of the earlier stages of life but at a higher level—reflecting Erikson's greater acknowledgment of the unity of human life.[43]

Erikson developed his theory on the basis of his wide experience as a clinical therapist. However, psychiatrist George Vaillant has attempted to test Erik Erikson's theory systematically with a vast array of data collected from a set of long-term psychological studies of human development. In these studies, men and women were interviewed at fixed intervals throughout their adult lives in an attempt to measure their successful adaptation to the challenges of life.[44] With this data from hundreds of adults over a period of seven decades, Vaillant explored the validity of Erikson's claim that adult development must proceed through this sequence: intimacy, career consolidation, and generativity (meaning parenting or mentoring of the next generation). According to Vaillant, much of the empirical evidence corroborates Erikson's sequence, as illustrated by this typical statement from one subject of the Harvard Grant Study: "From age 20 to 30 I learned how to get along with my wife; from age 30 to 40, I learned how to be a success at my job; and since 40, I have worried less about myself and more about the children." Not all subjects, of course, had this "almost embryological progression" through Erikson's stages of adult development.[45] Still, Vaillant claims to have found much evidence for the validity of the Eriksonian sequence.[46] One wonders, however, whether this sequence of marriage, career, and generativity reflects universal patterns of human maturation or just the customs of modern industrial society.

Erikson's theory of maturation permits arrested development but no reversals: we can get stuck in a stage but we cannot regress. According to Vaillant's empirical studies, subjects never revert to earlier stages, except in the presence of organic disease such as major depression, alcoholism, or Alzheimer's.[47] Vaillant adopts Erikson's scholastic language to describe life as a school of hard knocks.[48] In this school, once we have mastered a task and learned our lesson, we never forget, unless we are set back by disease. So Eriksonian maturation has an inherent ratchet effect: whatever we gain we do not normally lose.

If the sequence of Eriksonian stages were truly invariant, then we ought to be able to predict adult success. Mastery of intimacy should predict mastery of career competence, and mastery of career competence should predict mastery of generativity. Indeed, when the Grant Study was started in 1937, the hope was that it would permit prediction of individual developmental milestones. Yet human development turned out to be unpredictable and full of surprises: not only was the timing of the stages highly variable, but many men who failed at the earlier stages ultimately succeeded in later stages.[49] Speculating more widely about human achievement in history, Vaillant concedes that many individuals tackle developmental tasks out of order or even all at once—either because of great external pressure and/or because of inherent genius.[50] As Vaillant rightly concludes: "Clearly, adult development is not as orderly as embryology."[51] What is the value of the study of adult development if it lacks predictive power? According to Vaillant, his studies may not tell us where we will go, but they do help us to diagnose how we arrived where we now are. We thus return to Kierkegaard's observation that life must be lived prospectively but can be understood only retrospectively.

In Erikson's account of the stages of human life we see both development within each stage and development across stages. We thus commonly judge infants, children, adolescents, and the elderly by how well they meet the expectations we have for each stage. We also judge people by how close they come to our ideals of full adult maturity. According to the philosopher David Norton, however, there is development only within each stage of life, and there is no development across stages. Why? According to Norton, the principles that define one stage are incommensurable with the principles that define other stages.[52] The tasks and virtues of childhood share nothing in common, on his account, with the tasks and virtues of adulthood. Being a splendid child has nothing in common with being a splendid adult.[53] Norton describes a process of evolution within each stage and revolution between stages.[54] According to Norton, the change between stages is instantaneous.[55]

Norton's denial that development takes place across the whole of human life requires him to deny that there is any single goal for the whole of human life. Each stage of life has its own unique goal and is launched by the arrival of its own unique existential insight. For example, he defines adolescence as a period of experimentation in which a child becomes not just a problem to others but also a problem to himself. The instant a child becomes a problem to himself, he is surprised to find himself an adolescent.[56] As soon as an adolescent discovers that his experimentation must end because time is limited, he is surprised to find himself an adult. And when an adult first discovers that she has no future, then she is surprised to find that she is old.[57] The phenomenon of surprise reveals the sudden and revolutionary change in our lives when we exchange one developmental goal for a totally new one. We are so locked into the perspective of each stage of life that we cannot fail to be surprised when a new stage arrives.[58]

Norton can deny any developmental continuity to human life as a whole because he divorces moral life from bodily life. Even Norton concedes that our bodies grow and decline over the whole of our lives, and he does not deny lifelong development in a purely physical sense.[59] Norton here follows Augustine in arguing that we are not our bodies, we are our souls (our *daimones*, in his terms), and our soul's journey in life has little or no connection to our bodily maturation or decline. Norton explains the appearance of moral continuity in life by the illusion of memory or anticipation, which transforms other stages in accordance with the stage one occupies. Memory of childhood is distorted by the needs of adulthood, just as the hopes for adulthood are distorted by the needs of childhood. Here Norton acknowledges that we always live in relation to the whole of life, but a whole that always represents simply a projection of a particular stage. Each stage of life creates its own distinctive version of the whole of life.[60]

Norton's account of the stages of human life becomes more complex when he connects it to his account of human flourishing. Following the philosopher Friedrich Nietzsche, rather than Aristotle, Norton argues that self-actualization is the supreme ethical project of human life.[61] To be a human person, says Norton, is to be self-actualizing.[62] More precisely, Norton must say that self-actualization is the supreme ethical project of mature adulthood. Like Aristotle, Norton acknowledges that we can fully actualize our capacities only in the prime of adulthood. A child, he says, lacks the autonomy for *self*-actualization while an old person lacks the capacities necessary for self-*actualization*.[63]

By the principle of incommensurability, every stage of life is independent of every other stage; but by the principle of self-actualization, the prime of life has primacy. Norton offers two strategies for reconciling these principles. First, we can say that ethical development is limited to the prime of life and that the other stages of human life lack any ethical purpose. Second, we can say that each stage of life has its own unique kind of actualization, but that self-actualization is restricted to mature adulthood.[64] Norton defends this second option, in which "personal development" is "a succession of stages." But here Norton must surrender his doctrine of the autonomy and incommensurability of the stages of life because now he posits a goal for the whole of human life by which development can be measured across stages. The stages of life can be autonomous and incommensurable only if there is no overarching purpose in human life.

Norton insightfully notes that most accounts of human development simply identify the purpose of human life with maturation, judging all stages of life by the standards of the prime of life. This subordination of all stages of life to the imperatives of the prime of life is certainly true of Aristotle. It is also true of some advocates of juvenilization, who treat childhood as the prime of life.[65] If we define the human in terms of a particular stage of life, then we ignore the unique tasks and virtues of the other stages of life. Norton believes that by restricting self-actualization to mature adulthood, he is protecting the intrinsic values of the other stages of life. If childhood for Aristotle is only about preparation for adulthood, childhood for Norton has nothing to do with preparation for adulthood. But since Norton identifies the supreme human ethical project as self-actualization, it is difficult to see how he avoids the same disparagement of childhood and old age that we witnessed in Aristotle. Incommensurability does not entail that every stage of life is equally valuable, for equality is a form of commensurability. Yet incommensurability does entail that no stage of life is simply supreme.[66] Still, Norton unequivocally asserts the primacy of the prime of life.[67]

Norton does not seem to notice that, on his account, old age might precede adolescence. Since he defines the stages of life without reference to bodily growth and decline but with reference only to personal existential insights, the order of the stages of life becomes highly variable. If childhood is defined only by existential dependence on independent adults, then anyone reduced by illness or accident to such dependence returns fully to childhood. If adolescence is defined only by lack of awareness of one's own death, then adolescence might well extend into old age. And if old age is defined only by an awareness that one lacks a future, then a terminal illness at any age could trigger old age. Such are the paradoxical consequences of denying the reality of development across the whole of human life.

Norton is aware that at every stage of life we are concerned with love, freedom, justice, truth, and death. But he insists that the meaning of these existential ideals is incommensurably different at each stage of life.[68] Certainly Norton is right that each stage of life has its own conception of these common concepts, but are those various conceptions truly incomparable? Often adult understandings of these concepts are simply superior in the sense that they include and transcend a child's conception. The need-love of a child for his mother is certainly different from the gift-love of a mother for her child, but are these kinds of love totally incommensurable? The fact that these different meanings of common words are not univocal does not entail that they are purely equivocal. Aristotle would say that the ethical ideals and virtues of the different stages of life are neither identical nor incommensurable but analogous. There are real analogies between a child's conception of justice and an adult's conception of justice or a child's conception of death and that of an adult. Aristotle sees real analogies, as we noted, between the natural virtues of children and the full virtues of adults.

Norton's account of incommensurable stages of human life provides a foundation for the notion of age-relative goods and virtues. For example, philosopher Michael Slote argues that some goods and some virtues are appropriate only for particular stages of life. He says, for example, that striving for merit badges or sporting trophies might be goods for children but not for adults; similarly, he says that victory at shuffleboard might be a good for the elderly but not for someone in the prime of life.[69] But are these intrinsically valuable goods at any stage of life? Surely seeking trophies is a trivial pursuit at any age. By contrast, children and the elderly also often help each other manage the vicissitudes of life. Surely assisting the weak is a genuine good at any stage of life. Children are good at mastering technological devices, learning new languages, fantasy play, and asking metaphysical questions; the elderly are good at seeing life as a whole, accepting ambiguity, and foreseeing many dangers. These goods come more easily at various stages of life, but they are all goods of human life. Any genuine good is a good for any human being.

Slote also argues that some virtues are age relative. He says that prudence (by which he means "caution") is a virtue in adults but not in children. For example, he says, we would find it inappropriate, if not appalling, for a small child to save for his retirement or develop and conform to a life plan. We expect small children to be open and trusting about the future. By contrast, moral innocence, he says, is a virtue for children but not for adults. We would find it inappropriate, if not appalling, for an adult to be morally innocent and not to foresee obvious moral dangers. For a child to exercise financial prudence or for an adult to be morally innocent implies that something has drastically gone wrong in their lives.[70]

Slote is right that prudence and moral innocence take different forms in different stages of life, but are they truly restricted to one stage? The prudence of a child takes the form of learning to trust the right adults. This prudence is certainly different but also analogous to adult prudence. Is it true that children ought not to be prudent and adults ought not to be innocent? Perhaps Aristotle is right when he argues that there is only one set of virtues for a complete life and that those virtues take different but analogous forms at different stages of life. Children are innocent and trusting because they are ignorant of the full extent of human evil. Innocence in adults means what William Blake called "organized innocence": an awareness of evil but a deliberate choice to trust fully other people—at some personal risk—on the theory that trust usually brings out the best in others.[71] This kind of deliberate innocence is characteristic of Christian saints and the "holy fools" of many religious traditions. Moral innocence comes more naturally to children but can become cultivated by adults, while prudence comes more naturally to adults but can be partly learned by children.[72]

I believe Aristotle is right that in principle, an adult in the prime of life is capable of enjoying all the genuine goods and virtues of childhood and of old age.[73] But Aristotle's description of the stages of life is misleading because he neglects the fact that very few adults in the prime of life actually do preserve the childlike capacities for play and philosophical wonder or the elderly capacities for detachment and wisdom. Children are not alone in their capacity for play and for wonder, but these goods come more naturally to them and are more salient in childhood—salient in the senses of playing a larger role in their lives and in being more manifest to adults. The goods of childhood, though not limited to children, come more easily to them—partly because of the greater plasticity of their minds and partly because of their freedom from adult responsibilities.[74] Both by nature and by nurture, children have unique capacities and unique opportunities to participate in these goods. How many adults would be able to enjoy these goods if they did not experience them in childhood or observe them in children? While much is usually gained in the transformation of childhood potency into adult activity, some valuable capacities are usually lost. There are no goods unique to any stage of life; there are only human goods.

Many adults admire the instinctive, unreflective goodness of small children who are often impulsively generous, where adults are calculating and cautious. At the same time, adults often condemn the unthinking selfishness of children, which is sometimes mistaken for cruelty.[75] Aristotle might rightly insist that a fully virtuous adult could in principle unite the spontaneous generosity of children with the rational control of an adult. A virtuous deed certainly can be shaped by rational ideals without being calculating or cautious. Perfect virtue would unite the spontaneity of childlike impulse with the rationality of adult moral ideals. But this ideal of rational spontaneity in moral action is a high, even saintly ideal. The rest of us tend to lose our childlike spontaneity as we acquire adult prudence. Indeed, without the example of children, we might even lose sight of the value of their impulsive goodness. Aristotle may be right in principle that adults can retain the natural virtues of children. Yet in practice adults tend to lose those virtues, and we need children to remind us of them. To use Aristotle's own image of the bent stick, if adult life inclines us to be overly cautious, goal oriented, anxious, and busy, then we need to bend over backward to imitate children if we hope to get our lives straight.

Such is the astonishing imaginative freedom of prime-of-life adults that, with effort, they can cultivate the virtues distinctive of children and the elderly. Biological development is not destiny. With imagination and practice, adults can acquire the virtues of children and the elderly. Robert Pogue Harrison distinguishes two kinds of human intelligence. The first is the genius of youth that invents, experiments, discovers, imagines—and subverts the world of the old. The second is the wisdom of the old that selects, preserves, and curates the inheritance of human culture.[76] Individual and cultural vitality depend on our ability to balance these two very different kinds of human intelligence.[77] Even as we enjoy the prime of life, we do have good reason imaginatively to return to childhood and to journey ahead into old age—not because we prefer to live our whole lives in childhood or in old age, but because we need to learn from children and from the elderly about how to become complete human beings.

By relying on this bodily paradigm of development, philosophers from Aristotle to Freud have argued that psychological and moral development takes place only in childhood and in youth; in adulthood, they claim, we reach a stable plateau.[78] However, we now know from empirical study that this picture of psychological development is false.[79] Adulthood for most people is not a time of extended psychic equilibrium, because most adults continue to struggle with the basic issues of separation from their parents and attachment to new partners. Maturity itself is not a summit to be attained once and for all—maturity waxes and wanes throughout adulthood.[80] It takes a lifetime to grow up—indeed, in many respects we never grow up. Here we see the dangers of viewing physical development as an index to psychological or moral development.

Can anything be said in general about the best shape of a human life? Michael Slote made the insightful observation that in assessing the overall goodness of a life, we discount the successes and misfortunes of childhood compared to those of the prime of life. We much prefer childhood failure or unhappiness to be followed by adult success or happiness than the converse. We are not indifferent to the timing of goods and bads in our lives: we give greater weight to later goods and bads than to earlier ones.[81]

Philosopher David Velleman has generalized Slote's insights: "A life that gets better is, other things being equal, better than a life that gets worse." We want a life in which good fortune follows bad fortune, not because we discount childhood but because later events in life alter the meaning of earlier events—whenever they take place.[82] According to Velleman, the reason why later events alter the meaning of earlier ones is because we understand our lives as a narrative in which earlier misfortunes are compensated for or redeemed by later successes.[83] If our lives did not have a narrative structure, we would be concerned only with the balance of goods and bads in our life. But we do care deeply that earlier misfortunes be redeemed by later successes, because, in any narrative, what comes later determines the meaning of what comes earlier. The value of a life cannot be reduced to the sum of its goods and successes; a narrative sequence must create a pleasing whole.[84]

Aristotle, as we noted, insisted that a supremely happy life (*makarios*) must have the right narrative closure. Aristotle agrees with Solon that we should not call anyone alive happy, because a reversal of fortune might still spoil his life. Aristotle's example of such a dramatic reversal is the story of King Priam of Troy, who lost his son and his kingdom as an old man. Aristotle does not consider whether such catastrophes early in life might be redeemed by successes later in life. Aristotle is clear, however, that what happens near or at the end of life determines whether that life has a happy or unhappy shape. In stories, as in lives, the ending is all-important. Everyone prefers a life of promotion rather than a life of demotion, even if the life of demotion started at the top.[85] More surprising is that many if not most people would prefer a life with significant early misfortunes followed by significant later successes to a life with no significant misfortunes. What matters to us most is not the balance of pleasure and pain but the meaning of a life story. Whatever our early successes or failures, the future shape of our life is relatively undetermined. But as we age, we have fewer opportunities to redeem our misfortunes or mistakes: a life is spoiled by what happens late, not by what happens early.[86] Ironically, more human lives are spoiled by dramatic early success than by dramatic early failure.

Philosophers have noted that we care more about whether pain or pleasure happens in the past or in the future than we care about the total sum. We are strongly biased toward the future. We will accept much more pain if it happens in the past, and future pleasures count for more than past pleasures.[87] These biases seem irrational unless we recall that pleasure redeems pain in most narratives. The philosophical insight that what we value is not a mere sum of pleasure but the timing of when they occur is strongly supported by experimental evidence. Psychologist Daniel Kahneman reports that most people strongly prefer to experience a longer duration of pain with a happy ending to a much shorter duration of pain without one. The same narrative preferences apply not merely to particular experiences but also to the shape of a whole life. People prefer a short life with a meaningful closure to a much longer life without such a satisfying end. Whether individual episodes or a whole life, what people value are beginnings, peaks, and ends—not sums of pleasure or pain. According to Kahneman, every person is intuitively a storyteller.[88]

Kahneman thinks it is irrational to prefer a life with more total pain, even if that pain is redeemed by good closure. Here we see the contrast between a chronicle and a narrative view of a human life. A chronicle life is nothing more than the sum of its events; in a narrative life, by contrast, the whole of life is present at every moment in the form of memory and imagination. When we tell a story as opposed to listing a chronicle, the beginning foreshadows the end, and the end recapitulates the beginning. A narrative is much more unified than a chronicle. If a human life were a mere chronicle of discrete events, then Kahneman is right that we should prefer a life of maximal total pleasure. But if a human life is a narrative, then it makes sense to prefer good closure, even at the cost of more pain.

This contrast between a narrative and a chronicle can be seen in the distinction between three-dimensional and four-dimensional objects. A three-dimensional object *endures* through time by being wholly present at each moment of its life; a four-dimensional object, by contrast, *perdures* by passing through a series of temporal parts. A three-dimensional enduring object "sweeps through" a region of space-time, while a four-dimensional perduring object is "spread out" over a region of space-time.[89] Those who argue that a human life is four-dimensional say that just as a body has spatial parts, so a life has temporal parts.

Let us consider stages as temporal parts of a human life. On this view, my life is the sum of its various stages because my life is spread out across all of these temporal parts. Instead of saying that I passed through infancy, childhood, and adolescence, I would say that I have temporal parts, including all of these stages. I was not all there in childhood, only a part of me was. I did not develop through these stages, but one stage merely succeeded another. The theory of temporal parts treats change as a successive replacement of temporal parts. My life, on this view, is a succession of instantaneous temporal slices, none of which ever changes. Instead of being wholly present at every moment of my life, I am spread out over a spatiotemporal trajectory, and only a part of me is present at any moment.[90]

In a chronicle, the part is prior to the whole in the sense that the whole is nothing more than a sum of its parts. But in a narrative, the whole is prior to its parts in the sense that each part reflects the shape of the whole. The analogy between the spatial parts and the temporal parts of an organism is illuminating, so long as we recognize the explanatory priority of the whole over its parts. Just as my body is prior to its organs, my life is prior to its stages. Unfortunately, however, champions of four-dimensionalism often describe the whole of a human life as merely the sum of its temporal parts.[91] For example, many four-dimensionalists compare a person's journey through time with a road's journey through space.[92] Of course, a road is merely the sum of its spatial parts. As a road "journeys" through space, it merely adds new segments to old. Does a road look down the road at what is ahead? Every journey (as opposed to an adventure or saunter) has a subjective destination or goal, which could not be said of a road. Things get worse when a four-dimensionalist describes the act of touching a person. According to them, we never directly touch a whole person but only one spatial part of a person, such as her hand. Similarly, they say, we can only directly touch one temporal part of a person—say, his childhood—since the rest of him is not present to be touched.[93]

A human life cannot be reduced to its spatial or temporal parts. It makes no sense to contrast having my hand touched and having myself touched. To have my hand touched is to have myself touched. The only way I can be touched is to have one or more spatial parts touched. That I am touched is necessarily prior to any part of me being touched. The four-dimensionalist protests: "I did not touch you, I only touched your hand!" As for temporal parts, it is similarly absurd to suppose that you could touch my childhood or any other temporal part without directly touching me. Again, just as the whole of my body is present in all its spatial parts, the whole of my life is present in all its temporal parts.

Just as four-dimensionalists reduce the whole of a human life to the sum of its temporal parts, so they reduce a narrative to a chronicle. Philosopher Theodore Sider compares the temporal parts of a human life to the chapters of a story.[94] But he then says that the part of a life *just* consisting of childhood is like the chapter of a book *just* consisting of childhood.[95] But, of course, childhood is also about adulthood, just as adulthood is also about childhood. The chapter of a book on childhood cannot just consist of childhood, any more than actual childhood consists only of childhood. According to Sider, with enough detail, my life's story will have parts concerning only individual days, minutes, or even instants. Narrative unity gives way here to meaningless chronicle.[96] Here we see the logic of a stage conception of human life in its purest form, where each stage is a temporal part and a human life is just the sum of its stages.[97]

Biologists teach us that the whole organism is always prior to its organs, just as the whole life of an organism is always prior to any of its developmental stages. We cannot understand the function of any organ apart from the needs of the whole organism, just as we cannot understand any stage of life apart from the whole life story.[98] As we shall see, we cannot even identify the events of our lives apart from a life narrative.

CHAPTER 7

What Am I?

Human Beings and Human Persons

I have argued that important aspects of lifelong personal development can be well described by stories of individualization, preformation, neoteny, and recapitulation. Why should stories of development that emerged in biology apply so well, at least analogically, to moral, emotional, and spiritual development? Were these stories told about embryonic development because they already made sense of personal development? Did biologists just project inchoate stories of human personal development onto animal embryos? Or do the deep analogies between embryonic development and human personal development tell us something about what it means to be a human person? By contrast, we saw philosopher David Norton attempt to liberate "personal" development from the constraints of mere biological development. According to Norton, my "personal destiny" has no essential connection to my "biological destiny." Indeed, most philosophers since John Locke sharply distinguish a biological human being from a psychological person. Our stories of development, however, call into question any such contrast between our biological humanity and our psychological personhood.

Philosophical discussions of human nature often confound three quite different sets of questions. The first is the question of what kind of being is a human person. What qualities are essential, and which are merely contingent? What is permanent, and what changes in the development of a human life? How do we identify a human being? How does our humanity relate to our personhood? A second set of questions is about the persistence of human persons over time. Am I the same person I was as a child? Do I have an enduring self or am I merely a succession of selves? What markers ensure our re-identification over time? A third set of question is about how to characterize a human life. How do I relate to my own actions and experiences? How do I develop a sense of my own identity? What is the relation between understanding my life and leading it? What gives an individual human life meaning? Who am I?[1] In this chapter, I will address two questions: What am I? and How do I persist over time? In the next chapter, I will address the question of our sense of our own individual identity: Who am I?

Philosophers have multiplied the candidates for the title of human person. We are said to be either human beings or rational persons; we are said to *be* selves, souls, bodies, brains, or minds; we are also said to *have* selves, souls, bodies, brains, or minds. Philosopher P. M. S. Hacker rightly worries that the human vessel is "getting overcrowded or that there is some double counting on the manifest."[2] Some philosophers attribute this conceptual anarchy to grammatical confusion in the use of the first-person pronoun or to simple logical errors. I think these confusions have a deeper source in fundamental puzzles about the relation of the rational agency of persons to the biological powers of human beings.

Human beings have always been deeply puzzling to themselves.[3] The chorus in Sophocles's *Antigone* sings: "Wonders are many, but none is more wonderful than man."[4] Aristotle wonders how human beings manage to be both the best of all animals and the worst.[5] We have always felt a profound kinship with our fellow animals and yet deeply estranged from our natural family. We claim superiority over the beasts but then act in ways far worse than beastly. Our dominion over nature is full of anxiety about our rightful place. We are mortal but dream of immortality, finite but wrestle with the infinite.[6] We are bound up in the nexus of natural causes and yet radically free. For example, we share with every other animal an instinct for self-preservation but also possess a uniquely human power of willful self-destruction. We are born of this earth but are preparing to leave it; bound to this fragile body but planning a bionic or robotic future. Today, many philosophers are puzzled by how a mere physical brain could give rise to consciousness, let alone self-consciousness. Many linguists today are puzzled by how human language could emerge so suddenly from quite primitive forms of animal communication.[7]

How can we reconcile our kinship with the natural world and our uniquely human capacity to transcend that world in thought and deed?

Every human culture has attempted to answer this question by reference to the gods: the human being is somehow partly animal and partly divine. Our unique rational powers have long been attributed not to our animal body but to our divine soul. Even Socrates attributes his conscience to a divine spirit or *daimon*. As he dies, he claims to welcome the release of his immortal soul from the prison of his animal body. Socrates claims to have a share in the divine nature. Indeed, Socrates attributes many supreme human achievements to "divine madness" (*theia mania*).[8] And Aristotle, who usually adopts a strictly biological approach to human nature, sometimes insists that human reason (*nous*) is divine.[9] Here we find a paradoxical view of human nature: what most essentially human, our intellect, is also divine. Aristotle even says that we should strive to divinize ourselves.[10] Human nature is precariously suspended between the animal and the divine. In his famous *Oration on the Dignity of Man*, Pico de Mirandola describes a human being as the only entity who can choose whether to be a beast or a god: "To you is granted the power of degrading yourself into the lower forms of life, the beasts, and to you is granted the power, contained in your intellect and judgment, to be reborn into the higher forms, the divine." Shakespeare's Hamlet wonders whether a man is a beast or a god.[11] These appeals to the divine as a way to understand the uniqueness of human nature do not solve the problem of human being but merely sharpen the puzzle. The description of human beings as "persons" stemmed, as we shall see, from a comparison of human beings to God.

What am I essentially, a human being or a person? In ordinary discourse, we generally equate persons with human beings.[12] That is why most people chafe when lawyers describe corporations as persons or theologians describe God as a person. In the seventeenth century, John Locke broke with common sense and sharply contrasted the biological notion of a human being with the psychological notion of a person.[13] Locke denied that we can know or identify the real essence of human beings or, for that matter, of any substance.[14] Is human reason more essential to human being than skin color? Not according to Locke: "It is necessary for me to be as I am . . . . nothing I have is essential to me."[15] The differences between species of animals, he says, are based in our language not in reality. If a monkey or any animal had reason, we would call it a human being.[16] Indeed, so arbitrary are the distinctions among so-called species, says Locke, that humans can breed with monkeys.[17]

Although we can know nothing about who we really are, we can know what our descriptions of human beings mean. Our descriptions of human beings refer to our ideas of corporeality or rationality, not to aspects of real substances.[18] When Locke defines a human being as a "corporeal rational creature," he defines our nominal but not our real essence. Where Aristotle saw "rational" as a species of "animal," Locke insists that our idea of a rational creature is at odds with our idea of a corporeal creature. If we define human being as rational, he says, then, paradoxically, a child is not human; if we define a human being by corporeal form, then, equally paradoxically, a rational monkey would not be a human being.[19] Locke, unlike Aristotle, is widely thought to be a champion of human equality. Yet Locke explicitly compares a fetus to a vegetable, a child to a monkey, and a senescent old man to an oyster.[20] Locke may well assert the equality of all rational persons, but he explicitly denies the equality of all human beings. In this respect, as in others, most contemporary philosophers follow Locke closely.

To escape the paradoxes that emerge from our ideas of human being as both corporeal and rational, Locke distinguishes a human being from a person. Since we cannot have knowledge of real essences, we can only compare the persistence conditions of our ideas. As corporeal, says Locke, a human being has the same persistence conditions as any animal; as a rational person, says Locke, we persist through continuity of consciousness, especially the continuity of our memories of our past deeds.[21] A person, unlike a mere human animal, is a rational and moral agent.[22] A person, in his view, is an insubstantial ghost inhabiting an animal. Locke argues that a person, as a form of consciousness, might well switch animal bodies, just as one man may wear many suits of clothes.[23] Conversely, Locke argues, the same animal body might well contain several successive human persons.[24]

Locke decisively shapes modern theories of human nature in two ways. First, what Aristotle had joined, Locke rents asunder: he divides *Homo sapiens* into a biological animal and a psychological person—a division he illustrates with his thought experiments in which persons switch animals and animals switch persons. Second, Locke identifies his essential "self" with the psychological person rather than with the biological animal: I am essentially a conscious agent and only accidentally an organism.[25]

No philosopher is better known for his defense of human dignity than is Immanuel Kant. But Kant follows Locke in sharply distinguishing mere human beings from moral persons and in identifying the self with the moral person. Kant famously contrasts natural man, who is caught up in the nexus of causation, to a moral person, who is endowed with an "inner freedom."[26] Kant endorses the dignity not of human beings but only of human persons: "In the system of nature, man (*homo phaenomenon, animal rationale*) is a being of slight importance and shares with the rest of the animals, as offspring of the earth, an ordinary value (*pretium vulgare*). But man regarded as a person, that is, as the subject of a morally practical reason, is exalted above any price."[27] Kant contrasts the rational animal as phenomenal with the moral person as noumenal. Instead of defining human beings as both generically animal and specifically personal, Kant defines us essentially as persons who are only accidentally animals.

Yet Kant does speak of human dignity in relation to moral persons; we must, he says, respect the humanity within our persons by not, for example, killing or degrading ourselves. But Kant describes our humanity as a mere vehicle for our personhood, and our duties to our humanity as derivative of our duties to our moral personality. As moral persons each of us has a duty to protect and preserve our humanity.[28] Clearly, the person with an obligation to protect and preserve her humanity cannot be essentially human. If I feel a duty to protect my own body, then I cannot also be my body. For Kant, dignity stems only from our capacity for moral personality, and Kant denies that all human beings have this capacity.[29]

A person is a self-conscious rational and moral agent. Is every human being a person, or is every person a human being? Can there be non-human persons or human nonpersons? At bottom, do I think of myself as a human being or as a rational person? We often describe this distinction by contrasting a human body with a human mind. In some ways, we identify with our biological organism, as when we say "I am my body." But in other ways, we identify with our rational agency, as when we say "I have a body." Many philosophers agree about the twofold quality of our primordial experience of ourselves—as embodied and as an inner mental pilot.[30] There is no agreement among philosophers about how to define body or mind, let alone how they relate to each other. Most philosophers today follow Locke and Kant by sharply contrasting a biological conception of a human being with a psychological conception of a person.[31] Where philosophers mostly disagree is over whether our identity and our persistence conditions are basically biological or psychological, human or personal.

Unfortunately, philosophical analyses of this puzzle usually frame the inquiry in question-begging ways: "What is personal identity?" (assuming that we are persons) or "When does human life begin?" (assuming that we are organisms). The manner in which we frame the question deeply shapes our intuitions. If we begin by thinking of ourselves as persons, then we easily imagine ourselves occupying other kinds of bodies, physical, spiritual, or digital. But if we begin thinking of ourselves as human organisms, then we can imagine a succession of persons within our one human body.[32]

Human substantial unity means that we experience ourselves as organisms all the way down, such that any injury to any part of my body is an injury to me.[33] We experience an astounding integration of our intellectual and physical capacities so that our thought is expressed fluidly through the physical modalities of speech or writing. Everyone knows the location of her hands and feet without having to look. Each of us has a unique awareness of both our psychological anxiety as well as our physical pain.[34] The easiest way to understand our substantial unity is to see that when we say "I am thinking about you" or say "I am walking toward you," my first-person pronoun refers to the same entity. I would not normally say: "*I* am not thinking of you but my brain is" or "*I* am not walking toward you but my body is." We can imaginatively identify with any one of our biological or psychological powers, but we normally use "I" to refer to ourselves as an irreducible unity of physical and mental powers.

We are also able to withdraw our sense of ourselves into an inner center of psychological awareness in which our bodies appear to be mere instruments of a sovereign and indestructible rational person. Socrates famously argued that his body was only a prison and tomb of his rational soul; for him, salvation is the liberation of the immortal soul from the mortal body. Stoic philosophers counselled us to think of ourselves as an inner citadel of rational agency, where no bodily misfortune can threaten our moral freedom. It is tempting, especially for philosophers, to imagine ourselves as essentially mental commanders at the bridge of the mind, thinking and choosing in sovereign freedom from any biological or material constraint.[35] Dancers, athletes, and yogis, perhaps, are more likely to think of themselves as essentially embodied. A philosopher, I presume, is much more likely to imagine herself in another body than is a ballerina.[36]

Most philosophers since Locke have defined our essential identity not in terms of our biological animality but in the psychological terms of personhood.[37] In this diverse family of views, I am essentially a rational and moral agent who is only contingently related to a human organism. After all, what we value most in ourselves and other people is personhood, not mere humanity. We highly esteem the personal traits of memory, attention, and expectation; we honor a person's moral and intellectual virtues. Many philosophers and theologians have entertained the possibility of nonhuman persons, such as gods, angels, aliens, intelligent animals, and soon, perhaps, digital persons. If personhood can be sustained by many different kinds of substances, then a person cannot be identified with a human organism or with any biological organism. In these psychological views, personhood is not a substance at all but a quality that can arise in a variety of substances; personhood is not a noun but an adjective that qualifies its particular substance.

If not essentially a person, then what am I? One biological theory of human identity says that I am essentially an organism or animal. In this view, I came into existence as an animal embryo and I will remain in existence until the death of the organism that I am. Interestingly, as a human animal, personhood is also just one phase of my life. I was not born a person and I may die after losing my personhood to dementia. As a human animal, I care deeply about what happens to my organism, since what happens to my organism happens to me. I do not feel secure in an inner mental citadel but intensely vulnerable to disease or injury. I am pretty sure that I would not be me in another body. I am quite certain that my consciousness or memory cannot in principle be uploaded to a digital computer.

Locke, like most modern philosophers, equates his personhood with his "self." What does it mean to be or to have a self?[38] Champions of the psychological approach to personhood claim that our essential self must be the innermost part of us, unobservable by others. A self is thought to be the subject of our consciousness, the inner "I" that unifies and accompanies all conscious experience.[39] Already at around age three, children realize other people cannot read their minds, just as they cannot read other people's minds. We often feel as though we are alone in our heads.[40] A poet captures this widespread intuition eloquently: "A secret self I had enclos'd within / That was not bounded with my clothes or skin."[41] We seem to have a unique window on our own thoughts, desires, and memories, and it is natural to identify our private self with our true self. It does not follow from this, of course, that we know ourselves better than others know us or that we know others less well than they know themselves. A unique window is not a privileged vantage. Still, the private, interior self may well seem more truly mine than the public, bodily self.

In any philosophical debate, it is helpful to identify what the opposed views have in common. Advocates of the biological approach as well as advocates of the psychological approach largely agree that personhood is a psychological phenomenon.[42] That is why those who define humans as animals deny that we are essentially persons or even rational animals. They accept the view that personhood is merely a psychological phase in the life of a human animal.[43] Since I am essentially an animal, I existed before I developed personhood and I might exist after I lose my personhood. That is why some advocates of the biological approach curiously deny that we are essentially *Homo sapiens*. The biological interpretation of human identity rejects the specific difference, namely personhood, unique to human beings. According to these philosophers, we are essentially biological hominids with merely a contingent relationship to rationality and personhood.[44] In this view, I remain a human being whether or not I develop or lose my personhood. A human, they say, is essentially a biological *Homo* who might pass through a psychological phase of *sapiens*.[45] As for champions of the psychological approach to human identity, they also insist that rational and moral agency are psychological phenomena, which is why they argue that I was never an infant and that whoever dies of my dementia will not be me. If my identity is essentially psychological, then I might find it plausible to suppose that I could be erased, duplicated, transferred, or uploaded into other substances.

We must reject the common assumption that personhood is merely psychological. According to the biological approach, we are essentially animals and only accidentally rational persons; according to the psychological approach, we are essentially rational persons and only accidentally animals. In both approaches, a human life is divided into prepersonal, personal, and postpersonal phases or stages. A human life is a unified whole. Personhood is not a phase of life, like being an athlete or a teacher. We are not biological animals in whom psychological personhood somehow arises in late childhood and then disappears should we suffer dementia. Some philosophers today claim that personhood *supervenes on* the biological constitution of a human being, just as the wetness of water supervenes on the combination of hydrogen and oxygen. Yet whereas water cannot be identified with the elements on which it supervenes, personhood can be identified with the biological human being.[46] Human beings are not some combination of biological animal and rational agent. Rather, we are animals all the way up and persons all the way down. When we compose symphonies and create scientific theories we do so as human animals, and when we eat, forage, and mate we do so as human persons.

The notions of a human animal or a rational person are both philosophical abstractions remote from the lived unity of human life.[47] We must begin our inquiry with the concrete individual entity of a human person rather than with abstract ideas of animality or rational agency. The substance that we call an individual human person has a unity that is prior to any subsequent analysis into physical, chemical, biological, and psychological properties.[48] The concept of such a human person is primitive and cannot be reduced to either an ensouled body or to an embodied soul.[49] We derive the notion of a person from a human being; apart from a human being a person would not be an individual.[50] What is basic is the human person, not a body or mind. Aristotle's famous image of the relation of the human soul to the human body is that of a seal impressed into wax: it makes no sense to ask whether the we are the seal or the wax.[51] In Aristotle's psychology, the soul (*psyche*) refers to all of the powers of the living body. As such, the soul is no more separable from a body than vision is separable from an eye.[52]

What this means is that there is no inner, mental self who observes her own thoughts and memories. Our mind is not inside ourselves, and our thoughts are not observable by introspection.[53] Rather, a mind is a set of powers, and we can be aware of some of these powers. One power we have is the ability to give expression to our thoughts or sometimes to conceal them. This power does not entail that we can observe or have access to some mysterious inner realm.[54] When I refer to my "self" I refer only to myself, that is, to me, a human being.[55] What we call introspection is only a reflective awareness of our mental activities. To posit an inner self as a subject of my thought is to mistake reflection for another self, as in a mirror. Are my private thoughts more essentially me than my public utterances?[56] Anthony Kenny argues that really important questions about oneself are questions that can be settled not by private reflection but only by public discourse and deeds.[57] Even if an inner, mental self is an illusion, we can use expressions such as "my true self" or "my former self" correctly to refer to our most cherished individual commitments.

Ever since Locke, philosophers and theologians have devoted a great deal of ingenuity to attempting to pry apart human being from personhood. But I think we should affirm the commonsense view that to be a human being is to be a person. The expressions "human being" and "person" have different senses or meanings. To describe someone as a human being draws our attention to her biological reality as a uniquely rational animal of the genus of hominids. When we say "that is only human" or "all too human!" we intend to emphasize the weakness, folly, mortality, and other limits of our animal nature. To be human is to be a special kind of animal but an animal nonetheless. To describe someone as a "person," by contrast, draws our attention to rational and moral agency. The term "person" is an honorific that acknowledges the infinite powers of our rational nature. To be a person is to be a creature of inestimable dignity.[58] Words with different senses or meanings can refer to the same entity.[59] "The morning star" and "the evening star" both refer to Venus. In the same way, "human being" and "person" both refer to the same entity, namely, any individual member of *Homo sapiens*. Our paradigm for a person is a human being.[60]

The human beings we encounter are all persons, and the only persons we have ever met (outside of science fiction) are human beings. Our understanding of human beings is what informs our concept of personhood, and our understanding of personhood directs our attention to what gives unique dignity to all human beings. There is a "conceptual concordance" between our notions of a human being and of a person: a person is someone who can interpret a human being, and a human being is open to being interpreted by persons.[61] What about divine persons, alien persons, or even digital persons? Do these kinds of nonhuman persons show that the concept of person is only accidentally related to human beings? Not at all. The human being remains the sole paradigm of personhood.[62] The extension of the concept of "person" to other entities can only be by analogy. We would recognize as a person only an entity that shared essential features of our lives as human beings. The concept of person, then, articulates our understanding of what is essential to human beings.

∼

According to Aristotle, a living substance is an organism with an intrinsic essential nature; that is, a unique intrinsic principle of development and activity. A living substance, in short, is defined by its intrinsic and essential development and activity, whether merely potential or partially actualized.[63] Were we to define an organism by its actualized powers alone, then we could not explain why a caterpillar and a butterfly are the same substance—or a human fetus and an adult. Developmental change presupposes substantial permanence, and what is permanent is the intrinsic principle of activity. A living substance, then, is a temporal whole, not a mere series of phases or stages. If personhood is essential to human being, then we are always persons from the time we acquire our intrinsic principle of development until death. Being an athlete is a mere phase in human life; being a person is essential to human life.

As a biologist, Aristotle goes about defining human beings as he would any living substance, by locating our genus and species.[64] As for our genus, he consistently calls us an "animal," but as for our specific difference, he offers a range of descriptions. He calls us a civilized animal, a political animal, an animal capable of knowledge, a talking animal, and a rational animal.[65] Is there a way to unify these various descriptions? I think it is clear that they all focus on the unique human capacity for language. When Aristotle describes man as a rational animal, he usually uses a word (*logos*) that refers to both reason and speech.[66] And when he describes us as political animals, he elaborates by saying that we are political because we have the gift of speech and can debate what is just and unjust, whereas other animals are limited to expressions of pleasure and pain.[67] Our capacity for language rests on our nature as social animals and makes possible our rational nature. Aristotle is right: language is both unique to human beings and universal to all human beings. We are talking animals. Many contemporary philosophers agree that human capacities for rational and moral agency are inseparable from our unique linguistic capacities.[68]

The essence of a substance is often not observable but must be inferred in order to explain the visible properties of that substance. Locke, as we noted, denied that we could know the real essence of a substance, but he understood that such an essence, if known, would explain the visible qualities of that substance.[69] Following Locke, many contemporary philosophers define substances as bundles of properties. But only knowledge of the essence of a substance could explain why it possesses those particular properties. The necessary properties, powers, and capacities are determined by what a substance essentially is: what a thing is determines how it is. The essence or nature of a thing tells us what it is. What are called the laws of nature flow from the nature of substances: things behave the way they do because of what they are.[70]

Aristotle identified two paradigmatic classes of substances: the basic elements and living organisms.[71] When Aristotle claims that a living substance has its own intrinsic essence, he means, in modern terms, that a biological species is a natural kind.[72] Among modern philosophers, the paradigm of a natural kind is an element, such as gold. Aristotle assumed that gold had an intrinsic essence, but he had no idea what that essence might be. Thanks to modern physical chemistry, we now know what the essence of gold actually is: a metal with the atomic number (Z) of 79. Why is this the essence of gold? An essence serves two primary functions in explanation: first, an essence picks out those properties of a natural kind that are possessed by every member of that kind and by members of no other kind; second, these essential properties are intrinsic to the members of a kind and they explain the other properties of that kind. Any metal of atomic number 79 is gold, and only samples of gold have atomic number 79. Moreover, this unique atomic number explains the other properties of gold, such as its density, malleability, and color.

Many biologists and philosophers who accept that gold has an intrinsic essence deny that human beings do.[73] That is, they deny that a biological species is a natural kind. For example, they point out that a biological species is spatiotemporally restricted, while a physical element is spatiotemporally unrestricted. What this means is that a sample of metal with atomic number 79 would be gold, whether found a billion years ago or a billion years from now; it would be gold whether located on earth or in another galaxy; it would be gold whether discovered underground or created in a laboratory. A human being, by contrast, must be part of a specific lineage of primates descended from a common ancestor; that is, a historically particular segment of the genealogical tree of life. Were a creature identical to human beings to have evolved independently, or be discovered in another galaxy, or created in a laboratory, it would not be counted as *Homo sapiens*. In short, what defines our biological species is not some putative essence but a relation to a unique historical lineage.

A natural kind is a class of entities whose members share a common essence. But perhaps a species is not a class of entities but an individual whose parts are organisms. In this view, *Homo sapiens* is the proper name of a unique individual who was born in Eastern Africa two hundred thousand years ago, migrated throughout the earth, and will go extinct sooner than we like to think. Each human being, then, is not a member of a natural kind but a part of an individual species. Parts of an individual need not have a common essence, just as the organs of a human being do not have a common essence. According to these biologists and philosophers, because species evolve, there need be no essential properties in common among the parts of *Homo sapiens* from the time it emerged to the time it goes extinct. Indeed, we have no a priori reason to believe that the first human beings possessed the rational and moral agency that we now deem essential to human identity—or that our species will possess these properties in the distant future.

Biologists and philosophers who define *Homo sapiens* as a historical individual rely on one particular species concept: phylogenetic ancestry. On this view a species is defined by its relationship to its parent species. But there are other widely accepted concepts of species as well. Reproductive concepts define species in terms of communities of interbreeding organisms, while ecological concepts define species in terms of a shared environmental niche and lifestyle. All of these species concepts are widely used in contemporary biology. None of them is adequate to describe the weird diversity of life.[74] Phylogenetic species concepts must be supplemented by reproductive or ecological concepts in order to explain speciation: having a common ancestor does not explain why new species emerge.[75] Many biologists and philosophers argue that all of these species concepts imply only relational and not intrinsic properties. A species is defined, they say, by its relations to its ancestors, to its reproductive partners, and to its ecological niche. Any organism, no matter what its intrinsic essence, with the right ancestry, reproductive partners, and lifestyle will belong to a given species.[76]

I think these three kinds of species concepts are deeply revealing of our sense of what it means to be part of the human community. For example, those who deny the unity of the human species have always adopted one or more strategies based on these species concepts. First, they deny that all human beings have the same ancestors, asserting theories of polygenesis; second, they deny that human beings should form a single reproductive community, by banning miscegenation; third, they attempt to prevent human beings from sharing the same ecological niche by enforcing segregation. These complex cultural practices, widely practiced in the most diverse societies, thus have a simple, if misguided, biological rationale. The unity of the human species rests on sharing the same ancestors, the same reproductive community, and the same cultural environment. Were we to stop intermarrying or stop sharing the same cultural environment, then, over time, the human species would diverge into new species.

Does the fact that the dominant biological theories define species in relational terms imply that organisms have no intrinsic essences that sort them into species?[77] Let's consider two questions we might ask about species: (1) What is it to be a member of any group that happens to be a species? (2) What is it for a group to be a species? The species concepts I have discussed seem to answer the second question but not the first. They tell us that for a group of organisms to be a "species," it must have the right relations to ancestors, mates, and niches. But these relational concepts do not identify the intrinsic properties by virtue of which an organism participates in these relationships.[78] First, by sharing a common primate ancestor, human beings must also share certain intrinsic traits, which we inherited from that ancestor. Second, human beings can reproduce with other human beings (but not with members of other species) because of certain intrinsic properties we possess. Third, human beings occupy a unique ecological niche (including agriculture and culture) because we possess certain intrinsic traits, especially the capacity for language. Individual human organisms must possess some intrinsic properties which make it possible for human beings, but not organisms of any other species, to participate in these species-defining relationships. Indeed, the intrinsic traits by virtue of which we participate in these relationships must certainly be largely genetic. What have we inherited from our primate ancestors? What prevents us from reproducing with other species? What enables us to breathe terrestrial air and to make tools? There is certainly a genetic basis for all of these species-defining relationships.[79] These intrinsic properties are essential for defining what organisms belong to the species *Homo sapiens*.

Virtually no biologist or philosopher asks the truly basic question: Why are there species in the first place? Why is biological diversity not simply continuous, with no stable groups of organisms? Biologist Ernst Mayr believes that the answer must be the integrity of the genome.[80] By limiting variation into relatively stable groups of organisms who can breed only with conspecifics, evolution reduces the chances of bizarre genetic combinations that are unlikely to survive. Of course, species do evolve over time, but—within this stream of descent with modification—speciation creates islands of stability sufficient to constitute genuine natural kinds with species-specific essences. Some biological natural kinds, however, unlike gold, are spatiotemporally localized: an extinct species may never appear again.

A biological essence undoubtedly includes genetic as well as epigenetic properties. There are sharper boundaries between chemical kinds than biological kinds, and a biological kind does not have a single specific essence: there is no one gene for being human. Our essences are probably clusters of genetic and epigenetic traits.[81] What kinds of traits characterize biological essences? Each species is defined by an essential cluster of genealogical, reproductive, and ecological properties, partly genetic and partly epigenetic.

No one of these properties alone constitutes a biological essence, only a species-specific cluster.[82] Biological kinds, of course, admit of gradual change but, then again, so do unstable radioactive chemical elements. Just as uranium (Z 235 or 238) decays into lead (Z 82), so one biological species evolves into another. Such change is consistent with the possession of intrinsic essences.

Does it matter whether substances are defined by their necessary bundles of properties or by their essences? Being a sample of gold or being a human being is not matter of possessing certain properties but of being a substance of a certain kind. Being a metal is not a property of gold but partly constitutive of gold, just as being a mammal is not a property but partly constitutive of being a human. Being a metal or being a mammal is not a way to characterize something but tells us what it is. Properties tell us how something is; essences tell us what something is. Even if we know all the necessary properties of a substance we cannot know why these properties are necessarily correlated without knowing the essence. How something is characterized depends on what it is. To define a biological organism in terms of a species-specific cluster of genetic and epigenetic properties is not in itself explanatory. We want to know why these and only these properties necessarily correlate—that is, we want to know the essence of that species.[83]

Insofar as the essences of organisms are intrinsic, they are certainly largely genetic. Recall that essences define properties shared by all and only all members of a natural kind. Some biologists claim that there are no genetic features unique to each species. But genetic variation in the species-specific gene pool is compatible with unique genetic properties for each species.[84] What properties are shared by all and only all human beings? Now that we have sequenced the human genome we know that every human being shares a species-specific genetic profile, sometimes called the human "barcode."[85] Today, this genetic profile is merely a reliable diagnostic marker of our humanity; despite significant variation in the human gene pool, no geneticist would confuse a human genome with that of any other species. But we do not understand genetics well enough to identify the precise genetic basis for human personhood. No doubt, the full development of the human person involves many epigenetic factors, ranging from other aspects of the genome to human physiology and to human culture. Most biologists are confident that the linguistic, cognitive, and affective components of human personhood have a basis in the human genome.

Why does it matter that human beings belong to a natural kind with a specific essence? First, by virtue of our shared nature, we are constitutionally attuned to other human beings and are able to interpret them. We understand other human beings from the inside, so to speak. Were we to encounter nonhuman persons, we could understand them only insofar as we shared their biological nature. Wittgenstein famously said that even if a lion could speak we could not understand him. But perhaps we could understand a lion who expressed desires for food, sex, or domination since we share these desires with all mammals. We know what they feel like. How could we possibly understand an alien "person" who shared no biological desires with us? The barrier to communication would not be linguistic but much deeper. Second, sharing a common nature is the "precondition of the human solidarity (where present) that excoriates the treatment of a human being—of *one of us*—as a mere thing or a mere tool." Third, because we know that our own desires are infinite, we are able to respect the creative and unbounded quality of human aspirations in others.[86]

Despite skeptical worries about whether human beings could have an intrinsic essence, we have good reasons to affirm that a human being is a substance with a unique and intrinsic essence. What is that essence? What is human nature? We are sometimes called rational animals or linguistic animals or social animals. All of these concepts draw our attention to various aspects of rational and moral agency—that is, aspects of personhood. We are by nature personal animals. Some philosophers, however, deny that there is any coherent concept of a person.[87] If gods, aliens, and computers might be persons, then what traits could such diverse substances possibly have in common? Historians also often deny that there is any single or coherent concept of a person: they see only many culturally specific personae.[88] Historians enjoy showing that our modern concept of person is far from universal and is the unique product of the confluence of Greek and Christian thought. The word "person" ironically emerges from the word for a theatrical mask.[89] What is most authentically us, our personhood, originally meant the mask we wear on stage. Is a person the public mask or the private self? Truly, all the world is a stage and we persons are but players. *Persona* was also a term in ancient Roman law that could refer to human beings in general or to various legal roles (*personae*) defined by particular rights and duties, which could be played by individual human beings or various corporate bodies.[90] In modern law, even corporations are sometimes defined as legal "persons."

The modern concept of a person as a rational and moral agent stems from ancient Christian theological debates about the triune God, which Tertullian (ca. 220) defined as "one substance but three persons."[91] Boethius (ca. 520) defined a person as "an individual substance of a rational nature."[92] This definition was general enough to apply to divine, angelic, and human persons. Just as the Greek philosophers associated human intellect with divine intellect, so Christian theologians associated human rational and moral agency with divine rational and moral agency. The book of Genesis says that man was created in God's image. Christians interpret this to mean that human personhood stems from divine personhood. Thomas Aquinas sees rational and moral agency as the summit of all creation: "Person is that which is most perfect in all of nature."[93] According to Aquinas, we extend the idea of human personhood to the divine reality by analogy.[94]

Is there any coherence in this diversity of historical concepts of person, which evolved from a mask, to a legal status, to a moral agent? Cicero compares human life to a drama in which each of us must play several different parts. He distinguishes four roles (*personae*): the first is the universal and natural role of a rational animal; the second is the particular role each of us performs depending on our individual endowments and talents; the third is the role imposed by chance or status; and the fourth is the social office we choose for ourselves by our own decision. Isn't there a tension between being a person and adopting a persona? What gives all of these roles their unity, says Cicero, is that they all stem from our human capacity for rational agency.[95] The fact that human beings play so many roles in social life proves that we cannot be reduced to any particular role or set of roles. A person is the only entity who can adopt any number of personae.

Moreover, the Roman legal conception of a person as the bearer of rights and duties anticipates Locke's "forensic" conception of a person as someone morally responsible for his actions. Before Christianity, being a person was often regarded as a phase of a human life, like being an athlete. Roman law permitted legal persons to play various roles, depending on their status. After Christianity, being a person become the essence of human nature, not a mere phase of human life. Every human being was now regarded as essentially and inalienably a human person.[96] Yet, as we shall see, in our post-Christian world, many ethicists and philosophers are again arguing that personhood is merely a phase of human life.

Do even modern philosophers have a coherent concept of personhood? After all, some philosophers emphasize the autonomy of persons, while other philosophers emphasize the essentially social nature of persons.[97] These are not new worries. Personhood is a concept that attempts to capture the complex nature of human beings, who are both incommunicable and essentially self-communicating. We are incommunicable because we are integral wholes who are never merely parts of a larger whole; we are self-communicating because we are essentially social beings.[98] To be a person is to be both incommunicable and self-communicating, to be a complete world in relation to other complete worlds. Is there a tension between being incommunicable and self-communicating? Were we all merely parts of some larger social whole, we would have no need to be self-communicating, and were we not integral wholes, we could have nothing important to communicate. Our integral wholeness makes possible our uniquely intimate social relations.

To be a person is to be both self-possessing and self-giving. We are self-possessing because we are self-aware and self-determining. We are self-giving because we are self-communicating and receptive to others. How can we be both autonomous and social? To begin with, we cannot become self-possessing unless we first become open to others. As substances with a rational nature, we always have the capacity for personhood, but we cannot actualize our powers of self-awareness or self-determination except in response to the personal initiative of others. Unless someone else treats me as a "you," I will never wake up to myself as an "I." Like Sleeping Beauty, we are awakened to our personhood by the loving kiss of another.[99] For example, every human being possesses a biological capacity for language, but my ability to speak only emerges after I am spoken to. Our personal development spirals between inward self-possession and outward self-giving, between inward self-determination and outward receptiveness to others.

Personal development is not well described by ideals of self-actualization. We grow not merely by cultivating our own powers but by helping others cultivate their powers. Only in relation to others do we find ourselves. Self-possession must keep pace with self-expression. We lose whatever we don't share, and we gain whatever we give away: self-mastery, says Jacques Maritain, is for the purpose of self-giving.[100] A person is an intersubjective concept: all persons are interpersonal.

Recall that a species is defined by its unique relationship to its ancestors, its mates, and its niche. By virtue of an organism's intrinsic essence, it is able to participate in these species-specific relationships. What makes human beings unique is that all of these relationships are interpersonal. We build shrines to our ancestors and try to communicate with them even after their deaths. We form intimate friendships with our reproductive mates. Our ecological niche is primarily the society of persons into which we are born. But we even personify "mother nature" by seeing divine persons inhabiting the characteristic features of our environment. So powerful is the innate human orientation to persons that we even seek interpersonal relations to the wind, fire, the sea, storms, rocks, trees, and animals—by giving them all proper names, for example. We impute rational and moral agency even where we know there is none. To be human is to personify our ancestors, our mates, and our whole environment. We should be called *Homo personalis* rather than *Homo sapiens*.

What about divine, alien, or digital persons? These extensions of personhood are merely analogical; yes, extended that widely, the notion of personhood does become incoherent. I argued above that our concept of person shapes our concept of human being (human nature is defined as personal) just as our concept of human being shapes our concept of person (we mean by "person" a human person).[101] That there is no coherent concept of a person in the abstract does not mean that there is no coherent concept of a human person. The reason why history offers so many definitions of person is that the whole notion of a person is as open-ended as the aspirations of the human beings to which it refers. History is the unfolding of the creative possibilities of rational and moral agency, which characterize but do not delimit human persons. Personhood cannot be strictly defined but only characterized or elucidated.[102]

We are essentially persons not only because our rational and moral agency are uniquely and universally human, but also because they make sense of all the other important aspects of human biology. Human beings have uniquely long childhoods because actualizing our personal powers requires a very long apprenticeship of cultural learning. We have vocal cords because linguistic communication is essential to the full exercise of personal agency. Complex thought requires the subtle manipulation of objects, from tools to visual signs. Human beings are not uniquely dexterous only because we are so smart; we are so smart in part because we are uniquely dexterous. The human brain and the human hand have coevolved, making rational and moral agency possible.[103]

Recall that the ancient Greek word for person (*prosopon*) originally meant a theatrical mask and later, by extension, a face.[104] Many historians and philosophers claim that this fact reveals the incoherence of the whole notion of a person. But actually, in this case, etymology reveals the deeper truth: human personhood is expressed anatomically chiefly by the human face. To be a person is to be self-communicating, and the human face expresses a far wider range of thought and emotion than the face of any other animal.[105] We are the only animals who can laugh and who can cry.[106] Even our upright posture can be partly explained by the requirements of face-to-face communication, and we are the only primate who can copulate face-to-face. In all these ways, we express our personal agency through our uniquely communicative faces. The whole human face is marvelously expressive, especially the eyes. The eyes really are windows on the soul. No wonder most people identify the location of the "self" as close to the eyes.[107]

Personhood is expressed by the whole of the human body—especially the physiognomy of our faces and eyes. Did the fortuitous emergence of the human face, hand, and language make possible the emergence of rational and moral agency? Or did the survival value of rational and moral agency shape the evolution of human anatomy and physiognomy? Biologists and anthropologists see both processes at work. We know that in many respects human culture has shaped human evolution. Either way, human nature is essentially personal.

Before the rise of physical chemistry in the nineteenth century, we had no idea how to characterize the essence of gold—or any other element. Gold was defined according to its observable qualities such as color, density, and malleability. We now regard such definitions as ludicrously superficial, compared with defining gold as a metal with the atomic number of 79. With respect to the biological essence of organic species, we still lack the equivalent of the periodic table of the elements. Hence, we continue to define human beings by observable qualities, such as the exercise of our rational and moral powers. But these observable properties, like the observable properties of gold, rest on an unobservable essence which, when discovered, will explain why human beings and only human beings are persons.

What can we say about the human essence or nature? We can say that a human being is an organism with an intrinsic directedness toward personal maturity. By "personal maturity" I mean simply normal adult rational and moral agency. This intrinsic directedness is not a matter of degree; an organism either has it or not. If an individual organism, even one having human parents, lacked an intrinsic directedness toward personal maturity, then that individual is not a human being.[108] Indeed, our equality in sharing this directedness toward personal maturity is the only sense in which every human being is by nature equal. Our humanity is manifested only in the complete lifespan of typical members of our natural kind. Human nature, then, is best understood not as a static set of abilities but as a dynamic orientation. At any one stage of life, a human being, due to immaturity or impairment, might exercise abilities comparable to other animals, but no other organism possesses the typical human life trajectory. What is the biological basis for this directedness toward personal maturity? We do not yet know, but we do know that it is more than merely genetic. There are cells with a complete human genome but which lack intrinsic directedness toward a mature human person.[109] So human nature must require both genetic and epigenetic factors of development.

∽

Clarifying the relationship of humanity to personhood is of urgent moral importance. Many ethicists and philosophers today, following John Locke, sharply distinguish a human being from a moral person. The point of making this distinction is almost always to argue that killing human beings is permissible where killing moral persons is not.[110] As I have noted, we use the concept of "person" to honor the rational and moral agency of human beings. Human beings are widely thought to merit the special protection of human rights, especially the right not to be killed, because of the unique dignity of personhood. Yet, as I have noted, personhood is widely regarded among philosophers as a mere psychological phase of a human life—the phase ranging from late childhood up to senile dementia—in which we are normally able to exercise our rational and moral agency. If I am essentially a person (understood psychologically), then it follows that I was never an infant and that I will likely die before my human organism dies.[111]

If personhood is merely a stage of human life, then what we call "human rights" should actually be called "the rights of moral persons." After all, the "human" rights to free speech, assembly, free exercise of religion, travel, marriage, and so forth are rights that can be exercised only by rational and moral agents—that is, by actual persons. Many human beings cannot exercise rational and moral agency and are therefore not eligible for these rights.[112] Moreover, according to many ethicists, what is sometimes called "human dignity" should more precisely be called "the dignity of persons," since persons possess a higher moral status than nonpersons. Because many human beings, they say, do not possess the dignity of persons while some other animals arguably do, it is morally arbitrary to accord rights to human beings rather than to moral persons of any species. Instead of arbitrarily assigning special rights to all members of one (human) species, we should instead assign special rights to all persons of whatever species.

I agree that the special dignity we honor in human beings stems from their being persons. Indeed, we should honor personhood in whatever species it is to be found. The question is whether a human life can be divided into prepersonal, personal, and postpersonal stages. Many arguments about the moral rights of human beings rest on the premise that some human beings are not rational or moral persons.[113] I will not attempt here to adjudicate the complex normative questions about what moral rights, if any, are owed to all human beings. Instead, I will simply explore the assumption made by many ethicists that not all human beings are persons. If all human beings turn out to be persons, then this fact will have indirect implications for debates about human rights, but I will not explore those implications here.

Nicholas Wolterstorff rightly notes that many human beings are too immature or too impaired to exercise their rational and moral agency. He then concludes that such human beings lack the "capacity" for personhood.[114] Wolterstorff has shown only that some human beings cannot exercise their capacities for personhood; he has in no way shown that a human being could lack a capacity for personhood. To take one of many possible examples, when I was very young I could not speak any language, but it hardly follows that I lacked a capacity for language. Through illness or injury, I could very well lose my ability to speak or to sign without, of course, losing my capacity for language. Wolterstorff's argument fails by equivocation: a first-order capacity to exercise rational and moral agency must be distinguished from a second-order capacity to develop or restore rational or moral agency. A human being could possess a genetic capacity for rational agency without possessing the phenotypic capacity to exercise that agency now.

Many philosophers and ethicists strongly contrast a potential person with an actual person. But such a contrast ignores the reality of biological development. To be a living organism is always to be actualizing one's potential—even if only the metabolic potential for continued life. Every living creature has both potential and actual powers; no organism is fully potential or fully actual. So dividing human beings into potential and actual persons creates a dichotomy where there is only a spectrum.[115] An embryo or fetus is not a potential person but a person with potential. An embryo has the same intrinsic directedness toward the development of rational activity as any adult. Potentiality can range from remote to proximate: a tree is potentially a bookcase; Prince Charles is potentially the King of Great Britain; wine is potentially vinegar.[116] A tree and Prince Charles have no intrinsic directedness toward becoming a bookcase or a king, while wine does have an intrinsic directedness toward vinegar. This is not to say that there is no difference between potency and act or between a fetus and an ordinary adult, only that the differences are not sharp or dichotomous. Even adults vary hugely in their actualization of rational and moral agency due to illnesses, injuries, and disabilities. Many children are more actualized than many adults. Contrasting the "stages" of prepersonal, personal, and postpersonal lives creates very misleading dichotomies.

We actualize our powers of rational and moral agency over time and by degree. But we do not acquire our personal nature over time or by degree. As an individual substance with a personal nature, we become human persons simply by coming into existence. If a conceptus lacks this impetus to grow into a rational adult (as in the case of a complete mole), then it is not a human being, even though it has human parents.

Jeff McMahan asks whether this directedness toward rational maturity is truly intrinsic to an organism. After all, the growing embryo requires, at a minimum, external hydration and nutrition from its mother; at the other end of the spectrum we could imagine a primate embryo that "acquires" a rational nature by means of transplanted human genes. So perhaps there is no pure intrinsic directedness but only a spectrum of mixtures of intrinsic and extrinsic potentiality for rationality. Is there a difference only of degree between a human embryo, with a primarily intrinsic directedness toward rational maturity, and a primate embryo (with transplanted human genes), with a primarily extrinsic directedness toward rational maturity? No, the human embryo possesses an intrinsic disposition to make use of extrinsic supports from its mother; the human embryo is, so to speak, intrinsically programmed for particular extrinsic supports. No primate embryo, by contrast, possesses an intrinsic disposition to make use of transplanted human genes. If it were so disposed, then it would be a human embryo. McMahan fails to see that some (but not all) extrinsic factors in development belong to the intrinsic potentiality of each growing organism.[117]

When do we cease to be human beings or human persons? Because our capacities for personhood are radical, they are extremely difficult to eradicate. Diseases and injuries may block the exercise of our rational powers, but they do not remove our intrinsic capacity for restoring those powers. In the current state of medical science, not all injuries can be healed or all diseases cured. But we can be confident that advances in medical science will enable our bodies to restore the exercise of many rational and moral powers that are now blocked by disease or injury.[118] Regeneration of diseased or injured organs, including neural tissue, is possible because of the intrinsic powers already present in every human being.[119]

Because of advances in modern medicine, we now see an increasing number of cases in which an individual continues to live despite what is called "total brain death." It used to be thought that the brain was essential for controlling and integrating the functioning of all the organs of the body; but we now see that a human body can maintain basic functioning without a brain (but with the help of mechanical assistance for respiration and nutrition). Indeed, in an early embryo, bodily integrity is also maintained without the brain. It would appear, then, that in the case of total brain death we see the death of a human person arrive before the death of a human being. Does survival after total brain death show that not all human beings are human persons? Not necessarily. If a human being is defined as a rational animal, then total brain death ends the life of a human being. Because a brain is necessary (though not sufficient) for the exercise of any rational activity, total brain death marks the end of a human life.[120] Even here, human being and human personhood cannot be pried apart.

In the face of what philosopher Jeremy Waldron calls "profound disability" we are reminded of the fragility of human development. Biologists often express amazement that anyone reaches healthy maturity, given the innumerable ways in which development can go wrong—especially in the early stages. Although profoundly disabled persons are often compared to vegetables, nothing is more characteristically human than impairment. Disability shadows all our abilities. As Waldron eloquently reminds us, in the presence of even profound disabilities, our reflections on the fragility of human flourishing should lead us to the thought, "that could have been me."[121]

Ever since Locke, philosophers have attempted to answer the question of what we are by telling us how we persist.[122] But our "persistence conditions," while relevant to the question of what we are, do not specify what we are.[123] For example, champions of the biological approach to human identity describe the organic conditions (e.g., the continuity of metabolic self-regulation) that enable us to reidentify an organism (including a human organism) over time. But these persistence conditions apply to any living organism, so they tell us nothing about the specific essence of a human being. Generic organic persistence conditions do not specify the true persistence conditions of any actual organism, since those persistence conditions necessarily include species-specific conditions. These generic persistence conditions are necessary but not sufficient for genuine human persistence over time. They help us to define the generic properties of all organisms but not to define what is a human being.

As we saw in the case of total brain death, a formerly human body can survive the death of a human being. To say that the persistence conditions for a human being are merely those of any organism is like saying that Michelangelo's sculpture of David persists so long as the marble of which it is made persists. Yes, the persistence of the marble is necessary for the persistence of David but not sufficient. The melting or erosion of the sculpture over time could remove David even if the marble remained. A human person persists only so long as his or her rational nature persists.

Locke got things backward. He proposed that we find out what a human being is by identifying the criteria for how we persist over time. But we do not discover what we are by discovering how we persist; rather, only by knowing what we are can we know whether we persist over time. As David Wiggins shows, there are not two identity relations among substances, simple identity and identity over time. Rather, identity over time just is the simple or ordinary identity of things that persist over time.[124] Only when we identify human beings as having a rational nature can we identify when they come into existence and when they die.

This book adopts a resolutely developmental perspective on human nature, but development cannot be fully understood apart from evolution. And from an evolutionary perspective, the unique dignity of human nature looks much less metaphysically robust. Our species could lose its intrinsic directedness toward personhood through evolutionary change; whether such change necessarily implies the extinction of *Homo sapiens* depends on one's theory of speciation. Or another species might someday acquire that intrinsic directedness toward personhood, just as we acquired it long ago. An even more immediate challenge to the unique dignity of human nature will come from genetic engineering. Once we understand the precise genetic basis for personhood, we might gain the ability to remove it from some human beings or to transplant it to other species. Either by evolution or by engineering, personhood could become separated from human nature.

I have argued that "person" is an analogical concept: in the future, personhood might be analogically extended to include nonhuman primate, digital, or alien persons, just as in the past personhood has included divine and angelic persons. Because we understand human beings in light of persons and persons in light of human beings, if personhood becomes radically diversified, so will our understanding of human nature. Just as the idea of divine persons has shaped our understanding of human persons, so also might the idea of digital or alien persons.

What these speculations suggest is that we cannot define *human* persons merely in the abstract terms of rational or moral agency. Here our biological concepts of a species are helpful. To be a *human* person is to be descended from our same primate ancestors, to live in our same ecological niche, and to mate with our same reproductive partners. A rational or moral agent who does not participate in any of these communities (ancestral, ecological, and reproductive) might be analogically a person but surely not a human person.

I argued in the first chapter that human development does not proceed through an invariant sequence of qualitatively distinct stages. Human life is of a piece: development is continuous and not closely linked to age. Yet, for purposes of practical reasoning, we must sometimes draw sharp lines between infants, children, adults, and the elderly. Practical feasibility requires us to use chronological age as a proxy for developmental age. Infants do not possess all of the legal and moral rights of adults. The same is true of the alleged "stages" of prepersonal, personal, and postpersonal human lives. This contrast of human persons with human nonpersons falsely ignores the fundamental continuity of human development. No creature can "become" a person who was not already a person. Nonetheless, for many practical purposes, we must sometimes treat someone who cannot yet or who can no longer exercise her personal agency differently from those who can. Some very immature or very impaired human persons cannot be permitted the same degree of personal liberty and self-determination as fully-actual human persons. Indeed, in morality and law we assign different kinds of responsibility to adult humans who are asleep or otherwise unconscious from those who are not. Yet it hardly follows that by falling unconscious I lose my personhood. The practical necessity of categorizing human persons into various stages is fully consistent with the metaphysical continuity of human life.

CHAPTER 8

Who Am I?

A Storybook Life

A narrative can be told about anything, but not everything already has a quasi-narrative structure. Only a life unfolds like a story: the first narratives are biographies because both lives and stories develop. Even nonliving entities, such as a mountain or a planet, might have a beginning, middle, and end. What is different about life? What makes a life different is that the end (maturity or death) is already present at the beginning in the form of biological potential. This unfolding of what is already present gives a life a temporal unity unlike any other entity. The beginning foreshadows the end, and the end recapitulates the beginning. Moreover, good narratives require conflict between a protagonist and its environment. Unlike any inanimate entity, an organism is essentially distinct from its environment by means of a self-regulating metabolism. (Indeed, no inanimate entity has an environment at all, since the very word and concept refers only to the home of a living organism.) Every organism, like a Greek hero, comes into conflict with its surroundings and with other organisms, overcomes some of these challenges, and eventually succumbs. We can make sense of the mature organism only by knowing the unique path it has traversed. The dramatic whole of an organism's life is itself composed of smaller dramas: being born, building a nest, migrating south, finding a mate or a meal. In each event, we also see a goal at the beginning, striving and conflict, and, perhaps, fulfillment. The life of a species of organisms has the same narrative structure, beginning with birth (speciation), growth (propagation), and death (extinction). Every species, like each organism, is a biography. A life is a story composed of stories.

Does life intrinsically take the form of a dramatic narrative? Or do we merely project literary ideals of unity, suspense, crisis, and resolution onto a meaningless stream of time? Perhaps nature has no goals, no beginnings or endings, no striving, no conflict—merely necessity and blind chance. Human beings do tend to anthropomorphize nature, for example, by describing evolution as a "struggle for survival" or development as a "quest for maturity." We falsely impute agency to the weather, to landscapes, to accidents, and to many other natural phenomena. Perhaps one reason we anthropomorphize nature is precisely because of the real analogies between biological growth and human stories. Are literary narratives an escape from—or a compensation for—the sheer random meaninglessness of life? Or do we tell stories about human lives because life itself is already quasi-narrative? Some philosophers insist that "there are no beginnings or endings in the flow of events"—implying that narrative beginnings and endings are purely arbitrary.[1] True, there are no absolute beginnings or endings, but the birth of any organism or species marks the beginning of a unique entity that has never and will never be seen again. Conception is the closest thing to a true beginning in nature, which is why we associate hope with pregnancy. As for endings, only death and extinction are truly forever. Narrative is the natural mode for understanding the unique spatiotemporal trajectory of individual lives (organisms or species), which have true beginnings and endings. Perhaps novels develop and symphonic themes develop because lives develop?

What is a "narrative"? I define "narrative" as a mode of thought that unifies the past, present, and the future. Narratives need not be externalized in speech, writing, or any other medium.[2] As we shall see, most of our narratives are merely latent and become manifest only when we experience surprise or when we are asked to explain ourselves to others. There are degrees of narrativity based on the degree to which the past, present, and future are interwoven. Of course, narrative thinking is often expressed in stories, dramas, novels, and histories—even though not every novel or drama or history takes the form of a narrative.

How do narratives unify past, present, and future? Do narratives imply a causal connection between events? According to Aristotle, a narrative need not be unified by causation but only by meaning. He gives the famous example of a murderer looking up at a statue honoring his victim; the statue then inexplicably tips over and kills the murderer. Here events are unified by meaning (the justice of retribution) rather than by causation.[3]

Human beings find and create meaning primarily by relating the present to the past and the future—that is, by telling stories.

Human beings everywhere have always attempted to understand their lives by means of stories. Indeed, we make use of stories to explain everything and anything. We would not recognize as human a culture where storytelling was not the primary mode of human discourse. Even mathematical proofs and scientific theories must be translated into narratives to be comprehensible to most people. The biological stories of human development I have examined all take the form of narratives telling the story of human life in relation to the natural world or human history. Why? Alfred Korzybski, as I have noted, argued that plants bind chemicals together by means of photosynthesis; animals bind space together by means of perception; and humans bind time together by means of language. The use of language to interweave past, present, and future is called narrative.

There is no doubt that when we attempt to reveal who we are to someone we tell a story. We live in a sea of stories, and, like fish, we are often not even aware of that sea. As Barbara Hardy observes: "We dream in narrative, day-dream in narrative, remember, anticipate, hope, despair, believe, doubt, plan, revise, criticize, construct, gossip, learn, hate and love by narrative."[4] The pervasiveness of stories in our lives and the universality of narratives in all human cultures suggests that we might rightly be defined as "storytelling animals."[5] Who am I? I am a human person, which means that I am the narrator or, at a minimum, the subject of a set of stories about my life. The unique shape of a human life stems from the stories we tell about ourselves and that others tell about us.

No one doubts the ubiquity or salience of narratives in human life. But we must ask some basic questions about the relationship of narratives to lives. Some philosophers claim that we create our very selves by means of narratives. Do we really create ourselves by narratives or only our sense of ourselves? If the "self" is a narrative, then who or what is the narrator? I will argue that narrative is not the foundation of human personal identity, which is rooted in our biological capacity for rational and moral agency. We are embodied as well as ensouled, meaning that our identity is much deeper than our capacity for narrative. Narrative is not even the foundation of our sense of ourselves, since each of us has a bodily "memory" of our past. Rather, narrative is the characteristic expression of who we are as rational and moral agents.

Philosophers ask a descriptive question about whether narratives are the only way to understand a human life. Philosophers also ask a prescriptive or normative question about whether we should think of our lives as a narrative. Is the aspiration to narrative unity essential for leading a morally good life?[6] It is often said that these descriptive and prescriptive claims are logically independent, though rarely explicitly distinguished.[7] I will argue that both claims rest on a prior view of the relation between time and narrative, between life and art. Some writers see narrative as an arbitrary projection of form on a meaningless flow of time, while others see the human experience of time as already quasi-narrative; some see narrative art as an escape from life, and others see narrative as representing life.

Practical reasoning, I shall assert, rests on memory and imagination, on the capacity to bring the past and the future to bear on our choices in the present. Practically wise people always act in relation to the whole of their lives, a whole unified in thought by autobiographical narratives. Once we see that memory and imagination are already structured by narrative, we will understand why good practical reasoning depends on the truthfulness of the stories we tell about ourselves.

Many people aspire to lead what they call authentic lives, which literally means to be authors of their own lives. Is it possible to be the author of one's own life? Or do we all receive a life script from our societies, of which we are at most editors? Do we spin our life's stories or do they spin us?[8] The choice we face is not whether to tell a story but what kind of story to tell about our own lives.

As the basis of practical reasoning, narratives offer the promise of helping us lead better lives by helping us understand them. But can we truly understand our lives? And even if we could, would that knowledge lead us to live better lives? Kierkegaard famously offers reasons to doubt both of these claims: "It is perfectly true, as philosophers say, that life must be understood backwards. But they forget the other proposition, that it must be lived forwards. And if one thinks over that proposition it becomes more and more evident that life can never really be understood in time simply because at no particular moment can I find the necessary resting-place from which to understand it—backwards."[9]

Kierkegaard contrasts the prospective living of life from the retrospective attempt to understand it. Our human predicament, in his view, is one of attempting to drive a car forward by looking only in the rearview mirror.[10] Ironically, by seeking to understand our lives, we undermine our ability to lead them. Instead of looking backward for understanding, we should look forward even if in ignorance. To return to our image of driving a car, better to drive aimlessly than over a cliff.[11] Worse, Kierkegaard goes on to say, even if we look backward we still will not acquire true understanding, since a full retrospective knowledge of our lives is necessarily denied to us.

Kierkegaard is right that understanding our lives is not sufficient for leading them well. But he exaggerates the conflict between the understanding and the leading of a life.[12] Once we grasp the narrative structure of human life, we shall see why understanding our lives, no less than leading them, involves looking both forward and backward. Stories, both historical and fictional, are precisely devices for unifying the past and the future, so as to avoid, or at least to mitigate, Kierkegaard's stark predicament.

Are stories true to life? After all, calling someone a "storyteller" or a "teller of tales" can be just a polite way to call him a liar. Stories certainly give meaning to our deeds, experiences, and lives, but do they give us knowledge and truth? Stories often falsify. Does that mean that narratives are intrinsically falsifying? According to some philosophers and literary theorists, the whole idea of a narrative plot—as a device to unify past, present, and future—falsifies the temporal nature of human experience. In this view, human experience is either a totally unstructured sequence of moments, like a clock ticking (just one damn thing after another) or a uniform and unbounded stream of consciousness. This sequence or stream has no inherent structure or meaning, which is why we construct narratives in the first place. All narratives impose order on the otherwise meaningless sequence or stream of human experience. We tell stories to give our lives the meaning they would otherwise lack.

How do narratives create meaning? They gather events and actions into temporal wholes, or plots. Aristotle famously said that a plot (*muthos*) is a temporal whole with a beginning, a middle, and an end.[13] Perhaps a narrative cuts into the random sequence or stream of time and shapes it into artificial wholes called plots. A plot not only has a beginning, middle, and end, but these temporal phases are interwoven. The beginning foreshadows the end, and the end recapitulates the beginning. According to literary scholar Frank Kermode, the most basic plot is "tick-tock," which he describes as an arbitrary structure imposed on the meaningless sequence of a clock's ticking. "Tick-tock" has a beginning and an ending, which is much more pleasing to us than an unbounded and monotonous sequence of ticks.

But Kermode warns us not to confuse our literary device of "tick-tock" for the reality of the meaningless sequence of chronological time. Narrative, for him and many other literary scholars, creates rather than discovers meaning.[14]

If narratives were purely arbitrary, then it would be hard to explain why we frequently contrast true and false narratives. We see some narratives as misleadingly self-serving, the remedy for which could only be a more truthful narrative. If our lives did not already have a narrative structure, it would be hard to explain our practice of contesting the validity of other people's narratives. Moreover, we often feel strong emotions while we follow cinematic or literary narratives, emotions such as fear, pity, anxiety, and relief—the same (or at least analogous) emotions that we feel while we view the drama of real human lives. Again, if narratives were merely arbitrary impositions on real life, then these emotional analogies would be difficult to explain.

Aristotle was the first philosopher to insist that stories are lived before they are told and that literary narratives are a refinement of life stories. A literary drama, he says famously, is a representation (*mimesis*) of human life. What precisely is represented or imitated in a literary narrative? Aristotle explains that a narrative is a representation not of the qualities of individual men but of the events and actions that make up human life.[15] Narrative is the arrangement of the episodes of human life into a temporal unity.[16] According to Aristotle, human life is already an inchoate narrative; the poet or historian artfully selects, arranges, and refines the narratives we already live out. Human actions and lives were tragic or comic long before the dramatists arrived. A dramatic plot represents the inherent temporal structure of human life.[17] John Dewey follows Aristotle by claiming that the interactions of any organism with its environment is already a quasi-narrative. Time ceases to be mere stream or meaningless repetition and is instead structured into rhythmic patterns of action and reaction, learning, fulfillment, and growth.[18] David Velleman also follows Aristotle and Dewey by arguing that human emotional life follows a quasi-narrative plot of provocation, complication, and resolution. These affective patterns, he says, are biologically programmed: "we understand stories viscerally with our bodies . . . they are stored in the muscle-memory of the heart."[19]

What this means is that the essence of any narrative is the plot, since the temporal structure of events and actions is what reveals hidden human character.[20] Our actions are logically prior to our moral character, not only because actions alone reveal character traits, but also because our performance of chosen actions is what creates our traits of character. The supreme aim of life is happiness, and we are happy, says Aristotle, not because we have a certain character but because we engage in certain activities.[21] A narrative, he says, is impossible without a sequence of incidents, without a plot. Narratives require characters only to perform the actions that form the plot.[22] Moreover, as I have noted, the only way to understand or to reveal character is by means of a sequence of actions.[23] The unity of a plot, he says, rests on a unity of incidents not on the unity of one person.[24] A poet, he says, is above all the maker of plots, because his task is to represent human actions, and human action is already structured into plots.[25]

Literary narratives, whether historical or fictional, represent human life because human lives are already structured in simple narrative forms. Aristotle even says that fictional narratives are more philosophical than historical narratives because fictional narratives are more universal in scope.[26] How could fiction teach us more about human life than history? According to Aristotle, historical narratives may accurately represent the life of one or a few men, but fictional narratives may plausibly represent the life of many or all men. In history, we are bogged down in the biographical particularities of a single person. By contrast, a fictional character is an Everyman, and his adventures teach us not what did happen once but what might happen anytime to anyone. Fiction provides hypothetical plots that we can generalize to our own lives more easily than the highly particular plots in a work of history.

Philosopher Paul Ricoeur argues that Aristotle's theory of plots resembles his theory of metaphor. According to Aristotle, a metaphor is an analogy bridging two seemingly dissimilar things. It takes genius, he says, to see metaphorical relations. Similarly, a plot is a way to unify seemingly dissimilar events into a single story. In life, as in literary plots, the most trivial incidents can have the most profound consequences: "For want of a nail, the kingdom was lost." Both metaphors and plots rely on the capacity to discern deep analogies across seemingly unrelated matters. These insights can lead to genuine knowledge about human life. According to Ricoeur, good plots are characterized by a "discordant concordance." The poet turns conflict into harmony: the couple who fight at the beginning are sure to marry by the end. All human emotional response to the world follows the same plot of provocation, conflict, and resolution.

A plot unifies events and actions over time. We saw that Augustine could not understand human time until he first grappled with the idea of eternity. God sees past, present, and future simultaneously, as if arrayed on a landscape. According to Ricoeur, to narrate a plot, we must also attempt to see the sequence of events as a single whole, outside of time. Because a plot weaves past, present, and future together by means of foreshadowing and flashback, the narrator must be able to comprehend the whole temporal sequence at one moment. Here we see the narrator at his most omniscient and divine. How could our own lives be narrated when we seem stuck in the present? How could we possibly see our lives as a whole?[27]

The more we learn about the artfulness of the literary or historical narrative, especially the skillful interweaving of past and future, the more remote it can seem from our own lives. Perhaps this explains why so many literary scholars emphasize the chasm between literary narratives and ordinary human life. Mundane human experience seems so full of trivia, randomness, and noise that discerning a narrative structure seems at best quixotic. Perhaps narratives do not represent or imitate human life but merely cover it over with pleasing patterns. Is not any given sequence of events compatible with any number of plausible narratives? Are not the narratives we tell ourselves and others just post hoc rationalizations?

Jean-Paul Sartre's character Antoine Roquentin, in *Nausea*, famously argues that all narratives falsify the human experience of living: "There are no beginnings. Days are tacked on to days without rhyme or reason, an interminable monotonous addition." In this view, life is no more than a meaningless sequence of experiences. At best, we can calculate running tallies of these sequences, which have no beginnings, middles, or ends: "From time to time you make a semi-total." Experiences can be added up but not narrated. All narratives falsify: "As if there could possibly be true stories; things happen one way and we tell stories about them in the opposite sense." The retrospective stories we tell, says Roquentin, impose a false coherence on the dreary monotony of experience. "You seem to start at the beginning . . . and in reality you have started at the end." Roquentin is right that, in telling a story, we cannot know where to begin until we know how it ends. Yet, in life, he says, we cannot possibly know where our adventures will end, so we cannot know where they begin. Roquentin wants his life to unfold with the pleasing shape of a story: "I wanted the moments of my life to follow and order themselves like those of a life remembered. You might as well try and catch time by the tail."[28]

But Roquentin assumes that we tell stories only about the remembered past, whereas we also tell stories about the imagined future. To tell such stories, we need not have knowledge about how the adventures of our life will end, we need only have beliefs or expectations. As we revise our stories in the light of new experiences, often what seemed like endings turned out to be beginnings. There is a pathos in Roquentin's yearning to give his life the coherence and closure of a good story. But he ultimately rejects this yearning for the comforts of false stories and affirms the truth that life can only be added up, not narrated.

Many other philosophers today follow Aristotle by insisting that literary narratives represent human life because human life is inherently quasi-narrative.[29] After all, we commonly distribute actual human lives and actions into the literary genres of tragedy, comedy, epic, farce, or romance. Narratives cannot be arbitrary configurations of the events in our lives for the simple reason that what counts as an event in our life, as we shall see, is determined by the narrative told by ourselves or others.[30] Yet, before many philosophers jumped on the narrative bandwagon, there was the maverick literary scholar Barbara Hardy, who sounds like Aristotle when she says: "Nature, not art, makes us all story-tellers."[31]

Clearly there are many analogies as well as disanalogies between the stories we tell about our lives and literary narratives.[32] The important question is: What exactly is it about human experience, action, and rationality that gives our lives a narrative shape? As I have noted, narratives are devices to control time in order to unify human action. A narrator looks forward and backward in order to understand a course of conduct. True, human beings are in many ways ruthlessly subjected to time's arrow: we cannot literally return to the past or visit the future. Nonetheless, because of the unique structure of our memory and imagination, we are able to partly escape the tyranny of time.

One plot device, central to human life as well as to literature, is called "anticipatory retrospection." Here we imagine ourselves in the future, perhaps at our own funeral, and look back on the shape of our lives. Although, as many skeptics have noted, we do not actually experience our own deaths, we do know that we shall certainly die and we can even anticipate the circumstances of our death with varying degrees of reliability. We saw that Kierkegaard flatly denied that we could ever occupy a vantage point from which to understand our lives retrospectively. But by means of anticipatory retrospection, we are indeed able in some sense to find such a vantage point and at least draft our own obituary and eulogy. Nothing focuses the mind like the prospect of one's own death, so a memento mori is a common plot device to help us see the shape of our whole life.

The rational and moral agency of human persons rests on practical reasoning. And practical reasoning rests on three basic powers: memory, attention, and imagination. A wise person is experienced—he has a rich store of memories from which to draw lessons for the future; a wise person is also imaginative and can create new possibilities for conduct in the future; finally, a wise person is attentive and brings to bear memory and imagination, past and future, to the present occasion of choice. It is tempting but deeply misleading to associate memory with the past, attention with the present, and expectation with the future. We could not be the storytelling animals we are unless each of these powers could weave past, present, and future into a narrative unity. Yes, this means that memory unites our past experiences with our future dreams, just as imagination unites our future hope with our past experiences. We often remember the future, as when we recall something that we must do later; we often imagine the past, as when we consider what we might have done; and we are attentive to the present, as we shall soon see, only when we compare it to the past and the future. Memory, attention, and imagination are inherently narrative, which is why human practical reasoning rests on narratives.

Recall Augustine's discussion of the structure of human time-consciousness. He noticed that his attention to the present moment took him simultaneously into the past and the future. What is the past, he asks, except the present of memory? And what is the future, except the present of expectation? Augustine's present moment is thick with the past and the future. The mind, he says, stretches (*distentio animi*) from the past, through the present, and into the future. To illustrate how the present stretches between past and future, Augustine gives the example of reciting (i.e., singing) a psalm. He notes that we could not attend to the present tone of the psalmody without comparing it to the previous tone and without anticipating the subsequent tone. The course of singing a psalm is a landscape we traverse and we could not orient our present position except by simultaneously looking both forward and backward. The note I sing now is pregnant with the memory of past notes and expectations of future notes. There is no such thing as a bare now in time any more than there is a bare here in space. Cognition is always comparative. We also saw that Augustine compares the singing of a psalm to the course of a life, which begins full of expectation but ends full of memory. The present moment is itself a dramatic narrative with a beginning, middle, and end.

Edmund Husserl, the early twentieth-century philosopher, developed and refined Augustine's pioneering analysis of the subjective human experience of time.[33] Husserl even adopts Augustine's example of the experience of attending to the sequence of tone in a melody. Husserl argues that when I attend to the present tone, I also hear the echo or reverberation of the immediately prior tones.[34] Just as we cannot see a comet without also seeing its tail, so we cannot attend to the present tone without awareness of the immediately prior tones.[35] Similarly, our expectations of the future are as much a part of our present experience as is our memory of the past. We know how powerfully these expectations shape our experience of the present by the phenomenon of surprise. When the present tone does not conform to my expectations, I feel surprised, revealing how my present experience is already shaped by anticipation. Authors of literary narratives often deliberately violate our expectations so as to create surprise. Yet, this drama of defeated expectations is intrinsic to primordial human experience. Surprise surfaces our tacit expectations, without which we could not feel our way through the present.

Our experience of time is analogous to our experience of space. Just as we never experience space itself, apart from the objects contained in space, so we never experience time itself, apart from the events in time. As I walk along a trail, I cannot attend to my present location except in relation to what is behind me and what I see ahead. The horizon behind and ahead of me forms a shifting frame within which I am oriented. Confronting a boulder on my trail, I can experience it only one part at a time by walking around it, just as I can experience a song only one tone at a time. Wholes clearly are prior to parts, because I already know that the sides of a boulder are parts of the same boulder just as I already know that the tones I hear belong to the same melody.[36] Our experiences of spatial objects and of temporal events are both experiences of wholes, but wholes which must be explored part by part. Past, present, and future mutually determine one another in the experience of a spatial or temporal whole. We could not attend to the present apart from the frame provide by past and future.[37]

Augustine described the mind as stretching (*distentio*) from the past through the present and into the future by means of memory and anticipation. Husserl refines this analysis by distinguishing the reach of attention into the past (retention) from the reach of attention into the future (protention).[38] Moreover, Husserl distinguishes short-term memory (retention) from long-term memory (recollection): what is essential for attention to the present is only the immediate past. Similarly, Husserl distinguishes short-term expectations (protention) from long-term expectations (imagination): what is essential for attention to the present is only the immediate future. We now see that even our most primordial experiences are already a temporal unity of past, present, and future—a story with a beginning, middle, and end. This story is full of suspense because surprise is possible at any moment. The plot of human experience thickens.

What we call the present moment, then, is no such thing. It is at once an echo of the past and a glimpse of the future. All sensation and perception are comparative, as when we sense texture by running our fingers over a surface. Yet, the interweaving of past and future in the "thick" present moment is tacit, automatic, and inescapable. We have every reason to believe that other animals also make sense of the present by these tacit comparisons to memory and anticipation. As Wittgenstein famously observed, a dog expects to find his master behind a door but a dog does not expect his master to arrive next Thursday. What makes the human experience of time unique is our capacity to interweave the distant past and the distant future. Let's examine, then, memory and imagination to see if they also possess an intrinsic quasi-narrative structure. Recall that John Locke and the many philosophers who follow him define personal identity in terms of the continuity of memory, but the narrative view of our sense of ourselves reveals that we are defined by our anticipations of the future as much as by our memories of the past.[39]

Psychologists frequently distinguish episodic from semantic memory. Semantic memory, shared by humans and other animals, is simply the totality of all the facts, words, faces, and skills we have acquired over time—without knowing when we acquired them. We know and can do many things without recalling when and where we learned them. Semantic memory is timeless, like Freud's unconscious, and includes items from every phase of our lives. Episodic memory, however, is quite different and is probably unique to human beings. One kind of episodic memory is called "flashbulb" memory. Here I remember not just that President Kennedy was assassinated but exactly when and where I learned of it. Flashbulb episodic memories include such emotionally charged events as one's first day of school, graduation day, and wedding day, as well as personal or national traumas. I see the event unfold in time, as if I could rewind my life back to that point. With flashbulb memories, we are able to travel back in subjective time virtually to relive a page from our past. But not all episodic memories are flashbulb memories in which we recall an event from our own point of view and through our own eyes. Freud noted that each of us is necessarily present in all of our own dreams. The same can be said of episodic memories. Some episodic memories, including flashbulb memories, are recalled from our own first-person point of view through our own eyes; in other episodic memories, we observe ourselves from a third-person point of view.[40]

Because I am necessarily present in all of my episodic memories, these memories are obviously central to what we could call our "autobiographical" memory. But autobiographical memory also includes, of course, the semantic memories of what each of us has learned about his own life from others. Indeed, as our episodic memories fade, they become semantic memories: When I forget what I experienced on my wedding day I might still recall that my wedding was on a particular day. Many psychologists and philosophers see episodic memory as a foundation of personal identity—that is, our sense of ourselves over time.[41] These memories give us the personal sense of narrative time as we relive key events from our past.[42] But over time, our episodic memories fade into semantic memory, which can also provide a narrative sense of self.

It is now well known that episodic memories are not simple replays of past experiences; they are unconsciously revised, supplemented, and even censored over time.[43] Memory does not reflect the past alone; memory is constructed by the present in light of the needs of the future. If narratives were simply arbitrary impositions of art on life, it would be hard to explain the pervasive and totally unconscious revision of our memories over time. Episodic memory is not a video recording of past events; it is an ongoing narrative in which past events are massaged to fit the new plot.[44] Augustine was the first to distinguish the content of a memory from the act of remembering. He noted that we can recall in sadness the memory of a happy event—an experience known as nostalgia; he also noted that we can recall with pride or even joy the memory of past suffering—an experience of redemption.[45] What happens over time is that the past content of the memory and our present act of remembering become merged in our narrative imagination. The retrieval of a memory always reshapes that memory.[46]

Philosopher Peter Goldie shows that we can best understand the nature of autobiographical memory by reference to the literary device of dramatic irony. In the drama *Oedipus Rex*, for example, the audience knows that Oedipus has killed his own father, but Oedipus does not know. Dramatic irony is a contrast between the subjective beliefs of characters and audiences. In novels, dramatic irony often takes the form of what is called "free indirect style" in which the perspective of a character and the perspective of the narrator are merged.[47] A classic example of free indirect style is Tolstoy's description of Vronsky's moral code in *Anna Karenina*: "Vronsky's life was especially fortunate in that he had a code of rules which unquestionably defined everything that ought and ought not to be done. . . . These rules determined unquestionably that a card-sharper must be paid but a tailor need not be, that one should not lie to men but may lie to women, that it is wrong to deceive anyone but one may deceive a husband, that it is wrong to pardon insults but one may give insults, and so on."[48] Here Vronsky's voice is subtly merged with Tolstoy's. The content of this moral code reflects Vronsky alone, but the arrangement of the code reflects Tolstoy's ironic commentary.

In autobiographical memory, we see the same ironic contrast between our present self and our past self. With such memories, I will often combine memory of the past with the ironic perspective of the present: "I shamefully made a ridiculous fool of myself last night, getting up on the table and gleefully singing some stupid song."[49] Such dramatic irony is as central to autobiographical memory as it is to autobiographical narrative. We remember the past in light of the present: what was hilarious in the past is shameful in the present. Over time, hilarity gives way to shame. To return to *Anna Karenina*, had Vronsky matured into a wise man, he would have recalled his own youthful "moral" code with Tolstoyan irony and contempt. Goldie describes the inherently narrative structure of autobiographical memory: "I tell it the way I remember it, and I remember it the way I tell it." In grief, says Goldie, we remember not only the last time we saw our beloved—we remember it *as* the last time.[50] The content of the past memory becomes shaped and colored by present concerns.[51]

What about the future? A full narrative imagination requires that we unify past, present, and future. How could even episodic memory perform that feat? Philosopher Richard Wollheim argues that episodic memory indeed is the basis for our capacity to imagine our own future. Wollheim claims that all episodic memories are first-person or "field" memories. When we recall these salient past events, he says, we remember them as we experienced them. This capacity for first-person reliving of the past is widely thought to be the basis for our capacity to envisage our own first-person future. When we envisage our own future, say, to help clarify a choice we must make, we imagine ourselves in a future scenario on the pattern of remembering ourselves in a past scenario. What would it feel like to be married to this person? Or to become a doctor? Can I see myself in that future role?[52] We can preview our own future only because we are familiar with reviewing our own past. Just as episodic memory causes us to relive the emotional drama of the past, envisaging the future enables us to rehearse the emotional dramas of the future. Naturally, we cannot previsage our own deaths, though we can previsage a process of dying. Other kinds of imagination, of course, are not constrained by this first-person envisaging of a real-time future event. We are always free to construct fantasies about our own death.

Peter Goldie agrees with Wollheim that the narrative structure of our imagination of the future mirrors the narrative structure of our memory of the past. Imagination of the future involves a comparison of two selves, just as does memory of the past. As we previsage our own future, we necessarily infuse our imaginings with emotions from the present. In making decisions, for example, we imagine a future scenario in light of our current emotional response to it. What does it feel like now to see myself as a doctor in twenty years? To see the stark contrast between future and present emotions, I can imagine myself in the future, for example, blissfully falling asleep at the wheel; what I imagine might be fearful even though I do not imagine myself as afraid in the future. Imagination of the future reflects an interweaving of future and present selves, just as memory of the past reflects an interweaving of present and past selves. Similarly, I could imagine myself in retirement as a pathetic old man even though I know that I am not likely to feel pathetic when retired. Whenever we imagine the future, then, our imaginings are shaped and colored by our present perspective. Indeed, the structure of memory and imagination are so similar that is it not surprising that we often confuse remembering and imagining.[53]

Fifty years ago, literary scholars boldly proclaimed that autobiographical writing is not a mere chronicle but is always structured by literary conventions of dramatic irony. The truth about a life, they claimed, is always "distorted" by the art of the narrator.[54] We now realize that even memory and imagination are already structured by dramatic irony. Human experience is not distorted by literary conventions; rather, human experience is narrative all the way down. According to the ancients, memory is the mother of the muses: like her daughters, memory is artful.

Memory and imagination incorporate dramatic irony because human action is intrinsically ironic. With respect to what we intend, what we achieve is not consistently worse (tragic) or consistently better (comic) but often quite different. Actions are fraught with tension and suspense: ends and means interact so that what seem to be two means to the same end turn out to lead to different ends. As Mohandas Gandhi often pointed out, violence and nonviolence are not two possible means to the same future goal; they lead us to very different futures. Instead of a fixed future plan that simply unfolds over time, human action is full of vicissitudes, irony, and uncertainty because past, present, and future are all mutually determining. Not that the future somehow causally shapes the past, but our imagination of the future certainly shapes the present; and the actual future shapes our memories of the past. The only possible way to describe these vicissitudes and ironies—to understand them or to justify them—is by telling a story.[55] But the stories of our dreams, goals, and projects are lived before they are told. We do not wait for writers to teach us that all the world is a stage.[56]

To act, then, is to bring my past, my future, and my present into a productive relationship. All actions are a plot to manipulate time in order to achieve my goals. One difference between a literary narrative and our life's actions is the absence of an omniscient narrator in our lives. As we noted, a literary narrator can see all the events and actions of story as a simultaneous whole, and it is this vantage point that enables a writer to control time by looking forward and backward. It is often said that we cannot know the future.[57] But if we could not form any reliable beliefs about the future, we could never realize our goals. We do often achieve our goals, so we must be able to know something about our future. The knowledge of an omniscient narrator is a perfection of what we already possess.

Still, even if each of my complex actions, commitments, and projects takes the form of a story in which I am the narrator as well as the protagonist, it does not follow that my life as a whole could be a single story. Perhaps the diversity of my actions and projects defies any single narrative. Yet, surely a life is more than merely a random assortment of projects and commitments. Many of my actions form a nested hierarchy: I am writing this chapter because I am writing a book because I am a scholar. We typically understand our smaller projects in terms of our larger commitments.

But not all of our projects form a single hierarchy. I am a parent and a scholar because I wish to enjoy a range of the goods that make up a complete human life. How do I unify these two large and quite distinct commitments? I could tell a story about how being a parent has made me a better scholar or, perhaps less plausibly, about how being a scholar has made me a better parent. But I need not unify my life in this way. I could instead relate a very dramatic story about how I struggled but ultimately succeeded in reconciling the demands of being a parent and a scholar, giving my life a unity without unifying my major commitments.[58]

Surely the purely biological and economic dimensions of human life resist narrative unity. All the cyclical patterns of eating, sleeping, menstruating, cleaning, laboring, and the like seem to lack the dimension of meaning necessary for narrative interpretation.[59] Moreover, repetitive cycles lack the plot development over time we associate with good narratives. Philosopher Hannah Arendt, for example, following John Locke, strongly distinguishes "the labor of our bodies" from "the work of our hands."[60] In her view, the labor of our bodies belongs to the mute and purely biological cycles of animal life; the work of our hands, by contrast, creates a world of durable artifacts imbued with human significance. Work alone breaks out of the cycles of nature and turns mere life into a good human life. Are the cycles of human life mute realities external to the meaningful story of my life? Certainly, they are often politely ignored in biographical and autobiographical narratives. But even these cycles of repetitive labor and bodily needs can be made significant by narrative interpretation. The actions themselves might be cyclical and repetitive, but what I learn from them might form a developmental narrative. I might well say: "I used to resent all the time I spent preparing home-cooked meals for my family. But as I watched the rise of fast-food culture, I realized that I was creating a healthy culinary counterculture in my own home. I began to take pride in my kitchen labor."[61] In the same way, repetitive office or factory labor can become a story of sacrifice and service to one's family, firm, or nation.

We have explored some of the ways in which narratives capture the actual structure of the human experience of time. Aristotle was right that art imitates life. But Oscar Wilde was also right that life imitates art.[62] Stories imitate the plots of our lives, but in leading our lives we also imitate the stories we are told. In every society, children are presented with a culturally specific repertoire of stories. More than we like to admit, we end up living out some mix of those childhood scripts. Without a repertoire of stories, how could one possibly learn what to expect in life—what to avoid and what to aspire to?

We do not first lead our lives and then recount them. We begin life by first receiving a master narrative, or life script. This master narrative is tacitly internalized by every member of a particular society and tells us the sequence of all the most important events of a normative life and at what age we are expected to achieve them.[63] The purpose of the life script is to translate biological time into social time and chronological age into social age.[64] Because of this invisible but omnipresent master narrative, we all agree not only on the same list of milestones in a normative human life (in modern societies, this sequence includes starting school, finishing school, starting a career, getting married, having children, and retiring) but also in what age range we are expected to reach these milestones.[65] In many societies, the life scripts of men and woman differ; nonetheless, men and woman agree about each other's milestones.[66] We acquire this master narrative during childhood and into adolescence.[67] When asked to produce a life script, people always list the events in a forward chronological sequence, as we would expect for such a narrative.[68]

Whether or not our lives actually match this master narrative, or even whether we want them to, we understand what is expected. These cultural life scripts are called "master narratives" because they are compulsory and rigid. Everyone is painfully aware of whether her own life journey is on schedule. We are very rarely questioned by others when we conform to the master narrative; we are often questioned by others when we deviate from it. Although some of these milestones are required by law, others have only the force of custom. But we should not underestimate the importance of this master narrative: in general, lives that conform to it are happier than lives that do not.[69]

We have noted that our ability to compose our own life story rests on autobiographical memory, both episodic and semantic. It turns out that our autobiographical memory is itself deeply shaped by the master narrative of a life script. Life scripts are a form of semantic memory, but they structure our recall of autobiographical memory.[70] What this means is that we tend to remember the events specified by our life script: the life script provides us with the search descriptors for recalling past events.[71] Our life script shapes our life story by shaping our autobiographical memory. Our autobiographical memories are divided into life-stage chapters, and those chapters reflect the milestones of the cultural master narrative.[72] Understanding the master narrative of a life script seems to be a precondition for telling our own life story.[73] These social master narratives help to explain why our lives and life stories have so much in common with those of our peers.[74] Yes, we do lead our own lives, but those lives largely conform to our socially given life script. Yes, we do spin our life's story, but that story is itself largely spun by our life script. It makes no sense to wonder whether leading a life is prior to recounting it. Life and narrative can be separated no more than the dancer from the dance.[75]

∽

Even if our autobiographical memory and imagination are ineluctably shaped by our life script, are there normative reasons for attempting to reject the role of narratives in our lives? Just because a human life is inescapably narrative in structure does not mean that we ought to deliberately develop our own life story. Narratives are all about our relation to the past and to the future. But have not the great sages counselled us to live in the present? The sage of Ecclesiastes tells us to "eat, drink, and be merry, for tomorrow you shall die" (8:15). And Jesus tells us never to look back (Luke 9:62) and take no thought of the morrow (Matt. 6:34). How can we enjoy the present moment, if it is so freighted with the weight of the past and future? These counsels about living in the present must be interpreted as warnings about the wrong relation to past and future. We are prone to become mired or trapped in the past, so Jesus counsels us to look forward and put our hand resolutely to the plow. We are prone to become paralyzed by worry about the future, so Jesus counsels us to avoid futile anxiety: "sufficient unto the day is the evil thereof" (Matt. 6:34).[76] At the same time, Jesus reminds his listeners frequently to remember their past ("repent!") and to look forward to the kingdom ("watch out!").

Today's gurus of "mindful" meditation often claim that we can learn to live only in the present, but their therapies are actually aimed at avoiding only destructive and obsessive thoughts about the past and the future. The techniques of mindful meditation are narrative in structure and unify the immediate future and past into a thick present.[77] By focusing on stories of our thick present experience, we avoid the dangers of the stories we tell about remote past or future suffering. If I am in the grip of traumatic memory of the past or paralyzing dread of the future, then it makes sense to focus on the thick present moment. The present is usually safer than our most dire memories or fears. When we are perched on a precipice, it makes sense not to look up or down. But these are extreme situations and, as such, are a poor guide to ordinary human life. Who really wants to live only in the present? After all, much of the joy in life comes from eager anticipation and retrospective savoring. We live in the present well by having the right relation to past and future.

Some philosophers, inspired by their interpretations of Buddhism, claim that a human being could lead a nonnarrative and purely "episodic" life, in which each present moment is enjoyed on its own, with no comparisons to past moments or future moments.[78] But what is an episode? The word "episode" just means one part of a narrative plot. A life of episodes is by definition a narrative life. Imagine an episode of a TV show with no series. True, some series have more narrativity than others: an episode of a variety show is less integrated into its series than is an episode of a soap opera.[79] But the very notion of an episode implies a narrative series of some kind. A nonnarrative life, however, could be an incidental life, an accidental life, or a life of epiphanies.

An episode without a narrative is as nonsensical as a chronicle without a narrative. A chronicle is often described as the raw material for a narrative, as if we begin with a list of events and then weave them together in a narrative. Perhaps a given chronicle could be the basis for any number of narratives, just as a set of facts might be explained by many different theories. But every chronicle already presupposes a narrative; without a narrative, there are no criteria for selecting what to chronicle. A chronicle of average daily temperatures rests on a different narrative from a chronicle of major battles in history. What counts as an event in my life logically depends on the story I tell. It might seem as though some events in my life are so important that they belong in any narrative. Yet a historian and a poet might tell the story of the same life with no events in common.

Is a radically nonnarrative human life possible? In a strict sense, no animal can lead a nonnarrative life. Augustine and Husserl have demonstrated conclusively that any experience of the present logically rests on comparisons to the past and the future. So all experience of the present is ineluctably interwoven with the immediate past and future in what I have called a quasi-narrative. But what about the more distant past or future? Must we engage in deliberate acts of memory and imagination and weave those into a present story? A life without memory or imagination is possible for a human being but not for an actual human person. Infants, for example, and those with severe cognitive impairments may well live nonnarrative lives.[80] Recall that to be a person is to be a rational and moral agent, which means to make plans for one's future and to be responsible for one's past. The whole point of the Buddhist ideal of satori (the dissolution of the self) is to escape from the illusion of personhood as a stable center of desire. Accordingly, some philosophers claim that the whole idea of stable personal identity over time is an illusion; they claim that a human being is like a club or a nation, a collection of selves rather than a single self.[81] What they call a "club" or "nation" is better described as a "corporation sole," the succession of monarchs or of prime ministers. My future selves succeed my past selves. In a nonnarrative life, events that happened in my past did not happen to me, that is, they happened to my human being but not to my person.[82] I cannot make promises that bind future selves, just as I cannot accept credit or blame for the deeds of past selves. Hence, the irony of a nonnarrative theory of "personal" identity: it dissolves the very idea of a person.[83] This reductio ad absurdum nicely illuminates the essential relation between narrative and actual personhood. A nonnarrative person turns out not to be an actual person at all.

Many people deny that they live their lives in relation to any prospective narrative. They say things like "I had no idea what to expect when I left college . . . or got married . . . or had a baby . . . or retired." We know that these statements are not literally true because of the demonstrable reality of the life scripts we internalize by growing up in any human society. We all know what major milestones in life to expect. Indeed, we all possess lots of prospective ideas about what it means to leave school, to get a job, to get married, to have a baby, and to retire. How do we know that we possess all of these detailed life scripts? Because of the frequent experience of being surprised by life. We could not logically ever be surprised by what happens in our lives unless our expectations were defeated. Indeed, we say, "I had no idea what to expect" precisely when our expectations are overturned. Surprise is possible only when a life goes off script. The experience of surprise in life reveals that we are often not aware of the tacit narratives of our lives. We become aware of these narratives either when we attempt to explain ourselves to others or when our lives violate our tacit scripts.

The choice a human person faces is not between a narrative and a nonnarrative life but between kinds of life narrative. The critique of narrative understandings of our own life or of the lives of others should be directed at irrational and destructive narratives. Many of the narratives we tell about our lives and the lives of others are fundamentally irrational: we see events as omens of the future, we see people only as victims, we spin only catastrophic scenarios for the future, we see ourselves or others as trapped in the repetition of the past, we internalize destructive stereotypes, we see life as controlled by fate or the stars, and so on.[84]

Narratives can be hazardous to your health. In addition to these kinds of pathological narratives, there is another set of dangers associated with the attempt to model one's own life on literary narratives.[85] First, we cannot be the authors of our own lives, which are subject to many circumstances beyond our control. The attempt to author our own life can create illusions of autonomy, leading us to what philosopher Martha Nussbaum calls "the misanthropy of aestheticism."[86] The remedy for the overweening pride of pretended self-authorship is to see ourselves as the editors and narrators of life stories we largely inherit. Second, by placing our lives into one particular literary genre, we risk becoming trapped by the conventions of that genre. For Madame Bovary and Anna Karenina, that fatal genre was romantic melodrama, while for Don Quixote it was chivalric romance. The remedy for the dangerous illusions of self-dramatization is found not by avoiding literary models but by multiplying them: Don Quixote should have read not only chivalric romance but also *Don Quixote*.[87] Third, the contingent messiness of life means that we cannot achieve the kind of closure in our lives that we experience in literature. Philosopher David Velleman usefully distinguishes emotional closure from intellectual closure. In the narrative process of grieving, we often look for intellectual closure ("Why did she have to die?"), rather than settle for emotional closure.[88] The quest for intellectual closure about ultimate questions of suffering and justice is likely to be, well, quixotic. In many other contexts, however, we settle for emotional closure when we should seek intellectual closure. We find many narratives satisfying only because they provide emotional closure: we embrace stories of poetic justice, for example, no matter how preposterous.[89] Stories that feature bizarre but satisfying coincidences also provide emotional, but not intellectual, closure. Telling a story with good emotional closure is usually the best way to get people to believe crazy things.

As evidence of the ineradicable human quest for narrative, I claimed above that human beings are naturally and intuitively storytelling animals who value experiences based not on the sum of pleasure or pain but on their meaningful shape and closure. As psychologist Daniel Kahneman reports, experimental subjects consistently prefer more pain with good closure to less pain without it. What we value, he says, are beginnings, peaks, and ends—not sums of pleasure or pain. Kahneman, like philosopher Galen Strawson, finds these intuitive preferences to be normatively objectionable. Kahneman argues that we should care more about the sum and duration of pleasure and less about happy endings. We are too prone, he says, to accept long periods of mild unpleasantness if redeemed by a better future, and we are too prone to reject a long happy life with a sorry conclusion.[90]

Kahneman's preference for sums of pleasure over narrative closure—like Strawson's preference for an "episodic" life—rests on a deep-seated misunderstanding of human experience. Kahneman tells the story of a friend who reports listening to a beautiful symphony whose ending was ruined by cacophony caused by a damaged recording. His friend claims that the awful ending "ruined the whole experience." Kahneman objects to this evaluation on the grounds that the experience of listening to the symphony "was almost entirely good, and the bad end could not undo it, because it had already happened."[91] On this view, experience is just an accumulation of mutually independent moments. If 99 percent of those moments are pleasurable, then how can a painful finale remove all that accumulated pleasure? Kahneman is right that listening to a symphony is a lot like living a life—in both cases the whole is much more than the sum of its parts. We enjoy each moment of a symphony largely in relation to the whole. Every melody anticipates its own cadence, just as every harmony anticipates its own resolution. Without that cadence or resolution, there is no melody or harmony. Every note of a symphony creates expectations for its finale, and if those expectations are totally defeated, then the whole experience is indeed ruined. Cacophony at the beginning of a symphony or a life might be redeemed by harmony at the end; but how can a failed finale be redeemed? We rightly value the shape of an experience or life because we live each moment in relation to that expected shape.

A human life is not individuated into a sequence of events that can be summed; a human life is individuated into stories, each with its own cadence. We saw that Augustine and Husserl compare the temporal structure of time to singing a song. We perceive each note only in relation to the previous and subsequent notes. The melody is prior to any given note—after the first one. Life may be more like jazz than like psalmody, however, in the sense that we are always improvising. Is an improvised life a nonnarrative life? Not at all. In jazz we see the same priority of the story line to any given note. Miles Davis observed that in jazz, as in life, mistakes can be redeemed if seen as part of a story: "It's not the note you play that's the wrong note—it's the note you play afterwards that makes it right or wrong." In music, as in life, all's well that ends well.

Philosophers and psychologists have made a wide variety of claims about the importance of narratives in human life. Some claim that our "identity" rests on narratives or that we create our "selves" with narratives. How literally shall we interpret these claims? As I have argued, our literal identity rests on our being an organism with the biological basis for personhood and a unique journey through space and time. Narratives cannot create a "self" because there is no such thing other than the human person as a whole. Every actual self was created by its parents, not by a narrative. John Locke famously argued that personal identity is a forensic concept, used to assign praise or blame. If that is so, then we know from legal forensics that personal identity is established by one's unique genetic profile through DNA analysis.[92]

Even if narratives do not literally create persons or selves, do they give rise to our sense of ourselves, our sense of our own identity? Do I know myself over time because of my own ongoing autobiographical narrative? I have argued that narratives rest on the psychological powers of memory, attention, and imagination. What this means is that if I lose my powers of memory or attention or imagination, I necessarily lose the ability to tell my own life's story. Have I thereby lost my sense of my own personal identity? When we visit friends or relatives sunk in dementia, we often say "I didn't recognize him" or "she is no longer there" or "we have lost him." But are these assertions literally true? Do I lose my whole sense of self when I lose my memory?

We know who we are and who others are by many criteria quite independent of memory. Aside from sheer continuity of appearance, we identify ourselves and others by a robust set of unique traits that outlast our fragile memories. Narratives play an important role in our achieved sense of our own identity but not a foundational role. To see why narrative or even memory itself is not foundational to our sense of ourselves, we should consider what happens to our memories once we lose them—or rather, once we forget them, since nothing that happens to us is ever lost. Our loves and fears, our desires and aversions, our mannerisms, tics, moods, even our gait—these are all in part the residue of faded memories.[93] In my own case, I have always had a fear of large dogs even though I have no memory of ever being threatened by a dog. My mother, however, tells me that as a small child, I was terrorized by a neighbor's dog. I forgot the memory, but I am still shaped by the experience. Our most basic sense of ourselves is rooted not in conscious memories at all but in a distinctive mood (cautious or bold, depressed or confident, etc.), a set of desires and aversions, various bodily dispositions (supple or rigid), characteristic mannerisms, verbal tics, and so on. In part these are the product of innate temperament, but in part they are the product of experiences whose content may be long forgotten. Our bodies remember long after our minds forget.

The residue of all these former memories in our moods and bodily dispositions gives each and every person a unique existential style.[94] What this means is that we can sense someone's identity even if that person has lost virtually all conscious memory. Philosopher Mark Rowlands compares a person's identity to the identity of a book: even if virtually all the pages of a novel are lost, we can still identify what remains as written by Dickens based on his unique style.[95] What matters for our purposes is not whether a person's distinctive existential style derives from decayed memories or from innate temperament—or, more likely, both. What matters is that our sense of our own identity and that of others does not rest primarily on the survival of conscious memory—let alone our ability to tell the story of our own life.

This primordial sense of myself is the precondition and not the product of autobiographical narratives. Psychologist Jerome Bruner claims that individuals who have lost the ability to construct narratives have lost their very selves.[96] Assuming he means only "sense of self," is it true that someone sunk in dementia has lost all sense of himself? Not necessarily. We are aware of our own existential style and that of others quite apart from any conscious memories.[97] Is someone with dementia aware that the hunger or fear or fatigue or anger she experiences belong to her? Does she ascribe these experiences to someone else? There is no good reason to think that losing the ability to create narratives removes all sense of oneself as a subject of experience.[98] There are depths of degenerative dementia that do remove all sense of oneself by fundamentally altering one's character and temperament, but we should not confuse the mere loss of conscious memory with the loss of a sense of self.[99] We survive the shipwreck of conscious memory by means of a more primordial sense of self. Narratives do not create me nor even my basic sense of myself. But the full exercise of my rational and moral agency does require a coherent sense of my life's story.

The narrative conception of human life raises very pointed questions about whether we are essentially human beings or rational persons. Let us contrast two modes of personal narrative as ideal types: autobiography and biography. Narrative conceptions of personal identity often focus on the first-person story we tell of our own life.[100] An autobiographical narrative is the quintessential achievement of a self-conscious human person. Such a story, even if only implicit, exemplifies all the powers we associate with personhood. In my autobiography, I am both the protagonist and the narrator. What could be more godlike than to be author of oneself? Who else could possibly know my life as I know it? Surely my private happiness is as important as my public achievements. And I am uniquely motivated to understand my own life. Since I must lead my life, surely I must tell its story.

All of this may be true, but autobiography also has severe limitations. An autobiography is possible only for human beings who can exercise full rational self-reflection: there are many human beings who are too young or too old or too impaired to tell an autobiographical narrative. Moreover, no human life can be fully comprehended by autobiography. A first-person narrative can extend only as far as my first-person experience. No one can experience her own birth or death. An autobiographical conception of identity implies that I was never an infant and that I will never die of dementia.[101] Indeed, while telling his own life story, Augustine wonders whether he was ever an infant.[102] Autobiography extends only as far as my self-conscious personhood; it cannot comprehend a whole human life.

Moreover, as Bernard Shaw reminds us in the opening of his own life's story: "All autobiographies are lies." Even apart from deliberate and self-serving distortions, autobiographical memory is itself highly unreliable. Memory is constructive and reconstructive: we edit, bowdlerize, sanitize, delete, and italicize our past freely. We airbrush people and events completely out of our lives while we retouch other memories. It is often a shock—not usually a pleasant one—to discover pictures, letters, or diaries that document aspects of our past lives. These artifacts usually challenge the comforting narratives we construct of our past lives. As aging butterflies, we recall our days as young butterflies, only to be shocked when we discover that we were actually young caterpillars.¹⁰³ In relating the story of our own lives, we all turn out to be what literary theorists call "unreliable narrators."

A purely first-person narrative is an ideal type which is not possible in reality because there cannot be a wholly first-person person. The very idea of a person is social and relational.¹⁰⁴ I do not know who *I* am until other persons address *me*. I learn to be rational by being required to produce reasons, just as I learn to be responsible by being held responsible. In the same way, I learn to tell the story of my own life only because others ask me to do so—and, indeed, because my parents are already doing it for me. My birth and death cannot belong to my autobiography but only to the third-person stories we call biographies. Stories of any kind can be told only by human persons. But an autobiography can be told only about an actual person while a biography can be told about any living creature.

Telling biographical stories is how we incorporate all human beings into the world of human persons. At a minimum, we necessarily provide the biographical prequel and sequel to the autobiographies of the persons we love. But we also tell biographical stories of those who will never tell their own stories, and by doing so we bring all human beings into the personal society of storytellers.¹⁰⁵ These biographies root our autobiographies into the story of our family and nation. Third-person narratives not only extend the range of—and provide a context for—my autobiography, they also can serve to correct it.¹⁰⁶ A first-person narrative affords a unique source of knowledge of our own thoughts and feelings. But how could we understand our own virtues and vices were they not mirrored back to us by our friends and family—our informal biographers? A good autobiography incorporates many biographies.

The life of a human person can be understood only by a mix of first-person and third-person stories because our lives involve biological as well as personal dimensions. My birth and death belong to the stories told by others about me, usually my parents and children. These liminal events remind us that we are not truly the authors of our own life stories. We arrive into a world that contains an already established repertoire of familial and social roles, each rooted in a set of stories. We do not create our life stories as might an author; instead, we receive a life script which we accept, reject, or revise. Because of the intrinsically social nature of human persons, I cannot claim to be the author, or even the coauthor, of my life story.¹⁰⁷ At best, I can aspire to be the editor and teller of my life's story without being its author.¹⁰⁸

Yes, my autobiography will be subject to continual revision; but, then again, so will my posthumous biography. In my autobiographical narrative, what seemed like innocent fun in adolescence looks appallingly selfish in midlife. But this continuing revision does not stop at death. As Aristotle notes, the happiness or unhappiness of one's children casts a new light on the lives of their parents. The "successful" unification of Germany in 1870 looks quite different in the light of 1945. The meaning of my life, or of any human life, or of any event in history, will be subject to continuing revision until history itself ends. In this sense, my autobiography is no more provisional than any subsequent biography. There is no final vantage point for telling the story of our lives this side of Judgment Day.

One reason why narrative is at the root of practical reasoning is that any attempt to live up to an ideal necessarily takes the form of a quest narrative. To live up to any ideal means to see one's life as a quest to realize that ideal fully.[109] Of course, not every human being wants to live up to an ideal or is capable of doing so. But such a quest is essential to our notion of what it means to be an actual person. To live up to an ideal means to have second-order desires about one's first-order desires, so that our actual desires begin to conform to our ideal desires.[110] Such reflective self-evaluation must take the form of a quest, since it takes time for our actual desires to conform to our ideal desires. Philosopher Charles Taylor explains that to be a person means to make our choices by reference to a conception of the human good. Taylor points out that this orientation to the good implies a kind of moral "space."[111] The good is something to be sought not something ever fully realized. In order to seek the good, I must know where I am in relationship to it. To orient myself, I look back to where I have come from and forward to where I want to go. In this sense, the life of every fully rational human person is the story of a quest.[112] Clearly, autobiographical narrative is not essential to any merely human life—not everyone is capable of autobiography. Still, at a minimum, we might say that any human person who attempts to live up to an ideal necessarily lives in autobiographical relation to that ideal.

Every effort to live up to an ideal necessarily takes a narrative form. Yet some ethical ideas, such as utility maximizing, are not intrinsically narrative: it is possible to imagine simply being born or programmed to calculate utility perfectly. An ethics of virtue, however, is intrinsically narrative because a virtue, says Aristotle, is acquired only over time through practice. Virtue cannot be innate or externally programmed; a virtue is an acquired disposition. The only way to become virtuous is through trial and error. Aristotle observes that if we hope to become a just person, we must attempt to act now as if we were already just. Here we see the narrative structure of every virtue: I begin by imitating what I hope to become at the end. "Fake it until you make it" is the plot of every story of virtue. In my beginning is my end. The acquisition of virtue is a drama of repeated setbacks and occasional triumphs—a journey as unique as every person's life. If we ever do finally acquire virtue, that virtue is nothing more than the congealed story of our journey.

A life story should explain the meaning of a whole life, not merely a particular stage. If I endured a Dickensian childhood, I want a life narrative in which past suffering is redeemed by future happiness; if I experienced a Tom Jonesian youth, I want past folly redeemed by future virtue.[113] We have failed to make sense of our lives if we simply repudiate a particular stage.[114] Only a comprehensive life story will illustrate how our successes can bear the seeds of future failures and how our defeats can bear the seeds of our future victories.

Narrative embodies the human experience of time, and different kinds of time demand different kinds of narratives. Aristotle pioneered the cosmological conception of time as the numerical measurement of motion.[115] To this day, physicists think of time only in relation to physical motion. Cosmological time is measured by the motion of the earth in relation to the sun and the moon, or, today, the motion of atoms. Augustine pioneered the subjective conception of time as the thick temporal now, stretching between memory and anticipation. Our subjective experience of time leads us, as individuals and as cultures, to privilege moments of great import in which large swaths of past and future are gathered. A birthday or independence day are examples of these subjectively or intersubjectively significant moments. A calendar, says Ricoeur, is an attempt to bridge cosmological and subjective time. Calendars are anchored in culturally significant moments—such as the foundation of Rome or the birth of Jesus—but they measure time in relation to the sun or the moon.

How does historical narrative differ from fictional narrative? According to Ricoeur, historical narratives are always anchored in cosmological time, that is, in some calendar. Histories, like all narratives, weave together past, present, and future; but histories must also always be located on an objective timeline. Not only does history always begin with potentially datable events, but the intervals between historical events must also be potentially measureable. Fictional narratives, by contrast, need not be anchored in any calendar, and the intervals between fictional events need not be measurable. Fictional stories often pretend to be set in a historical moment, but they require only the psychological sense of time captured in the expression "once upon a time." History, then, is a narrative that bridges cosmological time with the subjective experience of past, present, and future.[116]

Autobiography and memoir are the two fundamental kinds of narratives we tell about our own lives, and each of these has a different relationship to time.[117] Autobiography, like history, necessarily makes reference to dates and measures intervals between events.[118] Memoir, like fiction, need not be anchored in any datable event and need not attempt to measure intervals between events. Memoirs unify the past, present, and future, but these need only be a subjective or psychological experience. Perhaps the structural similarity between memoir and fiction helps to explain why memoirs are so often fictional: once a story is liberated from the calendar, it will tend to lose all other connections to history. We should assume that memoirs are fictional until proven otherwise. In practice, of course, autobiographies usually incorporate memoir just as most memoirs are anchored in autobiography. The fact that memoirs are usually more fictional than autobiographies certainly does not mean that they are less truthful.

A narrative, of course, is not the only way to unify a human life. Philosopher John Rawls has sketched a conception of the rational unity of human life in terms of framing a life plan. Whereas I have defined an actual person as a human being with the capacity to tell a life story, Rawls defines a person as a man with a plan.[119] Rawls's conception of a life plan has been adopted by many contemporary moral and political philosophers.[120] I observed above that some philosophers claim that narratives are not mere tools for self-understanding but that our sense of ourselves is constituted by the ongoing stories we tell. Similarly for Rawls, our life plans are not mere tools for giving rational unity to our lives: we define who we are by our plans.[121] A rational plan, says Rawls, is one adopted after careful deliberation and informed by full knowledge of one's endowments and circumstances. Rawls is aware that we cannot know the future perfectly. A rational plan is actually a nested hierarchy of plans and subplans so that broad priorities can be fixed while allowing for ongoing revisions of the subplans.[122] Planning, he says, is partly scheduling; we organize our activities in a temporal sequence so that a diverse range of desires can be satisfied without unnecessary friction.[123] Rawls even goes so far as to say that if a person's plan is rational, then so is that person's conception of a good life.[124] Someone is happy, says Rawls, when his life goes according to plan.[125]

What are we to make of this planning conception of the unity of a human life? Certainly, planning is part of any life story: the hero of every story makes plans—though in good stories, those plans go awry. I have defined "narrative" as a device for controlling time, and making plans is certainly one way to attempt to control time so as to permit us to reach distant goals. But narratives are both forward-looking and backward-looking; indeed, they are forward-looking by way of being backward-looking. Rawls's planner is resolutely forward-looking: she leaves details to be filled in by her future self, but that self never looks back. Rawls does recognize that a good plan depends on adequate self-knowledge, but he fails to mention that self-knowledge comes only from retrospection. Rawls is clear that we must formulate our life plan when we are very young, since its central projects will include the choice of career and spouse. Rawls never notes the Kierkegaardian irony that by the time we attain the self-knowledge necessary to make rational plans, it is too late. As the French say: "If only youth knew and old age could."[126] Of course, there are ways to meet this paradox, but they involve anticipatory retrospection of a kind foreign to Rawlsian planning.

Indeed, Rawls's conception of planning almost escapes human temporality altogether. In order to form a nested hierarchy of plans and subplans, we must be able in some way to see our lives as a simultaneous whole. But the logical relation of means to ends is often subverted in the temporal relation of means to ends. College may well be a necessary means to my plan to become a lawyer, but by going to college I am likely to give up my original career goal. The tendency of our rational means to undermine our chosen ends in lived experience often makes a mockery of our youthful plans. Finally, Rawls's repeated assertion that a happy person is one whose life proceeds according to plan seems the very definition of naivety. The moral hazard of getting what we want is a central theme of many narratives, whether of literature or of life. The only thing worse than having our youthful plans fail is to have them succeed.

There are many dangers as well as many virtues in the youthful exercise of drawing up a plan of life. But before we do so, we should undertake the task of writing our own eulogy. By imagining our life's story as told by someone who can see it as a whole and who wishes us well, we might discover the underlying quest that could serve to unify our lives. Nothing brings life into focus as forcefully as the prospect of death. Plans lack moral gravity; plans can always be revised. Only death has the finality necessary to liberate our attention from the infinite distraction and dispersal of everyday life so that we might see our lives as a whole.

Ebenezer Scrooge, of Dickens's *A Christmas Carol*, is a cautionary tale of someone who resolutely attempts to live according to a plan. Fortunately, however, Scrooge suffers a catastrophe when the Ghosts of Christmas Past, Present, and Future reveal to him that his life story is headed toward a bad ending. Now, with the opportunity to make amends and to redeem his prior life, Scrooge abandons the life of planning and embraces the wisdom of narrative: "I will live in the Past, the Present, and the Future. The spirit of all three shall strive within me. I will not shut out the lesson they teach."[127] Storytelling looks backward and forward—or, more precisely, stories look forward by looking backward (foreshadowing) and look backward by looking forward (anticipatory retrospection). Narratives alone enable us to gather up the time of our lives into a whole. Yes, we will need to make plans, but, more importantly, we will need to tell stories to make sense of life, whether or not it proceeds according to plan.

What is a narrative conception of human development? Narrative psychologists often ask their subjects at different stages of life to compose autobiographical stories. The growing sophistication of these stories reflects the growth of autobiographical memory and then of autobiographical reasoning. There are important similarities in the structure of those stories at each stage of development. Children's stories tend to center on the roles they are learning to inhabit: how to be a good student, son or daughter, and friend. The stories of adolescents and young adults focus on establishing goals and making plans to achieve them. The stories of older adults are about making sense of life by seeing the past as foreshadowing the present and the present as redeeming the past. The autobiographical self, according to some psychologists, develops by sequentially adding the layers of actor, agent, and author.[128] At every age we relate to the whole of our lives, but our understanding of that whole develops.

What is a narrative conception of practical wisdom? Our failures of practical reasoning usually stem from a failure to relate important choices to the whole of our lives. We often make decisions in response to the felt urgency of immediate impulses and incentives without due regard for the larger story of our lives. That is why we call our mistakes "short-sighted" or "impulsive": they are not integrated into the narrative arc of our lives. Recall that in a metaphysical sense, we are wholly present at every moment of our lives: we endure through time, we are not spread out in parts over time. What happens in childhood does not affect only my childhood but affects me. Yet in a psychological sense—because of the dispersal of our attention—we are rarely if ever wholly present at any one time. We almost never respond fully to the challenge of any particular moment in our lives because psychologically we are only partly present. At any one time or even one stage of life, we can metaphorically say: "I was not all there."[129] This is why we are chronically belated. Like the French *"l'esprit d'escalier"* (wit of the stairwell), we think of what we should have said or done only when it is too late. But through the power of narrative we can gather up time and respond to every moment with the perspective gained by a life story. Only when forced to confront the whole of his life was Scrooge able to respond fully to the meaning of Christmas Day. Practical wisdom is the capacity to bring to bear the whole of our lives to the challenge of each moment.

What is a narrative conception of maturity? A mature person accepts that she can aspire to relate the story of her life but not claim to be the author. All autobiographies play two roles in forming a narrative identity. First, they integrate the childhood self with the adult self, usually by seeing the adult already in the child or by seeing the child in the ironic light of adulthood. Second, they integrate the private self with the public persona— "the private face in the mirror with the public face in the window."[130] We want to tell the story of our own life in order to correct the stories told about us by others. Autobiographies are written to challenge biographies. When we read the autobiographies of famous people, we are hoping to peek behind the public mask to see the true self—which, of course, is just another mask created by the author. Because we are essentially social animals, we cannot see ourselves accurately except in relation to how we appear to others: if you wish to see your private self, look through the public window.

Neither biography nor autobiography affords a privileged standpoint on the truth of a life. Autobiographies are just as unreliable as biographies, but each provides a necessary check on the other. Ultimately, of course, the veracity of either biography or autobiography depends on how conscientiously the narrator pursues the truth. T. S. Eliot may be right that "humankind cannot bear very much reality," but mature people do seek to tell a truthful story about their own lives. To do so, we must draw on a wide range of other narratives. First, we must acknowledge how much we owe to the ongoing stories already drafted by our parents and by our society: we are editors of our life story more than its creators. Second, we should listen carefully to the stories that other people tell about us, even uncharitable ones. Finally, we must attempt to assess our lives in relation to an ideal of a complete and infallible story told by an omniscient narrator. The only way to approximate the point of view of an omniscient narrator is by the literary device of anticipatory retrospection. We can attempt to preview not only the stories marking our own death but also the story of our lives from the vantage of the end of history.

A narrative conception of maturity, then, would rest on the degree of consistency between three life stories: the story I tell about myself, the story that virtuous others tell about me, and the infallibly true story told by an omniscient narrator when time—and, hence, narrative—come to an end.

Conclusion

A Practical Guide to Life Writing

I began this book by discussing recapitulation, preformation, epigenesis, and neoteny as the basic biological stories of human development. Although each of these stories divides growth into a series of stages, each story also unifies a human life by giving development a goal. By the end of this book, I was arguing that our lives are unified by biographical and autobiographical narratives. So am I a biological animal or a storytelling person? Surely biological growth is quite different from relating a narrative. Biological development happens to me willy-nilly whereas I must choose to construct and tell the story of my own life. Moreover, biological development is a generic process that happens to everyone whereas the story I tell about my own life is uniquely mine.

Certainly, there are contrasts between biological development and the telling of stories, but these contrasts are often exaggerated. Human biological development depends on cultural achievements, from midwives, to proper nutrition, to the acquisition of language. Without hearing and telling stories, we would not survive childhood. What about the role of choice? Biological development is not wholly involuntary: without choosing to take care of ourselves and to cooperate with other people, we cannot mature even in a physical sense. Nor is our storytelling wholly voluntary: we learn the stories of our culture and of our infancy whether we want to or not. Is biological development generically human while autobiography is uniquely personal? Biological development is partly generic and partly individual, just like every human genome. Similarly, the stories we tell about our own lives are much more generic than we would like to admit. In short, we are biological persons and storytelling animals.

I have argued that we are animals all the way up and persons all the way down. Our rational and moral powers are not accidental accoutrements of an essentially biological animal. We devote a lot of time speaking to and attempting to reason with our pets; if rationality could be taught, then dogs, cats, and horses ought to be rational. Rational or moral agency cannot be taught; it can only grow up in a human animal living among human animals. The lowest depths of our biological functions, such as eating, copulating, or defecating, reflect high cultural ideals just as the highest peaks of our intellectual and moral achievements never fully escape biological drives for status and reproduction. We eat food as rational persons and we write books as biological animals.

We often foolishly contrast the physical powers of our bodies with the mental powers of our brains. But, of course, our brains have nothing but physical powers while our minds extend well beyond our brains to the tips of our fingers and to the limits of our instruments. Instead of being partly physical and partly mental, we are all body and all mind. We often describe ourselves as "embodied," but it is equally true to say that we are "ensouled." All of our physical, biological, and psychological concepts attempt to capture aspects of a unity that escapes our powers of description.

I have noted that some philosophers claim that a human life has unity over time only insofar as we tell unified autobiographical stories. Other philosophers claim that a human life has unity because, from conception to death, we possess a single and unique genome. How can these accounts both be true? What does biological growth have in common with autobiographical narrative?

What unites our stories of biological growth with the structure of narratives is the idea of development. Something develops when potency becomes actual, when the end is present at the beginning, and when the beginning foreshadows the end. Our whole lives are implicitly present from the moment of conception. Development is more than a mere unfolding of organismic potential—the environment plays a crucial part—but development is partly an unfolding. As every storyteller knows, you cannot know how to begin a narrative until you know how it ends. Narratives unfold just as do lives. Biography is the original and paradigmatic narrative.

Even though sheer biological growth has a quasi-narrative structure, we cannot jump from biological development to the development of plots without passing through memory, attention, and imagination. We know that human memory and imagination are rooted in biology because many other animals also have powers of memory, attention, and imagination. Indeed, recalling past threats and imagining future threats have obvious survival value. Moreover, even the power of attending to the present, as I have noted, requires at least short-term memory and imagination: attention is stretched between memory of the immediate past and imagined expectation of the immediate future. Attention itself has a quasi-narrative structure, since a narrative is any device which unifies the past, present, and future. To be attentive is to see whether our expectation of the immediate future is borne out by the immediate past.

Memory also has a narrative structure. Far from being a mere record of the past, memories are constantly revised in light of the present. Later memories delete, italicize, and revise earlier ones in order to make the story more coherent—or more self-flattering. Our later "selves" add ironic commentary to the memories of our earlier selves. Imagination has the same narrative structure as memory: what we imagine about the future keeps changing in light of the past. The human mind is relentlessly editorial and never lets up from the work of revising our memories and imaginings—all with the aim of making the story more coherent.

The advent of language stabilizes the short-term recall and expectation of other animals into the long-term human powers of seeing our lives as a whole. We are the only animal that can "remember" our births (assisted by other storytellers) and imagine our deaths. Our powers of memory, attention, and imagination are undoubtedly rooted in our biological nature —which is why they emerge, develop, and fade over time. Without the linguistic ability to stabilize memory and imagination, we could not tell the story of our lives or the lives of others. A kitten does not look forward to being a cat; a dog does not fondly recall his puppyhood.

If our identities were founded on our narratives, then we would become a different person by telling a different autobiographical story. But surely that cannot be right. When it matters, as with criminal responsibility, we identify people by their genetic profile, not by their narratives or even memories. Whether I am the same person who performed a certain deed is decided by my DNA, not by my stories or even my recollections. Our autobiographical narratives are not the foundation but the capstone of our human identities, the highest achievement of our psychological powers of memory and imagination. The biological unity of our lives is foundational and ineradicable but lacks the marks of our personal aspirations. The psychological unity of our lives is not ineradicable, though many "bodily" memories do survive the shipwreck of our conscious memories. Still, psychological unity often lacks the full coherence of a well-told tale. Our memories are full of regrets and shame; our imaginings are full of conflicting fears and hopes. Only by telling a story in which past failures are redeemed by subsequent successes can we hope to reconcile our memories and our imaginings. The power of narrative to shape or distort a human life is especially evident when we adopt destructive narratives based on superstition, victimization, or illusions of grandeur.

Why give our lives a narrative unity? Because good practical reasoning depends on bringing to bear the whole of our lives on each decision. Most of our moral failures stem from acting in relation to immediate incentives and constraints. We lose perspective when we cannot see our lives as a whole—which is to say, when we forget who we really are. If every decision we made had to fit within a considered narrative of our entire lives—a narrative shaped by the eulogy we hope will mark our death—then our decisions would be wiser. Wisdom is the ability to bring to bear the whole of one's experience on the demands of each moment. Narratives alone enable us to gather up the time of our lives so that we might hope to live up to our own ideals.

Even if our identities are not founded on our life stories, narrative still provides the key for understanding a life. Genetic unfolding, memory and imagination, and stories are all devices for unifying the past, present, and future—that is, they are all kinds of narratives, or at least quasi-narratives. Human beings cannot escape time, but we can partially transcend time by gathering our past, present, and future into stories that both please and instruct. Is narrative an imitation of life, as Aristotle thought, or is life an imitation of narrative, as Oscar Wilde insisted? Both are true so long as we remember that stories were lived before they were told.

∽

Throughout this book, I have invited readers to reflect on the unity and shape of their own lives. I can attest from experience that the best way to bring your own childhood and adulthood into dialogue is to practice writing about your whole life. Each of the following writing exercises explores a basic theme in this book. Through this set of practicums, you will recapitulate not only the journey through this book but also the journey of your own life. You will discover: (1) whether your life conforms to the master narrative of our society; (2) whether your life mirrors the classical narratives of human life; (3) whether you see your life the way others see it; (4) whether your life is a story of redemption from suffering; (5) whether your life is guided by your own deepest values.

Just as it takes the whole of our bodies to heal an injury to any one part, so by understanding the whole of our lives we can bring healing to any one part. Socrates wisely told us that the unexamined life is not worth living. But, as someone who never wrote anything, he was not well positioned to teach us that the best way to examine your life is by writing about it.

First Practicum: Learning to Be the Editor of Your Life

Ever since Jean-Jacques Rousseau, modern Westerners have often aspired to be authentic. More than anything, we dread being "phonies," as Holden Caulfield memorably put it in J. D. Salinger's *Catcher in the Rye*. To be authentic means literally to be the author of one's own life. According to Rousseau and Caulfield, most people suppress their own individuality in order to please others: they let society write the story of their lives. But an authentic person rejects social expectations and bravely becomes the author of her own life.

Authenticity is a heroic ideal of individual self-fashioning. But can we truly be the authors of our own lives? I have already discussed some reasons for thinking that we cannot. To begin with, our stories begin with our parents, who write the first several chapters and haunt the rest of the book. Far from being the authors of our own lives, we spend much of our time trying to understand, erase, and revise the stories our parents have already written. Many of us never escape our parental narratives. An author can bring his characters into existence; only parents can bring us into existence. By the way, you also cannot be the author of your own death, though we shall attempt a draft obituary in a later exercise.

We have also discussed the master narrative or life script that each person inherits from her society. I once asked my students to write a list of the eight major milestones in the life of an American born in the year 2000. Each student independently came up with virtually the same milestones in a normative American life—and they even agreed at what age each milestone would be reached. So, yes, we all have internalized a life script. What makes this script a "master narrative"? First, everyone lists the milestones in chronological order, that is, as a narrative. Second, everyone understands that these milestones are considered mandatory. Even if we choose not to, say, get married, we know that we shall have a lot of explaining to do. No one will ever ask us why we decided to follow the master narrative, but we will often be asked why we deviated from it.

In this exercise, ask a friend to write a list of the eight major milestones of a normal life for anyone born in your country at roughly the same time. In some nations, the milestones will be partly different for men and women. Along with each milestone, have your friend specify the age range in which each milestone is normally expected to be reached.

Once you have this story of a normal life, compare it to your own life. To what extent have you followed your society's life script? Did you reach each milestone within the expected age range? Were you early or late? Will you simply reject some of the milestones? Do you have your own milestones? Through this focused comparison, you will discover to what extent you are the author of your own life. Is your own life uniquely yours? Or did you revise the master narrative of your society? I hope this exercise helps you to reflect on the relation between your own life script and the master narrative you have inherited. Are you an author or an editor of your life story?

Second Practicum: Learning from the Classics

We explored some classic stories of a human life. Aristotle focuses on the midlife prime of life, when our talents are most fully actualized. Childhood is just an unpleasant but necessary preparation for the adult prime, while old age is an even more unpleasant decline.

By contrast, Jesus asks adults to return to childhood and recapture the innocence and trust of small children. According to Jesus, adults tend to be status conscious, arrogant, mistrustful, and proud. We need to relearn how to be unselfconscious, trusting of others, and spontaneously generous. Is it possible to age without getting old?

Augustine insists that we never really change. Like the little homunculus hiding in a sperm cell, we just get bigger over time. From the time we are infants, we are selfish, impatient, and greedy. The objects of our grasping desire change over time, but not our essential lust for more. Our grownup tantrums are much worse than our toddler tantrums, but both reflect the same chronic frustrations. Are we basically the same person throughout our lives?

In this exercise, compare your own life to each of these classic models.

Aristotle: If you could choose to live in just one stage of life, would it be the prime? Does the prime of life include all the goods and virtues of life? Would you like to live your whole life in the prime?

Jesus: What have you lost by growing up? Do you wish that you were more innocent? Can you recapture the joys of childhood?

Augustine: Have you really changed much? Were you shy already as a child? Do you have the same basic temperamental style? Do you still get frustrated and want to tantrum? Are you morally better as an adult?

Third Practicum: Learning from Biographies

The aim in these exercises is to learn to write truthfully about our own lives. As noted above, however, autobiographies have severe limitations. Our autobiographies can extend only as far as our memories. We cannot recall our birth or infancy. So to understand the first chapters of our lives, we depend on the stories that others can tell us. Indeed, even what we "remember" about our own past is often shaped or even planted by the stories we have heard from others.

Moreover, as George Bernard Shaw observed, "all autobiographies are lies"—including, he admits, his own. We are all prone to tell our own stories in a way that is self-serving and less than fully frank. All good autobiographies rest on biographies. We need to check our version of events with more detached versions. Famous people write autobiographies mainly to challenge existing biographies. Which is more truthful, the story I tell about myself or the story that others tell? The best route to truth comes from comparing my own story with the stories about me told by others.

In this exercise, ask someone who knows you well, such as a friend, parent, or sibling (warning: not your spouse or partner!), to write your life's story (or the story of your recent life) in the form of a letter to you. Compare this biography to your own autobiography. Be prepared to have some cherished illusions shattered. Do other people see you as you see yourself? Do not get angry at your biographer: he or she is being very helpful to you even though sometimes the truth hurts.

Fourth Practicum: Stories of Redemption

If we were purely rational animals, then we would care only about the amount of suffering in our lives. A rational person wants a life of minimal total suffering, and does not care about the timing of that suffering. But we are storytelling animals, so we do care about whether our suffering comes early or late. In a good story, early suffering is redeemed by later wisdom and happiness. No one wants to be King Priam who lost everything too late for any redemption. We want a difficult childhood to be followed by a successful adulthood, not the reverse.

Indeed, the experiments in psychology discussed above suggest that most people choose to have more total suffering so long as that suffering is redeemed by later happiness. What we hate above all is meaningless suffering. How we think about suffering depends on whether it already happened or whether it might happen in the future. No one welcomes the prospect of future suffering, but many of us are grateful for past suffering. Amazingly, even most victims of horrible traumas, if they survive long enough, later report that they do not regret the terrible losses they endured—so compelling is our faith in the redemptive power of suffering.

In this exercise, describe your experiences of suffering, of having your heart's deepest desires crushed. What effects did that suffering have on your life? Did subsequent life experiences in some way redeem earlier suffering? Did you grow in wisdom or happiness because of what you suffered? Or was your suffering meaningless? Did your suffering come too late? Do you regret the misfortunes that arrived in your life? Or are you somehow grateful for them?

Fifth Practicum: Write Your Own Obituary and Eulogy

We have discussed the value of looking back on your whole life from the perspective of death—a literary device known as "anticipatory retrospection." Ancient monks would keep a human skull on their desks as a reminder of their own mortality. Throughout this book, I hope, each of us has attempted to bring his or her life into focus. Well, nothing focuses the mind quite like the prospect of death.

How does an obituary differ from a eulogy? Consider the difference between résumé values and eulogy values. A résumé tells what each of us has accomplished, while a eulogy tells what each of us stands for. Both reveal important things about our lives. An obituary is sort of like a final résumé: it relates the major milestones and achievements for which we want to be remembered. By writing your obituary now, you will have a better chance of actually realizing your own goals before it is too late.

Writing your own eulogy is more difficult, intimate, and revealing. That is why you should write your obituary first. Imagine your spouse or best friend at your funeral. What would you like them to say? What do you most wish to be remembered for? That you were president or that you were just? That you were a doctor or that you were compassionate? That you were a Christian or that you were prayerful?

Writing your own eulogy will help you to lead your life in a way that provides evidence of the virtues you want to be remembered for. Yes, people generally speak only good about the dead. But surely we want our eulogies to at least roughly match our lives. Tom Sawyer, in Mark Twain's classic book, enjoys the rare experience of actually attending his own funeral. The minister describes Tom's outrageous pranks as the noble and beautiful acts of a sweet and generous boy.

In this exercise, write your own obituary and then eulogy. If possible, compare your own eulogy to one written by a parent, friend, or child—though it may not be easy to convince someone to do this! If you wish to avoid the comic scene at Tom Sawyer's funeral, then write your own eulogy now.

NOTES

Epigraph: "Où est le commencement de nos actes? Notre destin, quand nous voulons l'isoler, ressemble à ces plantes qu'il est impossible d'arracher avec toutes leurs racines." Translated by Raymond N. MacKenzie (Lanham: Rowman and Littlefield, 2005), 37.

Chapter 1

1. Both ancient Epicureans and ancient Stoics developed the "argument from the cradle" to show that human nature could be accurately perceived in infants. See Jacques Brunschwig, "The Cradle Argument in Epicureanism and Stoicism," in *The Norms of Nature*, ed. Malcolm Schofield and Gisela Striker (Cambridge: Cambridge University Press, 1986), 113–144.

2. Psychologist Jerome Bruner judiciously concludes: "To understand the nature of any species fully, we need to know more than the ways of its adults." "The Nature and Uses of Immaturity," *American Psychologist* 27, no. 8 (August 1972): 687–708 at 687.

3. According to Plato, a real thing is nothing but its powers: "I'll take it as a definition that *those which are* amount to nothing other than capacity." *Sophist* 247E. According to Alan Gewirth, "there is a difference between what you now are and what you aspire to become or what you have the capacity to become." *Self-Fulfillment* (Princeton: Princeton University Press, 1998), 62 and 117. All translations of Plato are from *Plato: Complete Works*, ed. John M. Cooper (Indianapolis: Hackett, 1997).

4. *As You Like It*, act 2, scene 7.

5. "Decades of research have led to the conclusion that human development is more continuous and less discontinuous than stage theorists such as Piaget had proposed." Jeffrey Jensen Arnett, "Life Stage Concepts Across History and Cultures," *Human Development* 59 (2016): 290–316, at 312.

6. The leading theorist of life span development is Paul B. Baltes; see "On the Incomplete Architecture of Human Ontogeny," *American Psychologist* 52, no. 4 (April 1997): 366–380.

7. See Alison Gopnik et al., "Changes in Cognitive Flexibility and Hypothesis Search Across Human Life History from Childhood to Adolescence to Adulthood," *Proceedings of the National Academy of Sciences* 114, no. 30 (July 25, 2017): 7892–7899.

8. Biologist Melvin Konner describes recent studies of neonates: "the youngest infants can do some version of what only older children were thought to be able to do." *The Evolution of Childhood* (Cambridge: Harvard University Press, 2010), 214.

9. After acknowledging that human development is continuous, Arnett rightly asks: "Yet how do we account for an apparent human tendency to take continuities in development and

make them discontinuous, by introducing roles, status, and responsibilities that are distinctive to each life stage?" Arnett, "Life Stage Concepts Across History and Cultures," 312.

10. "There exists what might be called a prescriptive timetable for the ordering of major life events: a time in the life span when men and women are expected to marry, a time to raise children, a time to retire. . . . Age norms and age expectations operate as prods and brakes upon behavior." For empirical evidence of the social consensus on this life script, see Bernice L. Neugarten et al., "Age Norms, Age Constraints, and Adult Socialization," *American Journal of Sociology* 70, no. 6 (May 1965): 710–717, at 711.

11. Karl Rahner emphasizes this uniquely human capacity to imagine our lives as a whole in "Ideas for a Theology of Childhood," in *Theological Investigations*, vol. 8, trans. David Bourke (New York: Crossroads, 1971), 33–50, at 34–35.

12. I will not follow James K. Feibleman: "The human individual develops through the same set of stages as any other organism." *The Stages of Human Life: A Biography of Entire Man* (The Hague: Martinus Nijhoff, 1975), 14.

13. "It is not unusual—nor is it precocious—for a 10-year-old to express the insights and carry the gravity of a 50-year-old or to experience the loves and nostalgia of a 60-year-old. . . . At any given time, at any given age, we are all ages at once." Amélie Rorty, "Improvisatory Accident-Prone Dramas of (What Passes for) a Person's Life," in *Changing Conceptions of Psychological Life*, ed. Cynthia Lightfoot et al. (Mahwah, N.J.: Lawrence Erlbaum, 2004), 251–262, at 256 and 259.

14. Philosopher Kieran Setiya describes realizing at age forty that he will never be a doctor as one aspect of his own midlife crisis. Of course, he knew when he began to study philosophy at age twenty that he probably could not also be a doctor. Moreover, he *could* become a doctor at age forty, if he wished. He describes midlife as a time of lost opportunities, regrets and failures, and awareness of the finitude of life—all of which, he concedes, we experience throughout life. As for J. S. Mill's midlife crisis at age twenty, Setiya observes: "Mill was precocious." *Midlife: A Philosophical Guide* (Princeton: Princeton University Press, 2017), 56, 23, 30.

15. According to Aristotle's "homonymy principle," a severed hand or detached eye is a "hand" or "eye" in name only; similarly, a childhood with no anticipation of adulthood or an adulthood with no memory of childhood would be a "childhood" or "adulthood" in name only. On Aristotle's homonymy principle, see Ross Inman, *Substance and the Fundamentality of the Familiar* (New York: Routledge, 2018), 104.

16. In *Centuries of Childhood*, historian Philippe Ariès argues that in early modern Europe, childhood was invented: "there was no place for childhood in the medieval world." But logically, if childhood was invented, then so was adulthood. As Neil Postman effectively argues, if there were no children in the Middle Ages, then there were also no adults. What changes in history is the relationship between children and adults. The real subject of Ariès's book is not the invention of childhood but the history of family life, as evident in his original French title, *L'Enfant et la vie familiale sous l'ancien régime*. See Ariès, *Centuries of Childhood*, trans. Robert Baldick (New York: Alfred A. Knopf, 1962), 33; and Postman, *The Disappearance of Childhood* (New York: Delacorte Press, 1982). Postman is clear that the looming disappearance of childhood is also inexorably the disappearance of adulthood.

17. Alfred Korzybski defines human beings by their "time-binding" power. On plants, animals, and humans in Korzybski's thought, see *Manhood of Humanity* (New York: E. P.

Dutton, 1921), 58–59. Korzybski, however, ignores the continuity of life in relation to time: the biological growth of any organism binds time, and, as we shall see, animal perception also binds the immediate past and future into the present. So the unique human capacity to bind time with narrative rests on biological and psychological powers we share with plants and animals.

18. Kant, quoted in G. R. G. Mure, *An Introduction to Hegel* (Oxford: Clarendon Press, 1940), 6n. Our common words for describing change over time imply that nothing really changes. To "develop" originally meant to "unwrap": what develops was always there in the first place. The same is true of our word "evolution," which literally means to "unroll"—as if unrolling a scroll creates something new.

19. "It seems most distinctive of substance that what is numerically one and the same is able to receive contraries." Aristotle, *Categories* 4a 10.

20. On why a living organism is more unified than any artifact, see David Wiggins, *Substance and Sameness Renewed* (Cambridge: Cambridge University Press, 2001), 101.

21. "Even while each living thing is said to be alive and to be the same—as a person is said to be the same from childhood till he turns into an old man—even then he never consists of the same things, though he is called the same, but he is always being renewed and in other respects passing away, in his hair and flesh and bones and his entire body." Plato, *Symposium* 207D to 208B. Discussed in Helen Small, *The Long Life* (Oxford: Oxford University Press, 2007), 31.

22. James K. Feibleman neglects the difference between change and development: "Thus the life of man has a direction: it is indicated by the arrow of time." But the arrow of time does not provide a measure of development, which is the focus of Feibleman's theory. *The Stages of Human Life*, 14.

23. Psychologist Bernard Kaplan sharply contrasts "orthogenesis" as ideal development toward a goal from mere aging or "ontogenesis." This distinction, he says, frees us from the "unwarranted doctrine that Time was the mother of Perfection." "A Trio of Trials," in *Developmental Psychology*, ed. Richard M. Lerner (Hillsdale, N.J.: Lawrence Erlbaum, 1983), 185–228, at 195.

24. Richard Lewontin compares biological development to film in *The Triple Helix* (Cambridge: Harvard University Press, 2000), 5.

25. In his classic essay on biological teleology, philosopher Ernest Nagel distinguishes two criteria that define goal-directed processes. These are plasticity: "the goal of such processes can generally be reached by the system following alternative paths or starting from different initial positions"; and persistence: "the system has maintained its goal-directed behavior as a result of changes occurring in the system that compensate for a disturbance taking place (provided these are not too great) either within or external to the system, disturbances which, were there no compensating changes elsewhere, would prevent realization of the goal." Nagel, "Teleology Revisited," in *Nature's Purposes*, ed. Colin Allen et al. (Cambridge: Cambridge University Press, 1998), 197–240, at 208–209.

26. Biologist Ernst Mayr calls biological development *teleonomic* in contrast to intentional human goal seeking, called *teleological*: "The programs which control teleonomic processes in organisms are either entirely laid down in the DNA of the genotype (closed programs) or are constituted in such a way that they can incorporate additional information (open-programs)." Mayr, *Toward a New Philosophy of Biology* (Cambridge: Belknap Press, 1988), 49.

27. "According to Freud, the anatomical location and embryological trajectory of the mouth and anus in various animals was evidence for the oral-anal sequence in ontogeny." John R. Morss, "Against Ontogeny," in *Trees of Life*, ed. Paul Griffiths (Dordrecht: Kluwer Academic Publishers, 1992), 247–248. Erik Erikson explicitly claims that the sequence of stages in embryonic development applies to the whole of human life: "As I now quote what the embryologist has to tell us about the epigenesis of organ systems, I hope the reader will 'hear' the probability that all growth and development will follow analogous patterns." *The Life Cycle Completed* (New York: Norton, 1997), 27. Psychiatrist George E. Vaillant questions the biological basis of Erikson's theory of psychological development: "Immutable, clearly defined developmental stages belong only to biological embryology, not to adult development." *The Wisdom of the Ego* (Cambridge: Harvard University Press, 1993), 148.

28. Freud's and Piaget's famous theories of development were meant to apply only to children. Even developmental biologists are beginning to challenge the hegemony of reproductive maturity and to argue that development extends from conception to death. See Thomas Pradeu, "Regenerating Theories in Developmental Biology," in *Towards a Theory of Development*, ed. Alessandro Minelli and Thomas Pradeu (Oxford: Oxford University Press, 2014), 15–32, at 15.

29. "The dominant view among current biologists and philosophers is that developmental biology does not offer theories." Pradeu, "Regenerating Theories in Developmental Biology," 15. For a discussion of whether a theory of development is desirable or even possible, see the essays in Minelli and Pradeu, *Towards a Theory of Development*.

30. George Boas applied the biological theory of recapitulation to childhood in *The Cult of Childhood* (London: Warburg Institute, 1966), 61. Gareth B. Matthews offers three possible biological "models" for understanding childhood (preformation, the logical model or epigenesis, and recapitulation), though Matthews himself discusses only recapitulation. See Matthews, "Conceiving Childhood: 'Child Animism,'" *Nous* 16, no. 1 (March 1982): 29–37. Richard B. Miller then adds the theory of neoteny to Matthew's models in "Neoteny and the Virtues of Childhood," *Metaphilosophy* 20, nos. 3–4 (July–October 1989): 319–331. These writers were pioneers in seeing the value of applying biological models to human development. Unfortunately, they all saw their projects in terms of theorizing childhood rather than human life as a whole.

31. Psychologist Alison Gopnik champions this story of indirect development: "Children and adults are different forms of *Homo sapiens* . . . like caterpillars becoming butterflies. . . . The caterpillars and butterflies do different things well." *The Philosophical Baby* (New York: Farrar, Straus and Giroux, 2009), 9–11.

32. Philosopher Jerry Fodor described scholarship as the process whereby a butterfly transmogrifies into a caterpillar.

33. Jean-Jacques Rousseau and psychologist Alison Gopnik make this argument at length.

34. Nor are recapitulation theories a thing of the past. Paul MacLean's influential theory of the triune human brain is a classic example of recapitulation. He divides our brain anatomically into the reptilian brain (basal ganglia), the paleomammalian brain (limbic system), and the neomammalian brain (cerebral neocortex). See MacLean, *The Triune Brain in Evolution* (New York: Plenum Press, 1990).

35. Contemporary geneticist Richard Lewontin: "The very young embryos of terrestrial vertebrates have gill slits like fish and amphibia, which then disappear in later development. This is an example of the rule that 'ontogeny recapitulates phylogeny.'" *The Triple Helix*, 13.

36. Boas distinguishes biological from sociological recapitulation in *The Cult of Childhood*, 61.

37. For detailed textual proof of this claim, see Stephen Jay Gould, *Ontogeny and Phylogeny* (Cambridge: Harvard University Press, 1977), 135–164.

38. P. S. and J. S. Medawar, quoted in Jane Maienschein, "Preformation or New Formation—or Neither or Both," in *A History of Embryology*, ed. T. J. Horder et al. (Cambridge: Cambridge University Press, 1985), 73–108, at 101–102. According to geneticist Richard Lewontin: "It is usually said that the epigenetic view decisively defeated preformationism. . . . Yet it is really preformationism that has triumphed." *The Triple Helix*, 6. "Modern genetics is about as midway as it could be between the extreme formulations [preformation vs. epigenesis] of the eighteenth century." Gould, *Ontogeny and Phylogeny*, 18.

39. "The fetuses of humans and apes resemble each other much more than the adults do, and adult humans have morphological features that make them resemble fetal apes." Lewontin, *The Triple Helix*, 13.

40. For the continuing importance of all of these stories in contemporary biology, see Gould's *Ontogeny and Phylogeny* and Ernst Mayr's "Recapitulation Reinterpreted: The Somatic Program," *Quarterly Review of Biology* 69, no. 2 (June 1994): 223–232. The standard contemporary theory of evolution and development known as "heterochrony" involves elements of neoteny and of recapitulation; see Michael McKinney and Kenneth J. McNamara, *Heterochrony: The Evolution of Ontogeny* (New York: Plenum Press, 1991).

41. McKinney and McNamara argue something similar: "In short, humans show faster brain growth but delayed mental development. . . . It is not true that we are 'intended' to remain mentally youthful: we are in the youthful learning stage longer, but mental maturation continues . . . future evolution will probably involve a still greater prolongation of childhood and retardation of maturity"—not so that we remain children but so that we can surpass our primate ancestors. *Heterochrony*, 310–314.

42. Alan Gewirth says that a spiritual person transcends himself, that is, his better or more developed self supersedes or triumphs over his worse or less developed self. Saints and moral heroes, he says, transcend their self-protective instincts. *Self-Fulfillment*, 177–178.

43. In recapitulation, preformation, and epigenesis, the organism is defined *sub specie superioris*; in neoteny, the organism is defined *sub specie inferioris*.

44. Psychologist Jeffrey Jensen Arnett calls this new period of prolonged immaturity "emerging adulthood." *Emerging Adulthood* (New York: Oxford University Press, 2014).

45. Richard Lewontin attributes this maxim to Alexander Rosenblueth and Norbert Weiner. *The Triple Helix*, 4.

46. "If we had the complete DNA sequence of an organism and unlimited computational power, we could still not compute the organism, because the organism does not compute itself from its genes." Lewontin insists that the interaction between genotype, phenotype, and environment is intrinsically unpredictable in detail. *The Triple Helix*, 17.

47. Most developmental biologists agree that "development can be understood [only] with hindsight; there are still no formal predictors or rules as to what might happen." To understand by means of hindsight, of course, is to tell a story. Alessandro Minelli and Thomas Pradeu, "Theories of Development in Biology—Problems and Perspectives," in *Towards a Theory of Development*, 1–14, at 7.

48. Johan Huizinga points out, in his classic book *Homo Ludens*, that Heraclitus (frag. 70) compares human opinions to "child's play" and that Plato (*Laws*, book 7) describes play

as the most divine of human activities. Huizinga, *Homo Ludens* (Boston: Beacon Press, 1955), 211–212. Insofar as play is associated with children, Plato's endorsement of play seems at first as an endorsement of childhood. Yet, as we shall see in Chapter 2, Plato associates play with the gods and thus asks adults to imitate the gods, not children.

49. To my knowledge, the only other ancient sage who remotely approaches Jesus's praise of children is Mencius, who says only this: "A great man is one who retains the heart of a newborn babe." *Mencius*, trans. D. C. Lau (London: Penguin, 1970), IV B 12.

50. "Like the statue of Glaucus, which time, sea, and storms had so disfigured that it looked less like a God than a wild Beast, the human soul, altered in the bosom of society by a thousand continually renewed causes." Rousseau, *Discourse on the Origins of Inequality (Second Discourse)* (hereinafter *SD*), in *Collected Writings of Rousseau*, vol. 3, ed. Roger D. Masters and Christopher Kelly (Hanover, N.H.: University Press of New England, 1992), 12.

51. See the contrast of Rousseau and Aristotle on human nature in Roger D. Masters, *The Political Philosophy of Rousseau* (Princeton: Princeton University Press, 1968), 113–114. Speaking of Rousseau, Masters says: "This implies that a study of natural man must be concerned more with his beginnings than with his perfection" (198).

Chapter 2

1. The classic discussion of the hierarchy of nature in Aristotle is in the *History of Animals*: "Nature proceeds little by little from things lifeless to animal life." His ladder rises from minerals, to plants, to animals, to humans, to gods (588b 4ff). "And all things are ordered together somehow, but not all alike—both fishes and fowls and plants; and the world is not such that one thing has nothing to do with another, but they are connected. For all are ordered together to one end." *Metaphysics* (Meta.) 1075a 15. Aristotle also ranks animals in *Generation of Animals* (GA) 733a 33ff: (1) insects; (2) fish, cephalopods, and crustaceans; (3) birds and reptiles; (4) oviparous sharks; (5) mammals. For all of Aristotle's Greek texts, I have used the Oxford Classical Texts. For the English translation of the *Nicomachean Ethics* (NE), I have used Terence Irwin's (Indianapolis: Hackett, 1985). All other translations of Aristotle are from *The Complete Works of Aristotle*, ed. Jonathan Barnes (Princeton: Princeton University Press, 1984). In transliterating Aristotle's Greek, I have followed the usual convention of indicating long vowels by means of a macron.

2. NE 1177b 34.

3. Aristotle, *On the Soul* (*De Anima*, DA) 415a 32.

4. Aristotle, *Politics* (Pol.) 1252b 33.

5. Pol. 1335a 27. By marrying at these ages, husband and wife become infertile at roughly the same time.

6. Pol. 1335b 35.

7. *Rhetoric* (Rh.) 1390b 10.

8. Pol. 1329a 2–35.

9. Aristotle, DA 414a 29–b 19. Of these gradations of soul, Aristotle asks: "Is each of these a soul or part of a soul?" (DA 413b 14).

10. In his classic commentary, Hicks says: "In every case, the lower faculty can exist apart from the higher but the higher faculty presupposes those below it." R. D. Hicks, *Aristotle: De Anima* (Cambridge: Cambridge University Press, 1907), 335.

11. DA 414b 19.

12. Some eminent historians of biology describe Aristotle as a recapitulationist avant la lettre. Joseph Needham: "Aristotle has a good deal to say about the theory of recapitulation, as it was afterwards to be called. He thought there was no doubt that the vegetative or nutritive soul existed in the unfertilised material of the embryo." Needham goes on to say of Aristotle's contributions to embryology: "they are greater in number than those of any other individual embryologist." Needham, *Chemical Embryology*, vol. 1 (New York: Macmillan Co., 1931), 69 and 74. In his later *History of Embryology* (New York: Abelard-Schuman, 1959), Needham says of Aristotle: "He foreshadowed the theory of recapitulation in his speculations on the order in which souls came to inhabit the embryo during its growth" (55). In his standard English translation and edition of Aristotle's *Generation of Animals* (Cambridge: Harvard University Press, 1958), A. L. Peck endorses Needham's argument that Aristotle importantly foreshadowed the later theory of recapitulation (x). Stephen Jay Gould acknowledges Aristotle's many analogies between development and the ladder of nature, but he finds the label "recapitulationist" an anachronism when applied to Aristotle. See Gould, *Ontogeny and Phylogeny*, 15–16.

13. GA 736b 2–5.

14. GA 740b 35 to 741a 3: "nutritive soul in plants and animals . . . other parts of the soul present in some but not in others."

15. "The embryo, then, grows by means of the umbilicus in the same way as a plant by its root . . . for at first, all such embryos seem to live the life of a plant." Aristotle, GA 740b 9, 736b 11, cf. 736a 33, 740a 24, 745b 26, 774b 26; *Parts of Animals* 686b 36, 650a 21, 678a 10.

16. Perceptive soul is present potentially at conception (GA 741a 11–12) but actually present at birth (DA 417b 16).

17. Apart from those born with profound birth defects, whom Aristotle calls "monsters" (Meta. 1033b 22).

18. "For all three kinds of souls, not only the nutritive, must be possessed potentially before they are possessed in actuality" (GA 736b 14). Aristotle says that when animals are asleep, they live actually as plants: "indeed, at this time animals do actually live the life of a plant" (GA 779a 1).

19. Daryl McGowan Tress is right to emphasize that a developing human is never simply a plant or animal, since the "child, then, is always human." But Tress does not discuss the composite gradations of soul in a human being that include plant and animal souls. To be human is to develop "the powers of a soul" that include but transcend plant and animal souls. See Tress, "Aristotle's Children," in *The Philosopher's Child*, ed. Susan M. Turner and Gareth B. Matthew (Rochester, N.Y.: University of Rochester Press, 1998), 19–44, at 37 n. 8.

20. Aristotle, DA 412a 27.

21. "Thus Aristotle, evidently influenced by his doctrine of 'form' and 'matter,' decided against preformation." Needham, *Chemical Embryology*, vol. 1, 69.

22. "The life of the unborn child resembles that of the plant. . . . When the babe is brought into the world out of this vegetative state in which it exists in the womb, it passes into the animal mode of life." Hegel, *Hegel's Philosophy of Mind*, trans. William Wallace (Oxford: Clarendon Press, 1978), 58 *Zusatz*.

23. "For an animal does not become at the same time an animal and a man or a horse or any other particular animal. For the end is developed last, and the peculiar character of the species is at the end of the generation in each individual" (GA 736b 2).

24. "The nutritive soul must be possessed by everything that is alive" (DA 434a 24). For Aristotle's argument that there is no real genus of soul, see DA 414b 25. On the logic of classification that applies to numbers, figures, souls, and constitutions, see William W. Fortenbaugh, "Aristotle on Prior and Posterior, Correct and Mistaken Constitutions," in *Aristotle's Practical Side* (Leiden: Brill, 2006), 265–280.

25. Gould notices the difficulty of distinguishing individualization (epigenesis) from recapitulation in Aristotle, given that both development and the ladder of nature proceed from simple to complex. Gould, *Ontogeny and Phylogeny*, 16. However, Gould does not notice that Aristotle's denial of generic soul rules out individualization.

26. *Physis, ethos, logos*, at Pol. 1332a 38.

27. What this means for individual development is that there are three kinds of faculties or powers (*dynameis*): those that are innate (*suggenēs*), those that come by practice (*ethos*), and those that come from teaching (*mathēsis*; Meta. 1047b 31). These three faculties form a developmental hierarchy: "The contribution of nature clearly does not depend on us . . . while argument (*logos*) and teaching (*didakē*) surely do not influence everyone, but the soul of the student must be prepared by habit" (*ethos*; NE 1179b 21).

28. "The other animals for the most part live by nature (*physis*), though in some respects by habit (*ethos*) as well, while man lives also by reason (*logos*), for he alone has reason" (Pol. 1332b 2).

29. Aristotle: "a child is not happy" (*oude pais eudaimōn estin*) (NE 1100a 1); cf. *Magna Moralia* (MM) 1185a 2.

30. *Eudemian Ethics* (EE) 1215b 23.

31. "If he is called happy, he is being congratulated because of anticipated blessedness" (NE 1100a 3).

32. Gottfried Ramsauer accuses Aristotle of having disdain for children: "Nec notatu indignam est quam saepe parvulorum mentio cum contemptu fiat." *Aristotelis: Ethica Nicomachea* (Leipzig: B. G. Teubner, 1878), 661 n. 2. René Gauthier and Jean Yves Jolif then endorse Ramsauer: "Ramsauer a justement remarqué le mépris dans lequel Aristote tient l'enfance, mépris qu'il a explicitement affirmé." See René Gauthier and Jean Yves Jolif, *L'Ethique à Nicomaque* (Louvain: Publications Universitaires de Louvain, 1959), vol. 2, 75–76. Gauthier and Jolif also refer to Aristotle's late marriage: "Son mépris de l'enfance pourrait bien n'exprimer qu'une certaine sécheresse de coeur, celle de l'intellectuel tard marié qui ne s'est pas penché assez tôt sur un berceau" (76). Yet in his disdain for childhood, Aristotle is far from unique: he is simply echoing the nearly universal consensus of the ancient world. "In general the Ancients had a low opinion of children if they appraised them at all." Boas, *The Cult of Childhood*, 12.

33. The life of a plant is like the life of a person asleep: "Plants at any rate seem to possess this sort of existence, and similarly children" (EE 1216a 5). "It is impossible that plants should sleep, for there is no sleep which cannot be broken, and the condition in plants which is analogous to sleep cannot be broken" (GA 779a 1).

34. NE 1099b 33–35.

35. "None of the other animals is happy, since they in no way share in contemplation" (NE 1178b 28).

36. "For children and the other animals share in what is voluntary, but not in decision; and the actions we do on the spur of the moment are said to be voluntary, but not to express decision" (NE 1111b 8).

37. "Children and the brutes pursue pleasure" (NE 1152b 20).

38. Rh. 1371a 14–16 and 1384b 23.

39. "As the body is prior in order of generation to the soul, so the irrational is prior to the rational. The proof is that anger and wishing and desire are implanted in children from their very birth, but reason and understanding are developed as they grow older" (Pol. 1334b 20).

40. Pol. 1253a 33.

41. He says, "just as different things appear honorable to boys and to men, so it is reasonable that in the same way different things appear honorable to base and to decent people" (NE 1176b 23). Similarly, he says that what is pleasant for children and brutes is not really pleasant; only what is pleasant for good adults is truly pleasant: "as the child or brute is to the adult man, so are the bad and foolish to the good and sensible" (EE 1236a 2). Aristotle further compares the mental capacities of children to defective adults when he says that no one would call happy a vicious man "as feeble and false in mind as a child or a madman" (Pol. 1323a 34). Because of this mental fickleness, true friendship, he says, is impossible for "children, brutes, and bad men" (EE 1238a 32). In short, "the life we lead as children is not desirable, for no one in his senses would return again to this" (EE 1215b 23).

42. Aristotle frequently describes the child as incomplete or immature using the Greek word *atelēs* in contrast to the adult man, who is *telos*. The complete (*telos*) adult includes and transcends the incomplete (*atelēs*) child. In the *Politics*, Aristotle says that "the child has [the deliberative faculty], but it is immature (*atelēs*)" (Pol. 1260a 12), and "the child is imperfect (*atelēs*) and therefore obviously his excellence is not relative to himself alone but to the perfect man (*telos*)" (Pol. 1260a 31).

43. "For there must first be produced in us (as indeed is the case) an irrational impulse to the right, and later on reason must put the question to the vote and decide it. Once may see this from the case of children and those who live without reason" (MM 1206b 19–22). In the *Nicomachean Ethics*, Aristotle similarly compares the natural virtue of children with the true virtue of adults. He emphasizes that children's innate impulses to do good actions are not true virtues until they are guided by mature practical wisdom (*phronēsis*): "For these natural states belong to children and to beasts as well, but without understanding they are evidently harmful . . . full virtue cannot be acquired without prudence" (NE 1144b 8 and 16). On natural virtue and full virtue, see NE 1117a 4, 1127b 14, 1151a 18, 1179b 21.

44. EE 1229a 16, 1229a 29, 1230a 23.

45. See NE 1095b 20 and 1174a 1; EE 1215b 22.

46. "For there is no unconditional injustice in relation to what is one's own; one's own possessions or one's child until it is old enough and separated, is as though it were a part of oneself . . . hence there is no injustice in relation to them" (NE 1134b 10).

47. "Let there be a law that no deformed child shall live" and "if couples have children in excess, let abortion be procured before sense and life have begun" (Pol. 1335b 20).

48. NE 1161b 25.

49. EE 1241b 1–9.

50. NE 1167b 34.

51. EE 1241b 6.

52. As for why children and the elderly are not true citizens: "in the one case, they are not of age, and in the other, they are past the age" (Pol. 1275a 16; cf. Pol. 1278a 4).

53. NE 1170b 19.
54. EE 1238a 32.
55. NE 1158a 20.
56. EE 1240b 31.
57. NE 1155a 14.
58. NE 1158a 3.
59. Child (*pais*), to play (*paizo*), and education (*paideia*).
60. Pol. 1337b 41.
61. Pol. 1337b 32.
62. Pol. 1337b 33 and 1337b 9.
63. Pol. 1338a 37, 1339a 23, and 1340b 12.
64. Pol. 1339a 28 and 1339a 30.
65. Plato, *Laws* 803E, 804B, 644D, 803C.
66. Plato, *Laws* 803E.
67. Plato, *Laws* 716C. "All men of good will should put God at the center of their thoughts . . . man has been created as a toy for God" (*Laws* 803C).
68. In an unpublished lecture, "Childhood and Play," Malcolm Schofield argues that Plato may have been drawing on Heraclitus, who also compares gods, humans, and children: "Man is infantile in the eyes of a god as a child in the eyes of a man" (frag. 79); and "Human character does not have true judgment but divine character does" (frag. 78). See G. S. Kirk, J. E. Raven, and M. Schofield, *The Presocratic Philosophers* (Cambridge: Cambridge University Press, 1983), 191 n.
69. See Pol. 1333a 35 and 1337b 35. Referring to the *Protrepticus*, Stephen Halliwell says: "From one philosophical angle of vision, in other words, Aristotle was able to see a kind of absurdity in (ordinary) human existence. But that is not a vision that appears in any of his surviving treatises, let alone in the *Ethics*." *Greek Laughter* (Cambridge: Cambridge University Press, 2008), 309.
70. NE 1176b 32–33. Aristotle adds (NE 1177a 2): "The happy life is thought to be one of excellence; now an excellent life requires exertion, and does not consist in amusement. And we say that serious things are better than laughable things and those connected with amusements."
71. "Be careful what tales or stories the children hear, for all such things are designed to prepare the way for the business of later life, and should be for the most part imitations of the occupations which they will hereafter pursue in earnest" (Pol. 1336a 30).
72. NE 1177a 15.
73. Nonetheless, Aristotle does take one kind of adult play seriously, namely verbal humor. In this activity, Aristotle defines a virtue called "wittiness," which is the mean between being a buffoon and a bore. Aristotle says that wit is characteristic of the young, who love to insult people: "wit being educated hubris." For Aristotle, every joke is a form of abuse, subtle or not, so his praise of youthful wittiness is a rather backhanded compliment. Wittiness (*eutrapelia*) at NE 1128a 10. See also Rh. 1389b 11 and NE 1128a 29.
74. NE 1178b 20–32; Pol. 1323b 2; EE 1217a 26.
75. For him, "happiness (*eudaimonia*) is an activity of the soul expressing virtue" (NE 1099b 26). We are happy in our prime (*akmē*), not when we are young (*neotēs*) or old (*gēras*).

Chapter 3

1. According to Augustine, most human beings are eternally damned (*massa damnata*), but a few are eternally elected (*electi*) by God for salvation. Augustine was aware that this doctrine might weaken Christian moral resolve, so he does not emphasize predestination in his sermons and warns us not to worry about it or to teach it too widely. See Mathijs Lamberigts, "Predestination," in *Augustine Through the Ages: An Encyclopedia*, ed. Allan D. Fitzgerald (Grand Rapids: William B. Eerdmans, 1999), 677–679, at 678–679.

2. "Augustine is a biblical Everyman." Rowan Williams, *On Augustine* (London: Bloomsbury, 2016), 16.

3. "We can, if we like, read his *Confessions* as if it were the story of a man in search of God—and so it is, at one level. But more deeply it is a story of God in search of his lost child." Williams, *On Augustine*, 207.

4. After his "conversion," Augustine still feels crushed by the burden of his continual sinning: "Ground down by my sins and by the weight of my sorrow, I troubled my heart with thought of escape into the desert." *Confessions* 10.7.70. All translations of *Confessions*, unless otherwise indicated, are from Garry Wills, *Confessions* (New York: Penguin Books, 2006).

5. "We cannot ever be at rest within this temporal order. . . . Our holiness begins with our acceptance of restlessness." Williams, *On Augustine*, 19.

6. As James J. O'Donnell says of the *Confessions*: "And for all that it is a testimony of faith and confidence, it is permeated with anxiety." O'Donnell, *Augustine: A New Biography* (New York: HarperCollins, 2005), 36.

7. *Confessions* 10.6.64.

8. "The conversions of Augustine were many, and they did not end in the garden in Milan." James J. O'Donnell, *Augustine: Confessions*, vol. 1 (Oxford: Clarendon Press, 1992), xlii.

9. "Augustine probably never missed church on Sunday in his life." O'Donnell, *Augustine: A New Biography*, 53.

10. Among other reasons, consider that Aristotle ranked history even below poetry as a source of knowledge.

11. "Augustine never intended to write a literary classic—*Confessiones* may in fact be disunited—and, therefore, search for unity may be in vain." Frederick Van Fleteren, "*Confessiones*," in Fitzgerald, *Augustine Through the Ages*, 227–232, at 228. On the common refrain among scholars that "*Augustin compose mal*," see Robert J. O'Connell, *Augustine's Confessions: The Odyssey of Soul* (Cambridge: Harvard University Press, 1969), 9–11.

12. James J. O'Donnell says that some scholars believe that Book 10 was added later and "translators have sometimes abridged the work by omitting part or all of Bks. 11–13"; he also notes that Augustine is frequently charged with being an inept writer. O'Donnell, *Augustine: Confessions*, xxxii, xxxiv n. 45. Robert J. O'Connell also points out that many interpretations of the *Confessions* say little about Books 11–13. O'Connell, *Augustine's Confessions: The Odyssey of Soul*, 135 n.

13. "Augustine was bowled head over heels by his encounter with Platonism . . . while residing in Milan in A.D. 386, he came across some Platonist books in the Latin translation of Marius Victorinus." Richard Sorabji, "Time, Mysticism, and Creation," in *Augustine's "Confessions": Critical Essays*, ed. William E. Mann (Lanham, Md.: Rowman and Littlefield,

2006), 209–235, at 216. The best discussion of Augustine's *libri Platonicorum* is Pierre Hadot, *Marius Victorinus* (Paris: Etudes Augustiniennes, 1971), 201–210.

14. "The books of the Platonists did provoke in me a return into myself." *Confessions* 7.4.16.

15. Augustine discovers: "There can be no final clarity about who we are simply through introspection." Williams, *On Augustine*, 21.

16. "Grande profundum est ipse homo." *Confessions* 4.14.22; cf. 4.3.9.

17. Augustine prays to God: "Let me know myself; let me know you." (*Noverim me; noverim te*). This formula deliberately leaves open the question of the starting point. *Soliloquies* 2.1.1, quoted in Richard Sorabji, *Self* (Chicago: University of Chicago Press, 2006), 233.

18. *Confessions* 13.10.32.

19. "Heaven's knowledge is not now and then, but all at once, not subject to time's fluctuations." *Confessions* 12.2.16.

20. No time before creation: *Confessions* 11.2.15 and 11.3.17; no space before creation: *Confessions* 11.2.7.

21. Speaking of God's act of creation: "He does not will now this, now that. His will is singly, simultaneous, sempiternally all that he wills, not willing now and then, on this or that." *Confessions* 12.3.18. "But symbolically, as we have considered, you willed that creation be in a particular sequence, or be recorded in sequence; so that we can see that each thing taken separately is good, but all taken together are 'eminently good.'" *Confessions* 13.13.49.

22. We have only fragments of these early Greek philosophers, so all interpretations of their thought remains tentative. See G. S. Kirk, J. E. Raven, and M. Schofield, *The Presocratic Philosophers* (Cambridge: Cambridge University Press, 1983), 369 and 375. Gregory Vlastos: "A seed is a compound of all the essential constituents of the parent body from which it comes [the 'pangenesis' theory] and of the new organism into which it will grow [the 'preformation' theory]." W. K. C. Guthrie, *A History of Greek Philosophy*, vol. 2 (Cambridge: Cambridge University Press, 1965), 299. "The doctrine of seeds seems to be an important instance of the deliberate application and adaptation of a biological model to a general physical theory." G. E. R. Lloyd, *Polarity and Analogy* (Cambridge: Cambridge University Press, 1966), 247.

23. "Just as the sperm is enveloped in the seminal fluid, so god, who is the seminal principle (*spermatikos logos*) of the world, stays behind as such in the moisture, making matter serviceable to himself for the successive stages of creation." Diogenes Laertius 7.135–136, quoted in A. A. Long and D. N. Sedley, *The Hellenistic Philosophers*, vol. 1 (Cambridge: Cambridge University Press, 1987), 46B, p. 275.

24. Chrysippus: "Matter receives the seminal reasons (*spermatikoi logoi*) of god." Sometimes the Stoics simply called god himself the seminal reason of the cosmos: "god acts on matter, introducing the seminal reasons, with the result that the present cosmos comes to birth." These seeds contain the rational principles that govern the development of every entity. See David E. Hahm, *The Origins of Stoic Cosmology* (Columbus: Ohio State University Press, 1977), 62, 72, 75, 76.

25. On Augustine's reliance on the Stoics and Plotinus, see Hiro Hirai, "Logoi Spermatikoi and the Concept of Seed in the Mineralogy and Cosmogony of Paracelsus," *Revue d'Histoire des Sciences* 61, no. 2 (2008): 245–264.

26. See Augustine, *The Literal Meaning of Genesis*, trans. and ed. John Hammond Taylor (New York: Newman Press, 1982), vol. 1, 252 n. 67, and vol. 2, 9.17.32.

27. "For through Wisdom all things were made, and the motion we now see in creatures, measured by the lapse of time, as each one fulfills its proper function, comes to creatures from those causal reasons implanted in them, which God scattered as seeds at the moment of creation when 'He spoke and they were made, He commanded and they were created.'" Augustine, *The Literal Meaning of Genesis*, vol. 1, 4.33.51 p. 141.

28. Augustine, cited in Michael J. McKeough, *The Meaning of the Rationes Seminales in St. Augustine* (Washington, D.C.: Catholic University Press, 1926), 31–32.

29. "The concept of the *rationes seminales* allows Augustine to affirm that, in one sense, creation is completed simultaneously, once for all, and yet there is a real history of interaction between creator and creation, not just the playing out of a foreordained necessity." Rowan Williams, "Creation," in Fitzgerald, *Augustine Through the Ages*, 251–254, at 252.

30. *De Genesi ad Litteram* (http://www.augustinus.it/latino/genesi_lettera/index.htm), 1.9.15; 2.8.16; 6.1.2; 7.24.35.

31. "The work of creation, from the viewpoint of creatures as well as that of God, was completed at that instant when God made everything simultaneously. The fulfillment of the seminal reasons in individuals was not the completion of the creative act but a natural development of the inherent powers in matter under the same administrative activity of God as that which sustains and supports all natural movement today." McKeough, *The Meaning of the Rationes Seminales in St. Augustine*, 63.

32. *De Genesi ad Litteram* (http://www.augustinus.it/latino/genesi_lettera/index.htm): 5.4.9; 6.6.10; 6.11.19. On "seminal reasons" see Étienne Gilson, *The Christian Philosophy of Saint Augustine*, trans. L. E. M. Lynch (New York: Random House, 1960), 206–209.

33. Augustine, "On the Trinity," in *The Works of Aurelius Augustine*, trans. Arthur West Hadden (Edinburgh: T. and T. Clark, 1873), III, 8, pp. 90–91.

34. Although seeds have an intrinsic principle of development, Augustine insists that their growth is determined by divine will, not natural necessity: *Dei voluntas rerum necessitas est*. See Williams, "Creation," in Fitzgerald, *Augustine Through the Ages*, 252.

35. "Let us suppose that in the original works created simultaneously God also created the human soul, which in due time He would breathe into the members of the body." *The Literal Meaning of Genesis*, vol. 2, 7.24.35 and 10.6.9. According to McKeough, Augustine "preferred the opinion that the soul was created at the first moment of time and remained hidden until in the course of time it was united to the body." *The Meaning of the Rationes Seminales in St. Augustine*, 87.

36. Augustine himself lists four possible theories of the origin of the soul, here summarized by Ronnie Rombs: "1) *traducianism*, the theory that each soul was produced by the parents just as the body is produced; 2) *creationism*, whereby the soul was believed to be created directly by God at the time of conception; 3) the '*mission theory*,' according to which God created the soul and sent it at some subsequent time to a life to be lived in a body; 4) and the '*fallen soul*' theory, whereby the soul was believed to have existed precious in a higher, spiritual manner and to have fallen into the body and into corporeal existence only as the direct result of its sin" (xv–xvi). According to Rombs, "Augustine seems to have always vacillated between a theory of the fall of soul and some form of traducianism" (xvii). Rombs, *Saint Augustine and the Fall of the Soul: Beyond O'Connell and His Critics* (Washington, D.C.: Catholic University Press, 2006). James J. O'Donnell independently endorses Rombs's conclusion in *Augustine: A New Biography*, 299. On the relation of the seminal reasons to Augustine's theory of the soul, see Robert J. O'Connell, *The Origin of the Soul in St. Augustine's Later Works* (New York: Fordham University Press, 1987), 230.

37. Many scholars, however, deny that Augustine's theory of preformation involves any kind of preexistence. On the distinction between preformation and preexistence, see Justin E. H. Smith, *Divine Machines: Leibniz and the Sciences of Life* (Princeton: Princeton University Press, 2011), 170. Smith argues that Augustine's seminal reasons indicate a theory of preformation, not preexistence: "Augustine gives no real account of the ontological status of things prior to the 'proper opportunity for their appearance.'" 175. Gilson says: "Augustine never says anywhere that the soul exists before the body"—which is clearly false in the case of Adam's soul. See Gilson, *The Christian Philosophy of Saint Augustine*, 71.

38. Speaking of Adam, Augustine says: "his soul in its own proper being was already created with the making of the first day, and that thus created it lay hidden in the works of God until at the proper time He would breathe it into the body He would form from the slime of the earth." *The Literal Meaning of Genesis*, vol. 2, 7.24.35. This twofold creation of Adam corresponds, says Augustine, to the two accounts of the creation of man in Scripture: Genesis 1:26 and 2:7.

39. "In my memory, then, you have been lodged from the time I first learned of you. . . . But where in memory can you be lodged, Lord, where lodge you there?" *Confessions* 10.7.35–36.

40. "As the soul is immortal, has been born often and has seen all things here and in the underworld, there is nothing which it has not learned; so it is in no way surprising that it can recollect the things it knew before, both about virtue and other things." Plato, *Meno* 81C. Plato also discusses anamnesis in *Phaedo* 76C and *Phaedrus* 249C.

41. "As a philosophical neophyte many years earlier [than 404], he toyed with the doctrine [of anamnesis] but never definitely accepted it." Frederick Van Fleteren, "Plato, Platonism," in Fitzgerald, *Augustine Through the Ages*, 651–654, at 653.

42. "When they enter this life and submit to wearing mortal members these souls must also undergo forgetfulness of their former existence." *De Libero Arbitrio*, 3.20.57, cited in *The Literal Meaning of Genesis*, vol. 2, 281 n. Étienne Gilson assembles all the texts of the early Augustine which support Platonic preexistence and then concludes: "I am inclined to think that at first Augustine accepted the genuine Platonic doctrine. This opinion seems all the more probable if we bear in mind that he never rejects as certainly false the notion that the soul may exist before the body." Gilson goes on to say that he agrees with Johannes Hessen that Augustine, in his early writings, "leaned towards the doctrine of the pre-existence of the soul." Gilson adds: "This, it seems to me, is difficult to question." Gilson, *The Christian Philosophy of Saint Augustine*, 71 and 284 n. 11. For Hessen, see *Augustins Metaphysik der Erkenntnis* (Leiden: E. J. Brill, 1960), 53–59.

43. "Our souls, then, pre-existed, enjoyed the vision of God's supernal Truth and Beauty, but fell from that blissful state into the life we know as human beings . . . the real 'I' is a soul, fallen into a body, the resulting amalgam being a 'man.'" O'Connell, *St. Augustine's Confessions*, 23–24.

44. For the authoritative, though controversial, exposition of this view, see Robert J. O'Connell, *St. Augustine's Early Theory of Man, A.D. 386–391* (Cambridge: Harvard University Press, 1968). For a critique of O'Connell, see Gerard J. P. O'Daly, "Did St. Augustine Ever Believe in the Soul's Pre-existence?," *Augustinian Studies* 5 (1974): 227–235, and O'Connell's reply "Pre-existence in the Early Augustine," *Revue des Etudes Augustiniennes* 26 (1980): 176–188.

45. "Who then are you? And I answered myself: A man. Which brought to my mind two things belonging to me, body and soul, one external to me, one internal." *Confessions* 10.2.9.

46. *Confessions* 10.3.26. On this passage, see O'Connell, *St. Augustine's Confessions*, 126. Augustine continues in this Platonic vein of reminiscence: "We could not say we had found what was lost if we did not recognize it, and we could not recognize it without the memory of it, since it was lost to sight but not to memory." *Confessions* 10.3.27.

47. O'Connell's literal translation of "Tu assumsisti me ut viderem esse quod viderem et nondum me esse qui viderem." *Confessions* 7.4.16. Scholars disagree about how to translate this sentence. Garry Wills follows John K. Ryan's version, which O'Connell rejects: "In my early stage of knowing you, you lifted me far enough to see there is something to be seen, but also to know I was not capable of seeing it." But Ronnie J. Rombs endorses O'Connell's translation of this sentence in *Saint Augustine and the Fall of the Soul*, 34–35.

48. *Confessions* 10.3.29–30.

49. Robert J. O'Connell is unusual for insisting that even the late Augustine maintained the Plotinian theory of a fallen soul. See O'Connell, *The Origin of the Soul in St. Augustine's Later Works*. On the scholarly consensus in the wake of O'Connell's provocative work, see Rombs, *Saint Augustine and the Fall of the Soul*: "Contrary to his critics, I have attempted to show that O'Connell's first thesis is correct: the *young* Augustine embraced Plotinus's conception of man as a fallen soul. . . . Although he [Augustine] later rejects the Platonic epistemology of *anamnesis*, Augustine proposes learning to be identical to recollection in several early texts. To be sure, such a theory of knowledge depends upon the supposition of the preexistence and fall of the soul." According to Rombs, the later Augustine broke with Plotinus by arguing that the soul does not fall ontologically from higher to lower levels of being but that the soul falls morally and psychologically by sin. So Augustine maintains the Plotinian language of the fallen soul but with a moral or psychological interpretation of that fall. Rombs, *Saint Augustine and the Fall of the Soul*, 209, 38, 110, 211.

50. "We are dissolved into time." *Confessions* 11.5.39.

51. "Earthly things, you see, all pass away and are replaced by others, and their succession of parts makes up this lower universe." *Confessions* 4.4.16.

52. "Things rise and sink, and begin to be by rising, then progress toward being all they can, and when they have become all they can, they grow old and perish, though some things perish even without growing old." *Confessions* 4.4.15.

53. "So it is with every whole made up of parts, where all the parts cannot be present. The parts would be more pleasing if we could take them all in together, not singly." *Confessions* 4.4.17.

54. *Confessions* 13.14.52.

55. "In eternity there is no such succession of things, the entirety is present, and that cannot be a time." *Confessions* 11.2.13.

56. "Time is a mental perdurance, the mind is stretched" (*distentio animi*). *Confessions* 11.5.36. "Therefore, my life is stretched" (*Ecce distentio vita mea*). *Confessions* 11.5.39.

57. "Both past and future are constituted by the present they flow through. . . . The mind reaches at the present to transfer things from the future into the past. . . . What is anticipated passes through what observes it as it passes into what is remembered." *Confessions* 11.2.13, 11.5.36, and 11.5.37.

58. *Confessions* 11.5.38.

59. "It would not be an exaggeration to say that the narrative autobiographical voice of the *Confessions* is systematically blended with the voice of the psalmist." Williams, *On Augustine*, 25.

60. "Augustine famously articulates in the tenth book of the *Confessions* that his present situation in no way resembles a plateau of achieved virtue or inner calm." Williams, *On Augustine*, 36.

61. "In the creation of that narrative unity, we are not obliged to understand what cannot be understood, or to anticipate the judgment that can come only at the end of the temporal story. We must only continue to be faithful to the vocal 'register' of psalmody, with its personal address to God and its naked awareness of human need and failure." Williams, *On Augustine*, 36–37.

62. "Nor in your eternity do you see time simply as it develops. Then why do I arrange in sequence what I narrate for you?" *Confessions* 11.1.1.

63. *Confessions* 1.2.12.

64. *Confessions* 1.2.11.

65. Augustine plays on the literal meaning of *in-fans* (without speech).

66. *Confessions* 1.2.8.

67. *Confessions* 1.2.8 and 1.2.11.

68. "In this cry, the infant therefore reveals a nature which is, from the moment of birth, in an aggressive and hostile relation to the totality of creation." Colin Starns, "Saint Augustine on Infancy and Childhood," *Augustinian Studies* 6 (1975): 15–43, at 23.

69. "Augustine called this anxious grasping at objects in the anxiety that something will be missed, *concupiscentia*.... In future years the anxious grasping of the newborn will become the frenzied pursuit of sex, power, and possessions that Augustine will illustrate with his own story." Margaret R. Miles, "Infancy, Parenting, and Nourishment in Augustine's *Confessions*," *Journal of the American Academy of Religion* 50, no. 3 (September 1982): 349–364, at 352.

70. *Confessions* 1.5.30.

71. "And if I was conceived in evil, and my mother sheltered a sinful me in her womb, where, my God, I ask you, where, my Lord, was I, your servant, ever free from sin?" *Confessions* 1.2.12. "Who is there to remind me of my sin before I spoke?" *Confessions* 1.2.11.

72. James J. O'Donnell discusses Haeckel's theory of biological recapitulation and argues that Augustine interpreted human life as a recapitulation of biblical history: "For Augustine, the life of a human being merely retold on a smaller scale the story of all human history." O'Donnell then lists the parallels Augustine drew between the six ages of man and the six epochs of biblical history, from Adam (infancy) to Jesus (old age). Was Augustine a historical recapitulationist? In part, but each human life does not recapitulate Adam's fall since, unlike Adam, each of us is conceived in sin. See O'Donnell, *Augustine: A New Biography*, 303–304.

73. Philip L. Reynolds rightly says of Augustine: "his chief intention was arguably to show that *even* children were sinful, or that they were sinful *already*, and not to show that there was anything unusually or distinctively bad about the child." Reynolds, "Thomas Aquinas and the Paradigms of Childhood," in *The Vocation of the Child*, ed. Patrick McKinley Brennan (Grand Rapids: William B. Eerdmans, 2008), 154–188, at 162–163.

74. *Confessions* 1.2.11.

75. *Confessions* 1.2.11. "The behavior of the infant at the mother's breast is more or less adequately concealed but remains unaltered in adult behavior." Miles, "Infancy, Parenting, and Nourishment in Augustine's *Confessions*," 357.

76. Augustine's basic prayer never changes throughout his life: "My soul is 'too cramped for you to enter it—widen it out.' It is in disrepair—restore it." *Confessions* 1.1.6.

77. *Confessions* 1.2.7.

78. *Confessions* 1.2.12.

79. Augustine, *City of God*, trans. Henry Bettenson (New York: Penguin Books, 1984), 21.14, p. 991. Augustine quotes *Ecclesiastes* 40:1: "A heavy yoke is laid on Adam's sons, from the day they issue from their mother's womb until the day when they go for burial to the mother of all things" (991).

80. "From the outset of his work Augustine intends that our 'conversion' and 'return' to God shall take the form of a suckling child returning to the maternal breast." Robert J. O'Connell, *St. Augustine's Confessions*, 43.

81. "Was it really I who went onward from infancy and progressed to boyhood . . . Infancy did not leave me—for where did it go to?" *Confessions*, trans. Carolyn Hammond (Cambridge: Harvard University Press, 2014), 1.3.13.

82. "As for little children, I can only say that they will not rise again with the tiny bodies they had when they died . . . the infant at death lacked its perfect bodily development; even a perfect infant, to be sure, has not the perfection of full bodily development." Augustine, *City of God*, 22.14, pp. 1054–1055.

83. *Confessions* 1.4.19: "*tantillus puer et tantus peccator.*"

84. *Confessions* 1.3.14.

85. *Confessions* 1.3.15.

86. *Confessions* 1.4.23.

87. *Confessions* 1.4.23.

88. "Who, in these terms, was worse—my teacher, who writhed with bitter envy when caught in a solecism by a fellow pedant, or I, when I resented losing my ball game to a fellow player?" *Confessions* 1.3.15.

89. After relating his own vile machinations, Augustine asks with bitter irony: "Is this the innocence of children?" *Confessions* 1.5.30.

90. *Confessions* 1.5.30. See Carolyn Hammond's note at this passage: "Augustine means that Jesus defined the 'humility' of children as physical, not ethical or spiritual; not a convincing historical exegesis."

91. Here Augustine differs from his mentor Ambrose, who sees real humility in a small child: "It knows nothing as its own, it assumes no honors, it is unacquainted with self-advancement, it wishes for no revenge, nor can it. What insolence is, a pure a simple mind cannot understand." Ambrose quoted in George Boas, *Primitivism and Related Ideas in the Middle Ages* (Baltimore: Johns Hopkins University Press, 1948), 96.

92. Augustine, *City of God*, 21.14, p. 991.

93. "And the process of learning with its attendant punishment is so painful that children not infrequently prefer to endure the punishments designed to compel them to learn, rather than submit to the process of learning." *City of God*, 21.14, p. 991.

94. There is no necessary connection between the doctrine of original sin and the corporal punishment of children; nonetheless, it is fair to say in general that those Christian theologians and pastors who most strongly emphasize original sin (Calvinist, Lutheran) also endorse the harshest discipline for children. On Christian theology and child-rearing, see Marcia Bunge, ed., *The Child in Christian Thought* (Grand Rapids: William B. Eerdmans, 2001), 167.

95. *Confessions* 1.3.17.

96. O'Connell, *St. Augustine's Confessions*, 92.

97. Genesis 3:5.

98. See Augustine, *City of God*, 14.5: "We ought not, therefore, to blame our sins and defects on the nature of the flesh, for this is to disparage the Creator." He says of Adam and Eve (14.13): "Pride is the beginning of all sin."

99. *Confessions* 2.2.12 and 2.2.14.

100. "Someone has but to say, Let's do it!—and feeling shame becomes one's only shame." *Confessions* 2.2.17.

101. *Confessions* 8.3.10. His "will of the flesh" could itself be torn among many competing base desires (8.5.24).

102. *Confessions* 2.1.1, 2.2.15, 3.3.8.

103. "How can I boast of mastery in the arts and sciences, by which the knotty meanings of those books were teased out, when I was twisted about in my wandering from true piety into pestilent irreligion? Or how can your lowly ones regret their slower minds when they did not 'go far into exile' from you?" *Confessions* 4.6.31.

104. "And what am I, in my better state, but 'a child nursed with your milk,' feeding on the food that never fails?" *Confessions* 4.1.1.

105. "You took his life away early, but I am content, having nothing to fear from his conduct as a child or youth or (if he had become one) a man." *Confessions* 9.2.14.

106. "I did not call for baptism even in this perilous state, proving that I had been better in my youth, when I demanded it from my mother's piety, as I have recalled and testified (1.3.17)." *Confessions* 5.5.16.

107. "So I resumed provisionally the learner's status in the Catholic Church to which my parents had in the past assigned me." *Confessions* 5.7.25.

108. *Confessions* 6.2.5.

109. "Yet I stubbornly held to belief in Christ, our Lord and rescuer. . . . My faith was fuzzy still, was hazy about the standards of belief, yet my mind would not give it up." *Confessions* 7.2.7.

110. "As I thrashed about, stalling, I made bodily motions some persons might be incapable of, even if they wanted to perform them" (8.5.20). Compare to: "So I worked my limbs and voice energetically, trying to signal out something like my demands, to the best of my little (and little availing) ability" (1.2.8).

111. O'Connell, *St. Augustine's Confessions*, 63.

112. True, in the Milan garden, Augustine does commit himself to permanent celibacy—only to discover later that celibacy can itself lead to sinful pride.

113. *Confessions* 10.3.38.

114. *Conversio* in Latin means to turn completely around, back to the beginning, as in the cycles of the sun and the seasons. Augustine plays with this meaning as he describes his own wandering away from home (*aversio*), his sin (*perversio*), and then his return (*conversio*). See José Oroz Reta, "Conversion," in Fitzgerald, *Augustine Through the Ages*, 239–242, at 241.

115. "Perhaps *the* dominant and enduring image in Augustine's works is the depiction of man as sojourner, as a pilgrim wandering in a foreign land, waiting to be brought home." Rombs, *Saint Augustine and the Fall of the Soul*, 207.

Chapter 4

1. Aristotle's ladder of nature extends from the basic elements all the way to the gods; human development occupies only a part of this ladder.

2. Speaking of *Emile*, Robert Wokler says: "Rousseau here maps out a genetic account of the spiritual growth of the individual along lines which reflect his evolutionary perspective in the *Second Discourse*, of our passage from a savage to a civilized state, albeit in *Emile* around images of sentiment and sexuality rather than of reason and authority." Wokler, *Rousseau* (New York: Oxford University Press, 1995), 12. Roger Masters compares in detail Rousseau's account of development in *Emile* to his account of history in the *Second Discourse*. See Masters, *The Political Philosophy of Rousseau*, chaps. 1–4.

3. Rousseau, *Emile*, introduction, translation, and notes by Allan Bloom (New York: Basic Books, 1979), 37. Bloom's translation of *Emile* also appears in *Emile, or, On Education*, in *The Collected Writings of Rousseau* (*CW*), vol. 13, ed. Christopher Kelly and Allan Bloom (Hanover, N.H.: University Press of New England, 2010), 161. All quotations from *Emile* will provide page numbers from both the 1979 edition and the 2010 edition, separated by a slash.

4. Rousseau, *The Social Contract*, in *CW*, vol. 4, ed. Roger D. Masters and Christopher Kelly (Hanover, N.H.: University Press of New England, 1994), 131. As the editors point out (xiii), the French original is deliberately ambiguous between two meanings: *L'homme est né libre, et partout il est dans les fers*.

5. Rousseau, *Rousseau, Judge of Jean-Jacques: Dialogues*, in *CW*, vol. 1, ed. Roger D. Masters and Christopher Kelly (Hanover, N.H.: University Press of New England, 1990), 213.

6. "What! Must we destroy Societies, annihilate thine and mine, and go back to live in forests with Bears?" Rousseau, *Discourse on the Origins of Inequality (Second Discourse)* (*SD*), in *CW*, vol. 4, ed. Roger D. Masters and Christopher Kelly (Hanover, N.H.: University Press of New England, 1992), 79.

7. As Robert Wokler says: "Reversion to a natural state is no more possible for civilized man than would be the recovery of innocence or ignorance of vice." *Rousseau*, 23. Rousseau's famous *Discourse on the Sciences and the Arts* is devoted to arguing that the advancement of knowledge destroys innocence and moral goodness forever.

8. Rousseau, *Dialogues*, 213.

9. "If I had been the possessor of the ring of Gyges . . . I often asked myself what use I would have made of this ring. . . . One thing alone: that would have been to see every heart content." A moment later, however, Rousseau concedes that even he might be corrupted by such power: "All things considered, I believe I will do better to throw away my magic ring before it makes me commit some folly." Rousseau, *The Reveries of the Solitary Walker*, in *CW*, vol. 8, ed. Christopher Kelly (Hanover, N.H.: University Press of New England, 2000), 55–56.

10. "In order to judge the natural state of Man correctly, to consider him from his origin and examine him, so to speak, in the first Embryo of the species." *SD*, 20.

11. "Let us therefore take care not to confuse Savage man with the men we have before our eyes." *SD*, 24.

12. According to Hobbes, each man in the state of nature has a right to everything (*ius omnium in omnia*).

13. Of writers like Hobbes, Rousseau says: "they spoke about savage man and they described Civil man." *SD*, 19.

14. Allan Bloom's memorable phrase in his introduction to *Emile*, 5.

15. "Our needs bring us together in proportion as our passions divide us, and the more we become enemies of our fellow men, the less we can do without them." Rousseau, "Geneva Manuscript," in *The Social Contract*, in *CW*, vol. 4, 76.

16. As Arthur M. Melzer says, to transcend the contradiction between our selfishness and our selflessness, we must embrace either complete individualism or complete collectivism. See Melzer, *The Natural Goodness of Man* (Chicago: University of Chicago Press, 1990), 90.

17. Rousseau describes the requirements of civic virtue in his treatise *The Social Contract* as well as in his proposals for the constitutions of Poland and Corsica.

18. Rousseau describes his own journey within in his *Confessions, Dialogues*, and *Reveries*. Rousseau begins his *Confessions*: "I wish to show my fellows a man in all the truth of nature; and this man will be myself." See *Confessions*, in *CW*, vol. 5, ed. Christopher Kelly, Roger Masters, and Peter Stillman (Hanover, N.H.: University Press of New England, 1995), 5.

19. Rousseau describes the upbringing from birth of his imaginary pupil in *Emile*.

20. Of the education of Emile, Rousseau says: "I show the goal that must be set; I do not say that it can be reached." *Emile*, 95/228. Although Rousseau once described his native Geneva as a Republic of Virtue, he later came to the view that such a commonwealth was possible, if at all, only on the periphery of Europe, such as in Poland or Corsica. On Rousseau's political pessimism, see Graeme Garrard, *Rousseau's Counter-Enlightenment* (Albany: State University of New York Press, 2003), 111–115. By contrast, Rousseau seems very confident that he can recapture his own natural goodness in his autobiographical writings. He warns us, however, not to attempt to follow him: "It would not be good in the present structure of things that, avid for these sweet ecstasies, they ["most men"] should become disgusted with the active life their ever recurring needs prescribe to them as a duty." *Reveries*, in *CW*, vol. 8, 46.

21. *Emile*, 416/599. Rousseau describes *Emile* as his "greatest and best book" in the *Dialogues*, 23.

22. "This ignorance of the Nature of man," *SD*, 13; and "childhood is unknown," *Emile*, 33/157.

23. Rousseau also claims that childhood is unknown because "they are always seeking the man in the child without thinking of what he is before being a man." That is, we judge children by the inappropriate standards of adulthood; children are not merely imperfect adults. "The man must be considered in the man, and the child in the child." *Emile*, 34/157 and 80/210.

24. In his *Confessions* (5), Rousseau claims to find "the truth of nature" in himself and even to see himself as God sees him. In the *Reveries*, he asserts: "I am fully myself . . . I can truly claim to be what nature willed." *Second Walk*, 9.

25. Rousseau was a pioneer of the idea of "deep time" which is usually attributed to the geologist James Hutton, writing in the 1780s. For a discussion of Hutton's "discovery" of deep time (with no mention of Rousseau), see Stephen Jay Gould, *Time's Arrow, Time's Cycle: Myth and Metaphor in the Discovery of Geological Time* (Cambridge: Harvard University Press, 1987).

26. Rousseau speaks of "thousands of Centuries" of human history in *SD*, 29. In his narrative of primordial man, Rousseau says: "I cover multitudes of centuries like a flash." *SD*, 45.

27. Rousseau frequently insists that human evolution, like geological, proceeds by "imperceptible" changes over eons of time. *SD*, 65.

28. Rousseau: "nothing is so timid as man in the state of Nature." *SD*, 21. Rousseau also describes young Emile as timid: "He feels so weak that he fears everything he does not know." *Emile*, 63/191. As Masters says of the state of nature: "the crucial characteristic of this primitive condition is man's animal stupidity, his lack of reason, and his inability to speak." Masters does not observe how well this describes an infant. Masters, *The Political Philosophy of Rousseau*, 135 and 432.

29. "It cannot be denied that such was pretty nearly the primitive state of ignorance and stupidity natural to man before he learned anything from experience or his fellows." *Emile*, 61–62/189–190.

30. "To perceive and feel will be his first state, which he will have in common with all animals." *SD*, 27. Rousseau even hypothesizes that modern orangutans and pongos might actually be primeval human beings, *SD*, 83.

31. *SD*, 26.

32. "All children begin by walking on all fours." *SD*, 68.

33. "And if Infancy is longer among us, so also is life." *SD*, 23.

34. *Emile*, 38/162.

35. *SD*, 40.

36. Rousseau describes the state of nature as "your ancient and first innocence." *SD*, 79.

37. "Although the organ of speech is natural to man, speech itself is nonetheless not natural to him." *SD*, 82.

38. "Man's first language, the most universal, most energetic . . . is the cry of Nature." *SD*, 31. Emile's first language is also, of course, crying: "Since the first condition of man is want and weakness, his first voices are complaint and tears." *Emile*, 65/194.

39. "Whether there was a language natural and common to all men has long been a subject of research. . . . Let us study children, and we shall soon relearn it with them." *Emile*, 65/194.

40. "Onomatopoeia would constantly make itself felt." Rousseau, *Essay on the Origin of Language*, in *CW*, vol. 7, ed. John T. Scott (Hanover, N.H.: University Press of New England, 1998), 296. As for simple sentences: "they at first give each word the sense of a whole sentence." *SD*, 31. Rousseau even attributes to primordial man the childish habit of giving every object a proper name. *SD*, 32.

41. *Emile*, 160/90.

42. "His soul, agitated by nothing, is given over to the sole sentiment of its present existence without any idea of the future." *SD*, 28.

43. "To live is not to breathe; it is to act; it is to make use of our organs, our senses, our faculties, of all the parts of ourselves which give us the sentiment of our existence." *Emile*, 42/167, cf. 61/189.

44. For the human species, *amour de soi* in the state of nature becomes *amour propre* only when natural man enters society, see *SD*, 91. Speaking of Emile as an infant, Rousseau says: "natural man is entirely for himself." *Emile*, 39/164.

45. *Emile*, 68/197.

46. *SD*, 71. See Roger Master's discussion of vegetarianism in the state of nature in *The Political Philosophy of Rousseau*, 122–125.

47. "For as prey is almost the unique subject of fighting among Carnivorous animals, and as Frugivorous ones [e.g. humans] live among themselves in continual peace." *SD*, 71.

48. "One of the proofs that the taste for meat is not natural to man is the indifference that children have for that kind of food and the preference they all give to vegetable foods." *Emile*, 153/297.

49. Rousseau says in his own voice: "It is, above all, important not to denature this primitive taste and make children carnivorous. If this is not for their health, it is for their character . . . it is for certain that great eaters of meat are in general more cruel and ferocious than other men." *Emile*, 153/297.

50. On the theme of a bad man as an overgrown child (*malus puer robustus*) in Hobbes and Rousseau, see Susan Meld Shell, "Stalking *Puer Robustus*: Hobbes and Rousseau on the Origin of Human Malice," in *The Challenge of Rousseau*, ed. Eve Grace and Christopher Kelly (Cambridge: Cambridge University Press, 2013), 271–291. Shell rightly points out that Hobbes merely compares but does not equate a bad man to an overgrown child.

51. Rousseau says of Hobbes: "The evil man, he says, is a robust Child. It remains to be seen whether Savage Man is a robust Child." *SD*, 35.

52. Rousseau says of this overgrown child: "he would beat his Mother when she would be too slow in giving him her breast . . . he would strangle one of his young brothers when he would be inconvenienced by him." *SD*, 35.

53. "Let us not conclude with Hobbes that because man has no idea of goodness he is naturally evil; that he is vicious because he does not know virtue." *SD*, 35.

54. "When Hobbes called the wicked man a robust child, he said something absolutely contradictory. All wickedness comes from weakness. The child is only wicked because he is weak. Make him strong; he will be good." *Emile*, 67/196.

55. "Before the age of reason, we do good and bad without knowing it, and there is no morality in our actions." *Emile*, 67/196. Rousseau even attributes to divine providence the happy outcome that children are too small to do much harm with their aggression: "At the same time that the Author of nature gives children this active principle, by allowing them little strength to indulge it, He takes care that it do little harm." *Emile*, 67/197.

56. Rousseau says of primordial man: "His desires do not exceed his physical needs." *SD*, 27.

57. Rousseau says that the vital activity of a child "is superabundant and extends outward; he senses in himself, so to speak, enough life to animate everything surrounding him. . . . It is important to accustom him early not to give orders either to men, for he is not their master, or to things, for they do not hear him." *Emile*, 67/197 and 66/196.

58. "Let him see the necessity in things, never in the caprice of men." *Emile*, 91/223.

59. Rousseau says of primordial man: "Accustomed from infancy to inclemencies of the weather and rigor of the seasons, trained in fatigue, and forced, naked and without weapons . . . men develop a robust and almost unalterable physique." *SD*, 21. Rousseau says of raising children, like Emile: "Harden their bodies against the intemperance of season, climates, elements; against hunger thirst, fatigue." *Emile*, 47/173.

60. "Whatever injury a child may do to himself, it is very rare that he cries when he is alone, unless he hopes to be heard. . . . If he sees me run in agitation to console and pity him, he will consider himself lost. If he sees me keep my composure, he will soon regain his." *Emile*, 77/207.

61. "Savages as well as beasts struggle very little against death and endure it almost without complaint." As for Emile, because "he is accustomed to submitting to the law of necessity without resistance, when he has to die, he will die without moaning and without struggle." *Emile*, 82/213 and 208/359.

62. "The surest means of raising oneself above prejudices and ordering one's judgments about the true relations to things is to put oneself in the place of an isolated man and to judge everything as this man himself ought to judge of it with respect to his own utility." *Emile*, 185/332.

63. "He knows the essential relations of man to things but nothing of the moral relations of man to man." *Emile*, 207/358–359.

64. Speaking of Crusoe alone on his island, Rousseau says: "This state, I agree, is not that of social man: very likely it is not going to be that of Emile." *Emile*, 184/332.

65. In the state of nature, "natural man is entirely for himself." And of Emile: "The child raised according to his age is alone." *Emile*, 39/164 and 219/370. On Emile and his tutor, see *Emile*, 51/177–178.

66. "The most ancient of all societies, and the only natural one, is that of the family." *The Social Contract*, in *CW*, vol. 4, 132.

67. "There is a great difference between the natural man living in the state of nature and the natural man living in the state of society." *Emile*, 205/355, cf. 255/412.

68. As Roger Masters puts it in *The Political Philosophy of Rousseau*, 91. See also *Emile*, 205/356.

69. *Emile*, 94/227.

70. *SD*, 36–37.

71. "Thus is born pity, the first relative sentiment which touches the human heart according to the order of nature." *Emile*, 222/374.

72. In the state of nature, the only moral maxim is: "Do what is good for you with the least possible harm to others." *SD*, 38; Emile is told: "The only lesson of morality appropriate to childhood, and the most important for every age, is never to harm someone." *Emile*, 104/239.

73. "A being endowed with senses whose faculties equaled his desires would be an absolutely happy being." *Emile*, 80/211.

74. "Although this interval during which the individual is capable of more than he desires is not the time of his greatest absolute strength, it is, as I have said, the time of his greatest relative strength. . . . It is the most precious time of life, a time which comes only once, a very short time." *Emile*, 166/310.

75. "This period of the development of human faculties, maintaining a golden mean between the indolence of the primitive state and the petulant activity of our *amour propre*, must have been the happiest and most durable epoch . . . the best for man." *SD*, 48.

76. "As long as men were content with rustic huts . . . they lived free, healthy, good, and happy. . . . But from the moment one man needed the help of another, as soon as they observed that it was useful for a single person to have provisions for two, equality disappeared, property was introduced, labor became necessary." *SD*, 49.

77. *Emile*, 160/305.

78. "I agree that young people must be married when they reach the age at which they are nubile. But that age comes before its proper time for them. . . . It ought to be put off until maturity." *Emile*, 317/485.

79. "Each one began to look at the others and to want to be looked at himself" leading to "vanity and contempt, shame and envy." *SD*, 47.

80. "My child, there is no happiness without courage, or virtue without struggle. The word *virtue* comes from *strength*. . . . Virtue belongs only to a being that is weak by nature and strong by will." *Emile*, 444/633.

81. "Happy are the peoples among whom one can be good without effort and just without virtue." *Emile*, 193/342.

82. "The man who is only good is good only for himself." *Emile*, 444/633.

83. In cities, Rousseau says, we find "universal desire for reputation, honors, and preferences . . . making all men competitors, rivals, or rather enemies." *SD*, 63.

84. "Remove them from big cities where the adornment and the immodesty of women hasten and anticipate nature's lessons, where everything presents to their eyes pleasures they ought to know only when they are able to choose among them. Bring them back to their first abodes where rustic simplicity lets the passions of their age develop less rapidly." *Emile*, 231/384. For Rousseau's memorable *Adieu, Paris*, see *Emile*, 355/529.

85. "It is easily seen how the establishment of a single Society made that of the others indispensable, and how, to stand up to the united forces, it was necessary to unify in turn." *SD*, 54.

86. "Such was, or must have been, the origin of Society and Laws, which gave new fetters to the weak and new forces to the rich, destroyed natural freedom for all time, established forever the Law of property and inequality, changed a clever usurpation into an irrevocable right, and for the profit of a few ambitious men henceforth subjected the whole human Race to work, servitude, and misery." *SD*, 54.

87. "The most decent men learned to consider it one of their duties to murder their fellows; at length men were seen to massacre each other by the thousands without knowing why; more murders were committed on a single day than were committed in the state of Nature during whole centuries over the entire face of the earth." *SD*, 55.

88. "After having employed almost two years in roaming some of the great states of Europe and more of the small ones, after having learned Europe's two or three principal languages, and after having seen what is truly worthy of curiosity—whether in natural history, or in government, or in the arts, or in men." *Emile*, 471/665.

89. Rousseau teaches Emile (459–468/650–659) the principle of his later book, *The Social Contract*, which has been described as an appendix to *Emile*.

90. "It is certain that the greatest miracles of virtue have been produced by the love of fatherland. By combining the force of *amour-propre* with all the beauty of virtue . . . makes it the most heroic of the passions." Rousseau, *Political Economy*, in *CW*, vol. 3, 151.

91. "Now that Emile has considered himself in his physical relations with other beings and in his moral relations with other men, it remains for him to consider himself in his civil relations with his fellow citizens." *Emile*, 455/646.

92. Alan Bloom makes this observation in *Emile*, 3.

93. Who cannot hear the revolutionary call to arms at the conclusion of the allegedly "pessimistic" *Second Discourse*?: "it is manifestly against the Law of Nature, in whatever manner it is defined, that a child command an old man, an imbecile lead a wise man, and a handful of men be glutted with superfluities while the starving multitude lacks necessities." *SD*, 67. Perhaps Rousseau embodies Antonio Gramsci's ideal: pessimism of the intellect; optimism of the will. For Rousseau's praise of the civic virtue of the Romans, see *SD*, 94–95.

94. See Rousseau, *Emile and Sophie, or, The Solitaries*, in *Emile, or, On Education*, in *CW*, vol. 13, ed. Christopher Kelly and Allan Bloom (Hanover, N.H.: University Press of New England, 2010), 685–721. In his introduction to *Emile and Sophie*, Christopher Kelly claims that this unfinished sequel is essential to our understanding of *Emile*: "the sequel can be seen as the necessary complement of the original work" (xxv).

95. "Some readers have seen it as Rousseau's judgment of the ultimate failure of Emile's education . . . ; others have seen it as proof of the success of the education." Kelly, introduction to *Emile and Sophie*, xxiv. Kelly judiciously concludes: "at the very least, Sophie's infidelity shows the failure of her education [partly by Rousseau] if not that of her husband" (xxv). Judith Shklar sees the sequel as the true ending of the *Emile*: "The happy ending of *Emile* is false, especially to the tone of its opening pages, so full of dark foreboding. It is man, not the situation, that is being remade, and Emile's character cannot reveal itself until he *really* becomes a man, that is, a suffering victim." Shklar, *Men and Citizens* (Cambridge: Cambridge University Press, 1969), 235. Shklar is impressed by Emile's Stoicism, but Emile describes himself as "a stoic without virtues" and blames Rousseau for his travails "by abandoning it [my family] you have done more ills than you did me good in my whole life." *Emile and Sophie*, 689 and 687. Clearly, Emile, like *Emile and Sophie*, remains a work in progress.

Chapter 5

1. "I think that the Neoteny Model has much to offer by way of correcting the distortions introduced by the other models." Richard B. Miller, "Neoteny and the Virtues of Childhood," *Metaphilosophy* 20, no. 3–4 (July–October 1989): 319–331, at 324.

2. Like the other theories of development I have discussed, the role of neoteny in human evolution is highly controversial among biologists and physical anthropologists.

3. Louis Bolk (1925) famously defined human beings as "sexually mature, fetal apes." Bolk, "On the Problem of Anthropogenesis," *Proceedings of the Royal Academy of Amsterdam* 29 (1925): 465–475, at 469.

4. On evidence from fossil skulls, see Konner, *The Evolution of Childhood*, 137: "So human adults are objectively juvenilized."

5. Gould, *Ontogeny and Phylogeny*, 388.

6. Bolk distinguished the "fetalization hypothesis" from the "retardation hypothesis": "These two facts are closely related, for, after all, the fetalization is the necessary consequence of the retardation of the morphogenesis." Bolk, "On the Problem of Anthropogenesis," 471.

7. "Evolution occurs when ontogeny is altered in one of two ways: when new characters are introduced at any stage of development with varying effects upon subsequent stages, or when characters already present undergo changes in developmental timing. Together, these two processes exhaust the formal content of phyletic change; the second process is heterochrony." Gould, *Ontogeny and Phylogeny*, 4.

8. The study of these different developmental clocks, within and across organisms, is called "heterochrony." See McKinney and McNamara, *Heterochrony*.

9. Developmental biologist Walter Garstang famously said that "ontogeny does not recapitulate phylogeny; ontogeny creates phylogeny." McKinney and McNamara, *Heterochrony*, 10.

10. Paedomorphosis can also be caused by *progenesis*, the early termination of body growth and by *postdisplacement*, starting the growth process later. McKinney and McNamara, *Heterochrony*, 365.

11. "I believe that human beings are 'essentially' neotenous, not because I can enumerate a list of important paedomorphic features, but because a general, temporal retardation of development has clearly characterized human evolution." Gould, *Ontogeny and Phylogeny*, 365. For a critique of Gould's claim, see Brian T. Shea, "Heterochrony in Human Evolution: The Case for Neoteny Reconsidered," *Yearbook of Physical Anthropology* 32 (1989): 69–101, at 89–90.

12. "There is no placental mammal that remotely approaches the human in duration of infantile immaturity." Ashley Montagu, *Growing Young* (Granby, Mass.: Bergin and Garvey, 1989), 65.

13. Stephen Jay Gould, *Ever Since Darwin* (New York: Norton, 1977), 72. "Humans have a gestation period of 21 months. . . . At birth, our brains are still growing at fetal rates." Gould, *Ontogeny and Phylogeny*, 369 and 370.

14. "Humans should be born about twelve months later than we are, in terms of brain growth rate." Konner, *The Evolution of Childhood*, 126.

15. "Juvenile primates are more likely to starve to death or fall victim to predators than are adults." Tracey Joffe, "Social Pressures Have Selected for an Extended Juvenile Period in Primates," *Journal of Human Evolution* 32 (1997): 593–605, at 593.

16. "The newborn human child is about as dependent a creature as we find among placental mammalian infants." Gould, *Ontogeny and Phylogeny*, 400.

17. Gould, *Ontogeny and Phylogeny*, 401.

18. David F. Bjorklund, "The Role of Immaturity in Human Development," *Psychological Bulletin* 122, no. 2 (1997): 153–169, at 157.

19. "A longer care man's helpless kind demands / That longer care contracts more lasting bands." Alexander Pope, quoted in Gould, *Ontogeny and Phylogeny*, 404.

20. "Human faces resemble those of juvenile chimpanzees more closely than those of adult chimps . . . humans may be seen as ape-like animals that retained juvenile physical features." On neoteny in the evolution of the human face see Adam S. Wilkins, *Making Faces* (Cambridge: Harvard University Press, 2017), 297.

21. For a critique of Montagu's notion of behavioral neoteny, see Shea, "Heterochrony in Human Evolution," 94.

22. For the full list of twenty-seven "neotenous" traits in humans, see Montagu, *Growing Young*, 107. According to Montagu "the child is the possessor of all those traits which, when healthily developed, lead to a healthy and fulfilled human being and thus to a healthy and fulfilled humanity" (106).

23. "The constitutive character of man—the maintenance of active, creative interaction with the environment—is a neotenous phenomenon." Lorenz, quoted in Montagu, *Growing Young*, 230.

24. "The tame breeds in general not only show a degree of retention of juvenile physical features such as flatter faces and rounder heads but also exhibit prolonged periods of juvenile behaviors, in particular exploratory behavior and the high sociability and playfulness of the young." Wilkins, *Making Faces*, 298.

25. "Many adult dogs not only appear juvenile, they also act juvenile. They display a sort of behavioral paedomorphosis." Darcy Morey, "The Early Evolution of the Domestic Dog," *American Scientist* 82, no. 4 (July–August 1994): 336–347, at 344.

26. On neoteny in the domesticated silver foxes, see Lyudmila N. Trut, "Early Canid Domestication: The Farm-Fox Experiment," *American Scientist* 87, no. 2 (March–April 1999):

160–169. "In other words, they [the domesticated foxes] became childlike versions of their wild selves." Laura Hobgood-Oster, *A Dog's History of the World* (Waco, Tx.: Baylor University Press, 2014), 22.

27. "The modern human species can be seen as a 'self-domesticated ape,' one whose early social evolution put a premium on tameness and lack of aggression, thereby promoting cooperation and sociability." Wilkins, *Making Faces*, 301.

28. "If human evolution continued in the same direction as in the immediate past, the superman of the future would develop more slowly than we, and be teachable for longer. He would retain in maturity characteristics which most of us lose in childhood. Certain shades of the prison house would never close about him. He would probably be more intelligent than we, but distinctly less staid and solemn." Haldane, quoted in Montagu, *Growing Young*, 224.

29. Haldane, quoted in Montagu, *Growing Young*, 7.

30. For evidence demonstrating how much longer it takes young people to reach adulthood today, see Arnett, *Emerging Adulthood*, 3–25. Arnett describes this delay of adulthood not as the prolongation of adolescence but as the rise of a new and historically unprecedented stage of life that he terms "emerging adulthood" (4).

31. At the same time that sociological maturation is becoming prolonged, biological maturation is in at least some respects becoming accelerated, as with the age of menarche. See Stanley Shostak, *The Evolution of Death* (Albany: State University of New York Press, 2006), 135.

32. Erik H. Erikson, *Childhood and Society* (New York: Norton, 1963), 16.

33. Montagu, *Growing Young*, 237. For an argument that juvenile morphological and behavioral traits are not necessarily less specialized than adult traits, see Mary Jane West-Eberhard, *Developmental Plasticity and Evolution* (Oxford: Oxford University Press, 2003), 241.

34. "Human development has slowed down. Within this 'matrix of retardation,' adaptive features of ancestral juveniles are easily retained." Gould, *Ontogeny and Phylogeny*, 9.

35. "Underdevelopment (neoteny), however, would occur only if humans also experienced a slower rate of growth during each prolonged stage. But the rate of growth in humans is relatively unchanged compared with that of close living relatives and hominid ancestors. Life history delays thus produce overdevelopment, not underdevelopment, in both somatic and brain morphology." Michael L. McKinney, "Evolving Behavioral Complexity by Extending Development," in *Biology, Brains, and Behavior*, ed. Sue Taylor Parker et al. (Santa Fe: School of American Research Press, 2000), 25–40, at 28.

36. According to McKinney and McNamara, neoteny "is a process of paedomorphosis such that the descendant adult (us) *never attains behaviors* possessed by the ancestor. In stark contrast, hypermorphosis is a process of peramorphosis [overdevelopment] such that the descendant adult *goes beyond* behaviors of the ancestor." *Heterochrony*, 309. Emphasis in original.

37. "Mortality curves retain the lower values of youth while cohorts grow chronologically older. Thus, we stay younger and age more slowly while growing older!" Shostak, *The Evolution of Death*, 54.

38. For attempts by biologists to reconcile neoteny with peramorphosis (overdevelopment), see L. R. Godfrey and M. R. Sutherland, "Paradox of Peramorphic Paedomorphosis:

Heterochrony and Human Evolution," *American Journal of Physical Anthropology* 99 (January 1996): 17–42. Brian T. Shea, "Current Issues in the Investigation of Evolution by Heterochrony, with Emphasis on the Debate over Human Neoteny," in *Biology, Brains, and Behavior*, 181–213.

39. Erikson continues: "but it also leaves a lifelong residue of emotional immaturity in him." *Childhood and Society*, 16.

40. Newton: "to myself I seem to have been only like a boy playing on the seashore"; Einstein: "The gift of fantasy has meant more to me than my talent for absorbing knowledge." Quoted in Montagu, *Growing Young*, 103 and 138.

41. "I understand cultural neoteny as a highly variegated process of rejuvenation whereby older legacies assume newer or younger forms, thanks to a synergy between the synthetic forces of wisdom and the insurgent forces of genius." Robert Pogue Harrison, *Juvenescence* (Chicago: University of Chicago Press, 2014), 72. Harrison illustrates his theory of juvenescence with the example, among others, of the American founding.

42. J. B. S. Haldane facetiously described Jesus as the prophet of neoteny. See Gould, *Ontogeny and Phylogeny*, 401–402.

43. According to Runar M. Thorsteinsson, Jesus's claim that adults ought to emulate children has no parallel in Graeco-Roman philosophy: "becoming like a child was not a part of the process of becoming a true philosopher." Thorsteinsson, *Jesus as Philosopher* (Oxford: Oxford University Press, 2018), 97. Judith Gundry-Volf, speaking more generally of ancient culture, says: "This claim is striking, for nowhere in Jewish literature are children put forward as models for adults, and in a Greco-Roman setting, comparison with children was highly insulting." Judith M. Gundry-Volf, "The Least and the Greatest: Children in the New Testament," in *The Child in Christian Thought*, ed. Marcia J. Bunge (Grand Rapids: William B. Eerdmans, 2001), 29–60, at 39. We could qualify her sweeping generalization by pointing out that ancient religious cultures, both pagan and biblical, acknowledged a special ritual role for children due to their perceived purity. Moreover, Jewish law and custom honored all human life, including that of children, by prohibiting abortion and infanticide.

44. See Robert H. Gundry, *Mark* (Grand Rapids: William B. Eerdmans, 1993), 518–519.

45. Of course, efforts of deliberate debasement might be necessary for adults in order to reach the most profound kind of humility.

46. Gundry, *Mark*, 550.

47. See Judith M. Gundry, "Children in the Gospel of Mark," in *The Child in the Bible*, ed. Marcia Bunge (Grand Rapids: William B. Eerdmans, 2008), 143–176, at 153 (emphasis hers).

48. The New Testament word for belief or faith is *pistis*, which also means a primordial trust.

49. Robert H. Gundry, *Matthew* (Grand Rapids: William B. Eerdmans, 1994), 360.

50. Augustine, *Confessions* 1.5.30.

51. Fitzmyer continues about this passage (Luke 9:48): "The point is not that one has to have a childlike character to enter the kingdom (see 18:17), but rather to accept Jesus himself one has to be prepared to accept and esteem even the lowliest of human society." Joseph A. Fitzmyer, S.J., *The Gospel According to Luke I–IX* (New York: Doubleday, 1981), 816–817.

52. Joseph A. Fitzmyer, S.J., *The Gospel According to Luke X–XXIV* (New York: Doubleday, 1985), 1193.

53. Calvin's views on children are, of course, too complex to summarize here. In his commentary on Matthew 18:1–5, Calvin does actually mention some subjective attitudes of children that make them models of humility. Small children, he says, are "unacquainted with the degrees of honor, and with all the incentives to pride." Yet, in other places, Calvin is clear about the total depravity of children: "Even infants bear their condemnation with them from their mother's womb; for though they have not yet brought forth the fruits of their own iniquity, they have the seed enclosed within themselves. Indeed, their whole nature is a seed of sin; thus it cannot be but hateful and abominable to God." See Barbara Pitkin, "'The Heritage of the Lord': Children in the Theology of John Calvin," in Bunge, *The Child in Christian Thought*, 160–193, at 164 and 167.

54. About the Church fathers, George Boas says: "With the coming of Christianity, new literary material was available for the admirer of childhood, though it was seldom used. . . . The early Christian Fathers and ecclesiastical writers made little use of these New Testament verses which might induce them into an adoration of childhood as such." Of medieval theologians, Boas continues: "As one proceeds through Medieval Latin literature, one again fails to find any use being made of Matthew XVIII or similar passages. . . . The child as a model for adults never occurs in any of the writings that I have been able to examine." Boas, *The Cult of Childhood*, 15, 18, 19. Boas exaggerates the absence of patristic and medieval commentaries on Jesus's praise of children. Jerome set the general tone by observing that Jesus meant for adults to imitate the moral innocence of children, not their ignorance. For a brief survey of a range of ancient and medieval commentaries on Matthew 18:2–6, see Philip L. Reynolds, "Thomas Aquinas and the Paradigms of Childhood," in *The Vocation of the Child*, ed. Patrick McKinley Brennan (Grand Rapids: William B. Eerdmans, 2008), 174–188, at 171. Reynolds agrees with Boas that no ancient or medieval Christian commentator interpreted Jesus's words to imply that children possess unique goods and virtues that ought to be emulated by adults.

55. Friedrich Schleiermacher pioneered the Christian theology of childhood in the early nineteenth century.

56. On the tradition of speculation on infancy in Paradise, see Philip L. Reynolds, "The Infants of Eden: Scholastic Theologians on Early Childhood and Cognitive Development," *Mediaeval Studies* 68 (2006): 89–132, at 91–94.

57. "How could I have become wicked, since under my eyes I had only examples of gentleness, and round me only the best people in the world?" And then: "Despite the most decent education, I must have had a great penchant to degenerate." Rousseau, *Confessions*, 9 and 26. Augustine, of course, has an answer to Rousseau's questions.

58. Graeme Garrard observes that, according to Rousseau, a child before the age of reason "is, like Rousseau's *homme sauvage*, amoral and asocial." Garrard, *Rousseau's Counter-Enlightenment*, 106.

59. "A child wants to upset everything he sees: he smashes, breaks everything he can reach. He grabs a bird as he would grab a stone, and he strangles it without knowing what he does." Rousseau, *Emile*, 67/22. In contrast, Rousseau says that "nothing is so gentle as man in his primitive state." *SD*, 48.

60. Rousseau, *Emile*, 48/15.

61. "Of the children born, half, at most reach adolescence; and it is probable that your pupil will not reach the age of manhood. . . . What, then, must be thought of that barbarous education which sacrifices the present to an uncertain future." Rousseau, *Emile*, 79/209.

62. "Who among you has not sometimes regretted that age when a laugh is always on the lips and the soul is always at peace?" Rousseau, *Emile*, 79/209.

63. "They are always seeking the man in the child without thinking of what he is before being a man. . . . The man must be considered in the man, and the child in the child." Rousseau, *Emile*, 34/157, 80/210, and 90/222.

64. "Nature wants children to be children before being men. If we want to pervert this order, we shall produce precocious fruits which will be immature and insipid and will not be long in rotting. We shall have young doctors and old children." Rousseau, *Emile*, 90/222.

65. "Regard all delays as advantages." Rousseau, *Emile*, 94/227.

66. David Bjorklund discusses experiments in which early instruction interfered with a child's ability to learn later: "these data are suggestive of the possibility that not all learning experiences are necessarily good for infants . . . and sometimes may be actually detrimental to later learning and development." See Bjorklund, "The Role of Immaturity in Human Development," 160.

Chapter 6

1. "During development, and at all stages of the life span, both continuous (cumulative) and discontinuous (innovative) processes are at work." Paul B. Baltes, "Theoretical Propositions of Life-Span Developmental Psychology," *Developmental Psychology* 23, no. 5 (1987): 611–626, at 613.

2. See Aristotle, Rh. 1389a 2 to 1390b 10. I agree with Helen Small that this discussion is consistent with Aristotle's descriptions of old and young in his *Ethics* and *Politics*: "The *Rhetoric* is (deliberately) typologically reductive, but its view of ageing as a diminishment of character is less a betrayal than an addition to and intensification of the worries about old age that one finds in the *Ethics*." Small, *The Long Life*, 267.

3. "For Aristotle, old age is typically a state of disabusement with—and by—life. Its governing motivation is neediness; its predominant disposition fear." Small, *The Long Life*, 62.

4. "The painful and destructive evils are: death in its various forms, bodily injuries and afflictions, old age, diseases, lack of food." Aristotle, Rh. 1386a 7.

5. "The logic that leads him to the claim that children are 'not yet' capable of nobility might lead him to say also that the dependent elderly are 'no longer capable' of its most demanding forms. . . . But he does not say this. . . . Unlike children, the aged are not untrained or ignorant of what virtue requires." Small, *The Long Life*, 64.

6. "All the valuable qualities that youth and age divide between them are united in the prime of life, while all their excesses or defects are replaced by moderation and fitness." Aristotle, Rh. 1390b 7.

7. Aristotle, EE 1219b 6.

8. Aristotle, EE 1219b 4. "Since, then, happiness is a complete good and end, we must not fail to observe that it will be found in that which is complete. For it will not be found in a child (for a child is not happy), but in a man; for he is complete. . . . And a complete period of time will be as long as a man lives." MM 1185a 2.

9. Aristotle, NE 1098a 18.

10. "Pourtant la maturité ne fait encore que rendre possible cet exercice béatifiant de la vertu: l'homme mûr doit encore pouvoir disposer d'un espace de temps assez long pour que cet exercice de la vertu puisse s'y déployer largement . . . un homme heureux, ce n'est pas l'affaire d'un jour!" Gauthier and Jolif, *L'Ethique à Nicomaque*, at 1098a 18.

11. Anthony Kenny argues that a man might be happy (*eudaimon*) in his prime but only supremely blessed (*makarios*) if he avoids tragic reversals of fortune: "It will be true, then, that the word for supreme happiness, *makarios* or blessed, cannot be safely applied until a life is complete. . . . *Makarios*, we might say, is a proleptic predicate." Kenny, *Aristotle on the Perfect Life* (Oxford: Clarendon Press, 1992), 34–35.

12. "Aristotelian old age thus attacks the human capacity for *eudaimonia* at its core. It does this by damaging (progressively and ever more irretrievably) the virtuous character." Small, *The Long Life*, 63.

13. Aristotle, NE 1174a 1.

14. See Gareth Matthews and Amy Mullin, "The Philosophy of Childhood," in *The Stanford Encyclopedia of Philosophy* (Spring 2015 edition), ed. Edward N. Zalta, http://plato.stanford.edu/archives/spr2015/entries/childhood/.

15. "Because it is the soul that receives grace, and not the body, someone may achieve a spiritual perfection even in childhood as a special gift of the Holy Spirit." Philip L. Reynolds, "Thomas Aquinas and the Paradigms of Childhood," in *The Vocation of a Child*, ed. Patrick McKinley Brennan (Grand Rapids: William B. Eerdmans, 2008), 154–188, at 177.

16. "Now the soul, to which spiritual birth and perfect spiritual age belong, is immortal; and just as it can in old age attain to spiritual birth, so can it attain to perfect spiritual age in youth or childhood; because the various ages of the body do not affect the soul. . . . Consequently, even in childhood man can attain to the perfection of spiritual age." Aquinas, III, Q. 72, art. 8 *corpus* and *ad* 2. *Summa Theologiae*, ed. Thomas Gilby (New York: McGraw-Hill, 1964).

17. Philo, the eminent ancient Jewish philosopher, argued that the nudity of Adam and Eve was a symbol of their total lack of any virtues or vices, just like small children. For these ancient debates about Paradise in Genesis, see Boas, *Primitivism and Related Ideas in the Middle Ages*, 4. Rousseau also argued that man in the state of nature lacked all virtues and vices.

18. Augustine argued that Adam, like a child, is neither stupid nor wise. See Boas, *Primitivism and Related Ideas in the Middle Ages*, 47.

19. According to some ancient commentators, maturity, both for an individual and for our species, requires both knowledge and experience: "Before the sin, man knew good and evil: good through experience, evil by knowledge. After the sin, however, he knew evil by experience, good only through knowledge." Boas, *Primitivism and Related Ideas in the Middle Ages*, 79.

20. Lactantius, quoted in Boas, *Primitivism and Related Ideas in the Middle Ages*, 41. Boas summarizes Lactantius's ambivalence about paradise: "in so far as the first pair at their creation were merely innocent and wholly happy, they fell short of the full stature of man, and under such paradisiacal conditions the goal of human history could not have been attained" (41).

21. In his *Confessions*, Rousseau says: "I shall come with this book in my hands to present myself before the Sovereign Judge" (5). He also presents his entire life to his critics: "I could leave them my life to censure from one end to another" (536).

22. His life bounced "from one error to another, from one mistake to another, from one foolish act to another." However: "I never took pleasure in doing harm, damage, in accusing others, in tormenting poor animals." Rousseau, *Reveries of the Solitary Walker*, 3–4; *Confessions*, 9.

23. "I am fully myself. . . . I can truly claim to be what nature willed." *Reveries of the Solitary Walker*, 9.

24. "I have never become inured to my faults. . . . I will be happy if by the progress I make with myself I learn to leave life not better, for that is not possible, but more virtuous than I entered it." *Reveries of the Solitary Walker*, 29 and 27.

25. Boating in solitude "was enough to make me feel my own existence with pleasure." Rousseau struggled to live in the moment, like a child: "In our most intense enjoyments, there is hardly an instant when the heart can genuinely say to us: 'I would like this instant to last forever.'" *Reveries of the Solitary Walker*, 45–46.

26. "I consecrate my last days to studying myself and to preparing in advance the account I will give of myself before long. . . . Is the moment we have to die the time to learn how we should have lived?" *Reveries of the Solitary Walker*, 6 and 17.

27. *Reveries of the Solitary Walker*, 17.

28. "Of all the men I have known, the one whose character is derived most completely from his temperament alone is Jean-Jacques. He is what nature made him. Education has changed him very little. . . . He still maintains the same tastes, the same passions as in his younger years, and until the end of his life, he will not cease to be an elderly child (*vieux enfant*)." Rousseau, *Dialogues*, 107–108.

29. "Animals can slough off their highly specialized adult forms, return to the lability of youth, and prepare themselves for new evolutionary directions." Gould quotes Max Hilzheimer: "The adult stage is a rigid, unchangeable endform, adapted to specific conditions of life. New directions of development can arise only from the still changeable and adaptable youthful stages." Gould, *Ontogeny and Phylogeny*, 283.

30. Richard B. Miller uses this example of combining curiosity with persistence to illustrate the challenges of combining "the virtues of childhood with the virtues of adulthood." See Miller, "Neoteny and the Virtues of Childhood," 329–330.

31. On the psychology of habit interference, see James Bernard Murphy, "Does Habit Interference Explain Moral Failure?," *Review of Philosophy and Psychology* 6, no. 2 (June 2015): 255–273. Published online, 25 January 2015, http://link.springer.com/article/10.1007/s13164-014-0220-5/fulltext.html.

32. Gopnik, *The Philosophical Baby*, 11.

33. Jung, "The Stages of Life," in *The Structure and Dynamics of the Psyche*, trans. R. F. C. Hull (New York: Pantheon Books, 1960), 387–403, at 399.

34. "We have, in the last few decades, learned more about the development and growth of the individual . . . than in the whole of human history before us (excepting, of course, the implicit wisdom expressed in the Bible or Shakespeare)." Erik H. Erikson, *Identity and the Life Cycle* (New York: International Universities Press, 1959), 99.

35. Erikson calls his theory "epigenetic": "This principle states that anything that grows has a *ground plan*, and that out of this ground plan the *parts* arise, each part having its *time* of special ascendency, until all parts have arisen to form a *functioning whole*." Erikson, *Identity and the Life Cycle*, 52. A "ground plan" (*Bauplan*) is a technical term in embryology.

36. He describes "the proper rate and the proper sequence which govern the growth of personality as well as that of an organism." Erikson, *Identity and the Life Cycle*, 52.

37. "Society, in principle, tends to be so constituted as to meet and invite this succession of potentialities for interaction and attempts to safeguard and to encourage the proper rate and the proper sequence of their enfolding." Erikson, *Childhood and Society*, 270.

38. According to Erikson, the "eight ages of man" are each defined by a unique dilemma: (1) basic trust vs. basic mistrust; (2) autonomy vs. shame and doubt; (3) initiative vs. guilt; (4) industry vs. inferiority; (5) identity vs. role confusion; (6) intimacy vs. isolation; (7) generativity vs. stagnation; (8) ego integrity vs. despair. See Erikson, *Childhood and Society*, 247–274, at 270.

39. "A lasting ego identity, we have said, cannot begin to exist without the trust of the first oral stage." Erikson, *Childhood and Society*, 245.

40. Erikson, *Childhood and Society*, 258–259.

41. "Only in him may gradually ripen the fruit of these seven stages." Erikson, *Childhood and Society*, 268 and 272.

42. "Each [stage] comes to its ascendency, meets its crisis, and finds its lasting solution during the stage indicated. But they all must exist from the beginning in some form, for every act calls for an integration of all." Erikson, *Childhood and Society*, 271.

43. See Daniel Goleman, "Erikson, in His Own Old Age, Expands His View of Life," *New York Times*, 14 June 1988. George Vaillant also adopts Erikson's story of the spiral of development, in which we keep circling back to earlier stages: "Like the adolescent, the 40-year-old in crisis struggles with feelings; like the 10-year-old, the 60-year-old struggles to resist the changing times; and like the toddler, the 80-year-old is preoccupied with an unruly, unsteady body." Vaillant, *The Wisdom of the Ego*, 162.

44. These "prospective, longitudinal studies" include the Harvard Grant Study of men, the Lewis Terman study of women, and the inner-city men studied by Sheldon and Eleanor Glueck.

45. Vaillant, *The Wisdom of the Ego*, 142. "Of the 77 men who mastered generativity, 57 (74 percent) first mastered intimacy, then career consolidation, and only then generativity" (170).

46. "In general, the prospectively studied lives of the Grant Study men supported Erikson's hypothesis that the stages of the life cycle must be passed through in sequence." George E. Vaillant, *Adaptation to Life* (Cambridge: Harvard University Press, 1995), 207. Vaillant claims that this pattern was valid for women, as well. See Vaillant, *The Wisdom of the Ego*, 166–167. Of course, intimacy is not limited to one phase of life, even if it is learned in early adulthood: "Intimacy is not achieved once and for all, and the seeds of love must be eternally resown." Vaillant, *The Wisdom of the Ego*, 174.

47. See George E. Vaillant, *Triumphs of Experience: The Men of the Harvard Grant Study* (Cambridge: Harvard University Press, 2012), 146 and 180. Maturation "is the evolution of teenage self-centeredness into the disinterested empathy of a grandparent."

48. Vaillant tells us that "*developmental tasks* is more scientifically correct than *stage*." *The Wisdom of the Ego*, 148.

49. "The life cycle is more than an invariant sequence of stages with single predictable outcomes. The men's lives are full of surprises, and the Grant Study provides no predictable tasks." Vaillant, *Adaptation to Life*, 373. "Successful mastery of the task of integrity, Erikson's final stage of the life cycle, was not synonymous with having mastered all prior stages, although I am sure that mastery of the other tasks helped the mastery of integrity." Vaillant, *The Wisdom of the Ego*, 198.

50. "Alexander the Great, General Lafayette, Napoleon Bonaparte, and Joan of Arc were inspirational and generative leaders in their twenties." Vaillant, *The Wisdom of the Ego*, 199. If only Joan had lived to be twenty!

51. Vaillant, *The Wisdom of the Ego*, 199.

52. "By a 'stage of life' we mean a span of time in the life of the individual that is autonomous in the sense that its regulatory principles are intrinsic and unchanging in their application throughout. A given stage is preceded and followed by other stages, governed by sets of principles that are incommensurable with the principles of the given stage." David L. Norton, *Personal Destinies* (Princeton: Princeton University Press, 1976), 159.

53. "From the character of moral life in one stage, no inferences can be made concerning the character of moral life in other stages." Norton, *Personal Destinies*, 168.

54. Development within a stage is evolutionary while change between stages is revolutionary because it "consists in the exchange of incommensurable set of principles. The incommensurability of the sets of principles precludes intermediate positions." Norton, *Personal Destinies*, 159.

55. Some of the radical aspects of Norton's theory of stages appeared first in James K. Feibleman's (1975) work. Feibleman also describes each stage as "autonomous" and describes the exchange of stages as instantaneous: "Each [stage] has its own autonomy, and the transitions are definite and abrupt. . . . The passages between age-grades are swift, unnoticed, and decisive. All at once the infant is a child, the child an adolescent." Feibleman, *The Stages of Human Life*, 15–16. Feibleman's account, however, is more traditional because it allows for development both within each stage and across human life.

56. Carl Jung argues that in childhood we are a problem for others, in maturity we are a problem for ourselves, and in old age we become again a problem for others. See Jung, "The Stages of Life," 392 and 403.

57. "The perception of being fated to be misunderstood that opens adolescence, the perception of the death that is one's own that opens maturation, and the perception of the foreclosure of one's future that opens old age." Norton, *Personal Destinies*, 212.

58. "As late maturation is 'surprised' by old age, so adolescence is 'surprised' by adulthood and childhood is 'surprised' by adolescence. . . . Surprise arises from the discontinuities subsisting between stages, precluding anticipation of the stage to come." Norton, *Personal Destinies*, 202–203.

59. Norton says that physical continuity in human life is guaranteed by our human genome and our unique inborn potentialities. *Personal Destinies*, 213.

60. "Accordingly the continuity that appears in each stage is a product of a retrospective inference that *transforms* the previous stage in accordance with present principle, together with the prospective creation of a consonant future. Whether in feeling or idea, memory or will, the continuity that appears to each stage is only apparent, to be replaced by a different appearance in other stages." Norton, *Personal Destinies*, 213.

61. "Every person is both his empirical actuality and his ideal possibility, or *daimon*. . . . According to self-actualization ethics it is every person's primary responsibility first to discover the *daimon* within him and thereafter to live in accordance with it." Norton's account of self-actualization is much more individualistic than is Aristotle's. For Norton, the goal is to become uniquely oneself; for Aristotle the goal is to become supremely excellent. See Norton, *Personal Destinies*, 16.

62. "For the meaning of 'person' lies in the fundamental work of self-actualization." Norton, *Personal Destinies*, 348.

63. "Self-actualization entails a doctrine of stages of life because, by its cardinal terms, childhood and old age are exempted . . . it cannot be addressed to a child, for a child lacks

autonomy. . . . And old age, if judged by the actualization-criteria of maturity, appears as pure deterioration, thereby contradicting the basis of the self-actualization thesis." Norton, *Personal Destinies*, 158–159.

64. "Accordingly self-actualization theory has two options, each of which is a stage-doctrine. It can regard normativity as restricted to the period of life we term *maturity*; or it can conceive of personal development as a succession of stages each of which is (normatively) a law unto itself, exacting its own distinctive kind of actualization." Norton, *Personal Destinies*, 159. I think both of these alternatives are ultimately untenable. According to the first option, childhood, adolescence, and old age lack any normative dimension, making it impossible to define success in any of these stages. According to the second option, the other stages embody inferior kinds of actualization, making them commensurable with the prime of life.

65. "Most often it is maturity that is hypostatized, but alternatively the whole of life is represented as moral childhood by those doctrines that assert man's perpetual dependence—upon God, for example, or upon metaphysical necessity of one kind or another." Norton, *Personal Destinies*, 161.

66. Incommensurability is compatible with each stage of life having reciprocal superiorities with the other stages. On incommensurability, see Joseph Raz, *The Morality of Freedom* (Oxford: Clarendon, 1986), 322–340.

67. He defines "maturation, as the stage of life that claims theoretical priority for its explicit and normative rendering of the unique individuality of the person." Norton, *Personal Destinies*, 214.

68. "The meanings of such fundamental normative terms as love, freedom, justice, truth, and death are incommensurably different within the different stages of life." Norton, *Personal Destinies*, 211.

69. Michael Slote, *Goods and Virtues* (Oxford: Clarendon Press, 1983), 17–19.

70. Slote, *Goods and Virtues*, 46–50.

71. Aristotle observes that bad men are distrustful and good men trusting: "Therefore the good are more easily deceived unless experience has taught them distrust" (EE 1237b 29). So here Aristotle acknowledges that adult virtue requires some retention of childhood innocence. Ryan Preston-Roedder argues that this kind of trust is actually a virtue. See Ryan Preston-Roedder, "Faith in Humanity," *Philosophy and Phenomenological Research* 87, no. 3 (2013): 664–687; http://philpapers.org/rec/PREFIH-2.

72. If defined narrowly enough, some goods or virtues seem purely age relative. Michael Slote gives the example of financial prudence; Harry Brighouse and Adam Swift give the example of sexual innocence: "we think that innocence about sexuality, for example, is good in childhood, even though for most people it would not be valuable for their adulthood." Brighouse and Swift, *Family Values: The Ethics of Parent-Child Relationships* (Princeton: Princeton University Press, 2014), 65. Again, adults can never return to ignorance of human sexuality, but all adults have good reasons for cultivating a capacity in some contexts for treating all human persons as nonsexual beings. This valuable human capacity comes more easily to children.

73. Adults may not be able to enjoy the goods distinctive of childhood as fully as do children. "Even if we strived to preserve forever some of the features that make childhood valuable—such as the capacity to learn or to derive pleasure from play—we would probably not be able to enjoy them, as adults, to the same degree as we had enjoyed them as children."

See Anca Ghaeus, "The 'Intrinsic Goods of Childhood' and the Just Society," in *The Nature of Children's Well-Being*, ed. Alexander Bagotti and Colin Macleod (Dordrecht: Springer, 2015), 35–52, at 51. Note that Gheaus describes the differences between children and adults as a matter of degree, not kind.

74. "Other goods are just more readily available in childhood than in adulthood: the capacities to feel spontaneous joy, to be surprised, and to be thrilled seem to diminish a good deal with age; while they are valuable in adulthood as well as in childhood, it may be unrealistic to expect them to be experienced with great intensity much beyond childhood but entirely realistic to think that many children can experience them fully." Brighouse and Swift, *Family Values*, 65.

75. Cruelty requires the ability to understand the subjective perspective of the victim, a capacity only very gradually acquired in the course of maturation.

76. Harrison on the two kinds of *sapientia*: "One is linked to our genius, or the intelligence in us that experiences invents, discovers, imagines, calculates, and in general brings about wholesale change through knowledge and manipulation of the external world. The other is linked to that senile wisdom of humankind—arising from our awareness of mortality—that gave birth to the gods, the graves of the dead, the laws and scriptures of nations, the memory of poets, and the archives of scholars." Harrison, *Juvenescence*, 41.

77. "I understand cultural neoteny as a highly variegated process of rejuvenation whereby older legacies assume newer or younger forms, thanks to a synergy between the synthetic forces of wisdom and the insurgent forces of genius." Harrison, *Juvenescence*, 72.

78. "It is well for the world that in most of us, by the age of thirty, the character has set like plaster, and will never soften again." William James, quoted in Vaillant, *Triumphs of Experience*, 144.

79. "Cognitive development in adulthood is rich, complex, and dynamic, perhaps even more so than in infancy and childhood." Adults frequently show regression, as well as progression. Kurt Fischer et al., "Adult Cognitive Development," in *Handbook of Developmental Psychology*, ed. Jaan Valsiner and Kevin J. Connolly (London: Sage, 2003), 491–516, at 491.

80. "Maturation is not an inevitable by-product of aging; it can be derailed. . . . Separation and individualization are lifelong processes. . . . Adult development is a lifelong process." See Vaillant, *Triumphs of Experience*, 180, 151, 352.

81. Slote, *Goods and Virtues*, 9–15.

82. "The reason why later benefits are thought to have a greater impact on the value of one's life is not that greater weight is attached to what comes later. Rather, it is that later events are thought to alter the meaning of earlier events, thereby altering their contribution to the value of one's life." J. David Velleman, "Well-Being and Time," *Pacific Philosophical Quarterly* 72 (1991): 48–77, at 52–53.

83. "Learning from the misfortune confers some value on it, by making it the means of one's edification. . . . An edifying misfortune is not just offset but redeemed by being given a meaningful place in one's progress through life." Velleman, "Well-Being and Time," 54–55. Slote had also noticed how adult success might compensate for childhood misery. See Slote, *Goods and Virtues*, 15.

84. "Because an event's contribution to the value of one's life depends on its narrative relation to other events, a life's value can never be computed by an algorithm applied to bare amounts of momentary well-being, or even to ordered sequences of such amounts, in abstraction from the significance of the events with which they are associated." Velleman, "Well-Being and Time," 60.

85. "Any sensible person would prefer a life of promotion to a life of demotion, even if the life of demotion started at the top, and included the same total quantity of advantages." Sorabji, *Self*, 340. Sorabji attributes this time preference to natural selection: "Animals that minded past pain or danger more than future would not fare well in the evolutionary process" (340).

86. According to Velleman, the narrative structure of life "explains why we think that the value of someone's life remains almost entirely undetermined even after he has passed an especially happy or unhappy childhood; and why we are inclined to perceive some wisdom in Solon's refusal to declare Croesus happy without knowing how his life would ultimately turn out." Velleman, "Well-Being and Time," 61.

87. "It is fair to say, I think, that the rationality of future bias is an unsolved problem in philosophy." Setiya, *Midlife*, 115.

88. See Daniel Kahneman, *Thinking, Fast and Slow* (London: Penguin, 2011), 381–409. Kahneman discusses the experimental evidence in a chapter called "life as a story" (386–390). Experimental subjects, for example, preferred holding their hands in painfully cold water for ninety seconds (with some relief near the end) to sixty seconds without any relief (382–384). Other subjects preferred a short life that ends at a peak of achievement to a much longer life that simply trails off (387–388). As we shall see below, Kahneman finds these preferences to be less than rational.

89. On the contrast between three dimensions and four, see Theodore Sider, *Four-Dimensionalism* (Oxford: Clarendon Press, 2001), 3.

90. "Perdurantism seems to substitute the successive *replacement* of temporal parts for the notion of genuine change or alteration over time." Ross Inman, *Substance and the Fundamentality of the Familiar* (New York: Routledge, 2018), 165.

91. Yet, Sider claims: "Four-dimensionalism . . . merely implies the existence of temporal parts. It does not imply that temporal parts are in any sense prior to or more fundamental than the objects of which they are parts." *Four-Dimensionalism*, 60.

92. "A person's journey through time is like a road's journey through space." Sider, *Four-Dimensionalism*, 2.

93. "When you touch a person, you only directly touch a part of that person—the hand, say. According to the four-dimensionalist, there is another sense in which you only directly touch a part of the person. Even if you could somehow touch all of a person's spatial parts at once, you would still fail to touch all the person, for not all the person is *there* to be touched." Sider, *Four-Dimensionalism*, 2–3.

94. "Think of your life as a long story. . . . Like all stories, this story has parts. We can distinguish the part of the story concerning childhood from the part concerning adulthood. Given enough details, there will be parts concerning individual days, minutes, or even instants." Sider, *Four-Dimensionalism*, 1.

95. "Just as my story has a part for my childhood, so I have a part consisting just of my childhood." Sider, *Four-Dimensionalism*, 1.

96. "Just as my story has a part describing just this instant, so I have a part that is me-at-this-very-instant." Sider, *Four-Dimensionalism*, 1.

97. "A four-dimensionalist regards the world as a world of stages." Sider, *Four-Dimensionalism*, 7. Eric Olson comments: "If it belongs to the concept of a person that people ordinarily persist in the strict philosophical sense, then people cannot be stages." Eric T.

Olson, *What Are We?* (Oxford: Oxford University Press, 2007), 127. Ross Inman describes "stage theory" (exdurantism) as a distinct variant of four-dimensionalism: "On stage theory, in contrast to perdurantism, ordinary material objects are identical to a single stage that is wholly present at each moment it exists; it turns out, however, that each stage is instantaneous and maximally short-lived." *Substance and the Fundamentality of the Familiar*, 166.

98. "In biology we cannot escape from the dialectical relation between parts and wholes. Before we can recognize meaningful parts we must define the functional whole of which they are the constituents." Lewontin applies this spatial holism to a temporal holism: "It is impossible to understand the situation of living organisms without taking into account their history." Lewontin, *The Triple Helix*, 81–82 and 88.

Chapter 7

1. Marya Schechtman, in *The Constitution of Selves* (Ithaca: Cornell University Press, 1996), distinguishes "re-identification" from "characterization" (77); Amy Kind, in *Persons and Personal Identity* (Cambridge: Polity Press, 2015) distinguishes all three kinds of questions (3).

2. P. M. S. Hacker, *Human Nature: The Categorial Framework* (Oxford: Blackwell, 2007), 261.

3. "Man has always been his own most vexing problem." Reinhold Niebuhr, *Human Nature and Destiny*, vol. 1 (New York: Charles Scribner's, 1964), 1.

4. *Antigone*, line 332.

5. Aristotle, Pol. 1253a 32–36.

6. "I am dust and ashes, frail and wayward. . . . Dust I may be but troubled dust, dust that dreams." Richard Holloway, former bishop of Edinburgh, quoted by Graeme Finley, "The Emergence of Human Distinctiveness: The Genetic Story," in *Rethinking Human Nature*, ed. Malcolm Jeeves (Grand Rapids: Eerdmans, 2011), 107–148, at 134.

7. For current debates surrounding the puzzle of the sudden evolutionary emergence of human language, see Robert Berwick and Noam Chomsky, *Why Only Us* (Cambridge: MIT Press, 2015).

8. Plato, *Apology*, 40B–C; *Phaedo*, 78B–81B; *Phaedrus* 230A and 245B.

9. "The actuality of thought (*nous*) is life, and God is that actuality." Aristotle, Meta. 1072b 22–27. Aristotle wonders how reason (*nous*) enters the embryo: "It remains, then, for the reason alone so to enter and alone to be divine." GA 736b 26–30.

10. "We must not follow those who advise us, being men, to think of human things, and, being mortal, of mortal things, but must, so far as we can, make ourselves immortal." NE 1177b 31.

11. "What is a man / If his chief good and market of his time / Be but to sleep and feed? a beast, no more. / Sure He that made us with such large discourse, / Looking before and after, gave us not / That capability and godlike reason / To fust in us unus'd." *Hamlet*, act 4, scene 4.

12. The *Oxford English Dictionary*, for example, defines a person (2a) as: "an individual human being."

13. Even Locke concedes: "I know that, in the ordinary way of speaking, the same person, and the same man, stand for one and the same thing." *Essay Concerning Human Understanding*, edited by Alexander C. Fraser (New York: Dover, 1959), II, 27.15. All quotations of Locke are from this edition of this book. Plato, Descartes, and other philosophers have also offered

dualistic accounts of human being, but Locke's contrast of a "man" and a "person" has been especially influential.

14. "The real essence of that or any other sort of substance, it is evident, we know not . . . and so far are we from certainly knowing what a *man* is." We can describe, however, our idea of human being, what Locke calls our "nominal essence": "we mean nothing by man but a corporeal rational creature: what the real essence or other qualities of that creature are in this case is no way considered." *Essay Concerning Human Understanding*, III, 6.27 and III, 11.16.

15. Locke goes on to compare losing his color to losing his reason. *Essay Concerning Human Understanding*, III, 6.4.

16. "For, were there a monkey, or any other creature, to be found that had the use of reason to such a degree . . . he would no doubt be subject to law, and in that sense be a *man*." Locke, *Essay Concerning Human Understanding*, III, 11.16.

17. "If history lie not, women have conceived by drills." Locke, *Essay Concerning Human Understanding*, III, 6.23.

18. "Our ranking and distinguishing natural substances into species consists in the nominal essences the mind makes, and not in the real essences to be found in the things themselves." Locke, *Essay Concerning Human Understanding*, III, 6.11.

19. "And, therefore, whether a child or changeling be a man, in a physical sense, may amongst the naturalists be as disputable as it will, it concerns not at all the moral man." In short, says Locke, a defective child and a man are just as different in reason as a monkey differs in body from that same child: "Nobody will doubt that the wheels or springs (if I may so say) within are different in a rational man and a changeling: no more than that there is a difference in the frame between a drill and a changeling." Locke, *Essay Concerning Human Understanding*, III, 11.16 and III, 6.39.

20. "A foetus in the mother's womb differs not much from the state of a vegetable." Locke, *Essay Concerning Human Understanding*, II, 1.21. "How far such an one [a senescent old man] . . . is in his knowledge and intellectual faculties above the condition of a cockle or an oyster, I leave to be considered." II, 9.14.

21. Locke defines "the identity of man" as "nothing but a participation of the same continued life, by constantly fleeting particles of matter, in succession vitally united to the same organized body." This metabolic unity, he says, is no different from that of any animal. The idea of man, he says, "is nothing else but of an animal of such a certain form." See *Essay Concerning Human Understanding*, II, 27.6 and 27.8. By contrast, says Locke, "personal identity can by us be placed in nothing but consciousness (which is that alone which makes what we call self)." II, 27.21. "And as far as this consciousness can be extended backwards to any past Action or Thought, so far reaches the Identity of that Person." II, 27.9.

22. "A person," Locke famously says, "is a forensic term, appropriating actions and their merit; and so belongs only to intelligent agents, capable of a law, and happiness, and misery." *Essay Concerning Human Understanding*, II, 27.26.

23. Locke wonders why there could "not be one person in two distinct bodies, as much as one man is the same in two distinct clothings." *Essay Concerning Human Understanding* II, 27.23.

24. Locke, *Essay Concerning Human Understanding*, II, 27.23.

25. "Person, as I take it, is the name for this self." Locke, *Essay Concerning Human Understanding*, II, 27.26.

26. "Now, man as a natural being that has reason (*homo phaenomenon*) can be determined by his reason, as a *cause*, to actions in the sensible world, and so far the concept of obligation does not come into consideration." In other words, according to Kant, man as a rational animal is not yet a moral creature. "But the same man thought of in terms of his *personality*, that is, as a being endowed with *inner freedom* (*homo noumenon*) is regarded as a being that can be put under obligation, and, indeed, under obligation to himself." See Kant, *Metaphysics of Morals*, trans. Mary Gregor (Cambridge: Cambridge University Press, 1991), [418] 215. Bracketed page numbers refer to the standard German edition of Kant's works.

27. Kant, *Metaphysics of Morals*, [434] 230.

28. "Humanity in his person is the object of the respect which he can demand from every other man, but which he must also not forfeit. . . . Consequently, disposing of oneself as a mere means to some discretionary end is debasing humanity in one's person (*homo noumenon*), to which man (*homo phaenomemon*) was nevertheless entrusted for preservation." Kant, *Metaphysics of Morals*, [435] 230 and [423] 219.

29. Kant denies that killing an illegitimate newborn baby constitutes murder in *Metaphysics of Morals*, [336] 144–145.

30. Philosopher Galen Strawson, in *Selves* (Oxford: Clarendon Press, 2009), distinguishes two senses of "I": "the inner-self use and the human-being-considered-as-a-whole use"; these two uses rest on our experience of "an inner entity, an inner presence that is not the same thing as the whole human being" (23). Philosopher Norman Ford agrees: "The self can both identify with the body and withdraw somewhat from the body by way of having it." Ford, *When Did I Begin?* (Cambridge: Cambridge University Press, 1988), 68.

31. "Psychological theorists begin with the assumption that we are essentially persons. Animalists, in contrast, begin from the assumption that we are essentially animals." Animalism is one kind of biological approach. See Kind, *Persons and Personal Identity*, 83.

32. Locke thus gets the credit or blame for inspiring a huge philosophical literature devising fantastical thought experiments about persons being transplanted, teleported, replicated, and divided. These thought experiments are intended to reveal whether we intuitively identify with our bodies or with our minds. For a detailed comparison of these philosophical thought experiments to scientific thought experiments, see Kathleen V. Wilkes, *Real People* (Oxford: Clarendon Press, 1988). Her conclusion: "we cannot extract philosophically interesting conclusions from fantastical thought experiments" (46). Bernard Williams argued long ago that our intuitions about persons switching bodies or bodies switching persons are highly sensitive to how the problem is framed. For empirical evidence that our intuitions about these scenarios are highly unstable and unreliable, see Shawn Nichols and Michael Bruno, "Intuitions About Personal Identity: An Empirical Study," *Philosophical Psychology* 23, no. 3 (June 2010): 293–312, at 303.

33. According to the biological approach, "damage to my body is damage to me, not merely damage to a possession of mine." Kind, *Persons and Personal Identity*, 79.

34. According to Ford, this unity of all bodily and mental experience reveals the impossibility of conceptually separating the biological and psychological dimensions of the human person. See Ford, *When Did I Begin?*, 72.

35. Galen Strawson insists that we live primarily in our heads: "Which stand out most for us, in daily life: our mental features or our bodily features? Most of us find that our moods and emotional feelings are a great deal more present to our attention than our bodies, most of the time." *Selves*, 25. Note the assumption that our moods and emotions are not bodily.

36. Galen Strawson insists that our background awareness of our bodies is compatible with a focal awareness of our inner psychological self: "Our background awareness of our bodies is important, but this is wholly compatible with our regularly experiencing ourselves primarily and centrally as inner conscious presences who are not the same thing as a human being considered as a whole." *Selves*, 28. He quotes William James (29): "We feel the whole cubic mass of our body all the while, it gives us an unceasing sense of personal existence. Equally too we feel the inner 'nucleus' of the spiritual self."

37. "Locke's view has gained wide acceptance. Indeed, one might say that it is part of the current orthodoxy concerning personal identity." Mark Thornton, "Same Human Being, Same Person?" *Philosophy* 66, no. 255 (January 1991): 115–188, at 115. Jeff McMahan also observes that most philosophers embrace the psychological account, according to which "personal identity consists in non-branching psychological continuity." See McMahan, *The Ethics of Killing* (Oxford: Oxford University Press, 2002), 39–40.

38. Although many philosophers say that I am a self and that I have a self, Hacker rightly insists that "a person cannot both *be* and *have* a self." *Human Nature*, 261.

39. Galen Strawson describes the self as "a subject of experience that is a single, persisting, mental thing . . . that is, an agent that has a certain personality and is not the same thing as a human being considered as a whole." See Strawson, *Selves*, 3.

40. Hacker insists, by contrast, that "a human being is not 'alone in his head,' since he is not in his head, and he is not alone, although he can be lonely." *Human Nature*, 263.

41. Thomas Traherne, quoted in Anthony Kenny, *The Self* (Milwaukee: Marquette University Press, 1988), 1.

42. "It is often assumed that personhood is some sort of psychological concept . . . the difference between a person and a nonperson is a difference in psychological capacities. Something is a person just in case it is smart enough, in the right way, to be one." Eric T. Olson, *The Human Animal* (New York: Oxford University Press, 1997), 103.

43. "According to the Biological Approach, person . . . is not a substance concept, but a phase sortal like athlete." Olson, *The Human Animal*, 30. In other words, being a person is just one phase of life, like being an athlete.

44. David DeGrazia says: "I will argue that we human persons are essentially (living) human animals. . . . The important claim here is not species membership per se, but membership in some biological kind. Perhaps we are not essentially *Homo sapiens* but essentially hominids or members of some other biological kind." *Human Identity and Bioethics* (Cambridge: Cambridge University Press, 2005), 28 and 48. Eric Olson, who refers to human beings consistently as animals or primates, does also call them *Homo sapiens* in *What Are We?*, 23.

45. Olson, for example, points out that Aristotelians "argue that each human animal is essentially rational, which ordinary animalism denies." *What Are We?*, 173.

46. David Wiggins says: "I seek to show that there is no non-vacuous sense in which one can say 'the ordinary further facts of human personality *supervene* upon the facts of mental and physical continuity and connectedness.' (*Pace* the philosophers who say that sort of thing, those mental and physical facts are *already* identity-involving)." Wiggins, *Sameness and Substance Renewed* (Cambridge: Cambridge University Press, 2001), xiv.

47. "When we encounter a human person we do not proceed and act as if there are two loci—a person and an animal—but treat and perceive her as a complex, multi-dimensional, integrated being." Marya Schechtman, *Staying Alive* (Oxford: Oxford University Press, 2014), 186.

48. What does it mean to say that the concept of a person is "primitive"? "What I mean by the concept of a person is the concept of a type of entity such that *both* predicates ascribing states of consciousness *and* predicates ascribing corporeal characteristics, a physical situation, etc., are equally applicable to a single individual of that single type." P. F. Strawson, *Individuals* (London: Methuen, 1959), 101–102. As Harry Frankfurt pointed out, since this definition applies to nonhuman animals as well as to human beings, Strawson should have specified those states of consciousness unique to human persons. See Frankfurt, "Freedom of Will and the Concept of a Person," *Journal of Philosophy* 68, no. 1 (January 1971): 5–20, at 5.

49. "The concept of a person is not to be analysed as that of an animated body or of an embodied anima." P. F. Strawson, *Individuals*, 103.

50. "The concept of a person is logically prior to that of an individual consciousness." P. F. Strawson, "Persons," in *Body and Mind*, ed. G. N. A. Vesey (London: George Allen and Unwin, 1964), 403–423, at 413 and 421 n.

51. "The question of whether the *psuche* and the body are one thing or two, Aristotle taught, is as meaningless as the question of whether the wax and the impression made upon it are one thing or two (DA 412b 6–7)." Hacker, *Human Nature*, 254.

52. "Suppose that the eye were an animal—sight would have been its soul." Aristotle, DA 412b 18.

53. "The conception of consciousness or introspection as a form of inner vision is misconceived. . . . To feel angry or ashamed, to feel compassion or pity, to feel jealous or envious, is not to perceive or observe anything. . . . Introspection is a form of reflective thought not a form of perception." Hacker, *Human Nature*, 91 and 89.

54. What we call introspection "is not to have *access* to anything, it is to be able to *give expression* to something . . . introspection is a form of *reflection*, not a form of *observation*." Hacker, *Human Nature*, 246–247.

55. "When, outside philosophy, I talk about myself, I am simply talking about the human being, Anthony Kenny, and my self is nothing other than myself." Kenny, *The Self*, 4. "To speak of myself is not to speak of a self that I have, but simply to speak of the human being that I am. To say that I was thinking of myself is not to say that I was thinking of my *self*, but that I was thinking of *me*." Hacker, *Human Nature*, 266.

56. "What is wrong with the doctrine of the self is that it identifies the fundamental with the private . . . the fact that I suppressed certain remarks is often a more important fact about me than the fact that they came into my mind in the first place." Kenny, *The Self*, 30–31.

57. "Do I love her? These questions receive their definitive answers not in a private colloquy with oneself in the imagination, but in the testing conditions of life in the real and public world." Kenny, *The Self*, 31.

58. "The notion of a human being is a notion of a biologically defined entity; the notion of a person is, however, normatively and sometimes ideologically charged. It expresses a view about what is important or valuable about being creatures like us." Amélie Rorty, "Persons and Personae," in *Person and the Human Mind*, ed. Christopher Gill (Oxford: Clarendon Press, 1990), 21–38, at 36. "That human beings are persons is not a trivial tautology, but a fundamental claim about our moral status and our singularity in the order of nature." Hacker, *Human Nature*, 285.

59. "For different names with the same reference may be annexed to different conceptions of that reference, to different ways of thinking about it, and to different ways of presenting it." David Wiggins, *Continuants* (Oxford: Oxford University Press, 2016), 73.

60. "One may or may not want to say that to be a person is the same as to be a human being. But in practice the *extensions* of these concepts will coincide, and it will be no accident that they do." Wiggins, *Continuants*, 82. "A person is not just any sentient or conscious being. A person is one of us." David Wiggins, "Identity, Individuation and Substance," *European Journal of Philosophy* 20, no. 1 (2012): 1–25, at 16–17.

61. "Our grasp of what it is to be a human being gives matter and substance to our conception of persons ... and our apprehension of persons ... is what directs and animates our search for those marks of human beings in virtue of which we have to see them as the bearers and sources of value." David Wiggins, "The Person as Object of Science, as Subject of Experience, and as Locus of Value," in *Persons and Personality*, ed. Arthur Peacocke and Grant Gillett (Oxford: Basil Blackwell, 1987), 56–74, at 74.

62. "The only *stereotype* we can have of a person—and the only effective conception we can have of what a person is—is the conception of a human being, a fellow creature, *our* fellow creature. A person is a rational being with a distinctive and particular animal nature, origin, and physiognomy, namely ours." Wiggins, *Continuants*, 87.

63. "Nature in the primary and strict sense is the substance of things which have in themselves, as such, a source of movement ... and processes of becoming and growing are called nature because they are movements proceeding from this. ... And nature in this sense is the source of the movement of natural objects, being present in them somehow, either potentially or actually." Aristotle, Meta. 1015a 13. For a contemporary philosophical defense of Aristotelian substance, see Wiggins, *Continuants*, 41–70, and *Sameness and Substance Renewed*.

64. "Nothing, then, which is not a species of a genus will have an essence." Aristotle, Meta. 1030a 11–12. "Therefore there is an essence only of those things whose formula is a definition." Meta. 1030a 6.

65. See Aristotle, *Topics* 132a 8 and 20; NE 1097b 11, 1178a 7, 1166a 17, 1169a 1; *Problems* 899a 1; Pol. 1332b 5.

66. In Latin, this twofold reality of reason and language is captured by the play on *ratio/oratio*.

67. "Man is the only animal with the gift of speech. And whereas mere voice is but an indication of pleasure or pain, and is therefore found in other animals ... the power of speech is intended to set forth the expedient and the inexpedient, and therefore the just and the unjust." Aristotle, Pol. 1253a 9.

68. "We are language-using animals—*homo loquens*, not *homo sapiens*. Stripped of language, we are but killer apes. All the distinctive powers [of human beings] are either constitutive of or corollaries of our mastery of a developed language." Hacker, *Human Nature*, 238.

69. "For, since the powers or qualities that are observable by us are not the real essence of that substance, but depend on it, and flow from it, any collection whatsoever of these qualities cannot be the real essence of that thing." Locke, quoted in Inman, *Substance and the Fundamentality of the Familiar*, 38.

70. "The order of explanation runs from dispositional properties to laws, not the other way around." Inman, *Substance and the Fundamentality of the Familiar*, 36.

71. "We call substances the simple bodies, e.g., air, fire, water and all of that sort, and in general bodies and the animals." Aristotle, Meta. 1017b 10.

72. "That is why there is always a kind—of men and of animals and of plants." Aristotle, GA 732a 1. The classic analysis of natural kinds is Hilary Putnam's "Is Semantics Possible?,"

Metaphilosophy 1, no. 3 (July 1970): 187–201. "Natural kinds are *kinds* (rather than mere arbitrary collections) because the entities so grouped share a set of intrinsic properties—and essence—and *natural* (rather than conventional or *nominal*) because that essence exists independent of human cognition and purpose." Robert A. Wilson, "Realism, Essence, and Kind: Resuscitating Species Essentialism," in *Species: New Interdisciplinary Essays*, ed. Robert A. Wilson (Cambridge: MIT Press, 1999), 187–207, at 188.

73. Biologist and philosopher Michael T. Ghiselin has pioneered the contemporary argument that a species is not a natural kind but a metaphysical individual. See Ghiselin, *Metaphysics and the Origin of Species* (Albany: State University of New York Press, 1997). Ghiselin has persuaded biologists such as Ernst Mayr and philosophers such as David Hull of his central claim. For a development of Ghiselin's argument to the effect that there is no such thing as human nature, see David J. Buller, *Adapting Minds* (Cambridge: MIT Press, 2005).

74. For a guide to the bewildering variety of biological species concepts, see John S. Wilkins, *Species: A History of the Idea* (Berkeley: University of California Press, 2009).

75. "Indeed, a phylogenetic concept will have to rely on a concept of one of the other types [reproductive or ecological] to yield an account of speciation events." Samir Okasha, "Darwinian Metaphysics: Species and the Question of Essentialism," *Synthese* 131 (2002): 191–213, at 201.

76. "On all modern species concepts (except the phrenetic), the property in virtue of which a particular organism belongs to one species rather than another is a relational rather than an intrinsic property of that organism." Okasha, "Darwinian Metaphysics," 201.

77. "For most organisms the essential intrinsic properties are probably largely, although not entirely, genetic." In this paragraph I adopt the argument of Michael Devitt for "Intrinsic Biological Essentialism" in Devitt, "Resurrecting Biological Essentialism," *Philosophy of Science* 75 (July 2008): 344–382, at 347. For a critique of Devitt, see Matthew Barker, "Specious Intrinsicalism," *Philosophy of Science* 77 (January 2010): 73–91. For other defenses of species as natural kinds, see Paul E. Griffiths, "Squaring the Circle: Natural Kinds with Historical Essences," in *Species: New Interdisciplinary Essays*, ed. Robert A. Wilson (Cambridge: MIT Press, 1999), 209–228; and Martin Mahner, "What Is a Species?," *Journal for General Philosophy of Science* 24 (1993): 103–126.

78. "What enables the organism to have certain relational properties is precisely . . . the intrinsic constitution of the organism." David S. Oderberg, *Real Essentialism* (New York: Routledge, 2007), 222.

79. "Essentialism is committed simply to the view that in the pool of variation among the members of a species there are shared intrinsic, probably largely genetic, properties." Devitt, "Resurrecting Biological Essentialism," 372.

80. "Why do we not find in nature simply an unbroken continuum of similar or more and more widely diverging individuals? . . . It is now clear that the isolating mechanisms of a species are a protective device for well-integrated genotypes. Any interbreeding between different species would lead to a breakdown of well-balanced, harmonious genotypes, and would quickly be counteracted by natural selection." Ernst Mayr, *Toward a New Philosophy of Biology*, 319.

81. "I conclude that biological species are paradigmatic natural kinds, their historicality and lack of sharp boundaries notwithstanding. . . . I conclude that individual species have (homeostatic property cluster) essences, so that a form of 'essentialism' is true for species."

Richard Boyd, "Homeostasis, Species, ad Higher Taxa," in Wilson, *Species: New Interdisciplinary Essays*, 141–185, at 141–142. For an argument that a biological species has an essence but that individual organisms do not, see Joseph LaPorte, *Natural Kinds and Conceptual Change* (Cambridge: Cambridge University Press, 2004).

82. "Particular species taxa are natural kinds defined by a homeostatic cluster of morphological, genetic, ecological, genealogical, and reproductive features. This cluster of features tends to be possessed by any organism that is a member of a given species, though no one of these properties is a traditionally-defined essential property of that species and no proper subset of them is a species essence." Wilson, "Realism, Essence, and Kind," 199. David S. Oderberg insists, however, that "homeostatic clusters must be unified by a metaphysical principle in order to yield an essence." Oderberg, *Real Essentialism*, 237.

83. On this distinction between properties and essences, see Inman, *Substance and the Fundamentality of the Familiar*, 29–32.

84. "Species are genetically variable, but that is compatible with their having diagnostic features." Peter Godfrey-Smith, *Philosophy of Biology* (Princeton: Princeton University Press, 2013), 106.

85. "All or most species do have genetic profiles that enable us to sort the organisms that exist at a time into one species or another. . . . There is no reason to think that a genetic profile characteristic of a species at one time will stay fixed within a lineage." Godfrey-Smith, *Philosophy of Biology*, 106.

86. "We see ourselves not as things with a function—what on earth could a person, as a person, be *for*—but as autonomous, self-moving, animate beings," In this paragraph I have developed three reasons offered by David Wiggins, *Continuants*, 91.

87. "There is no such thing as 'the' concept of a person." Amélie O. Rorty, "Persons and Personae," 21; in the same collection, see Adam Morton, "Why There Is No Concept of a Person," in Gill, *Person and the Human Mind*, 39–59.

88. Historians have also attempted to dissolve the notion of person into myriad personae; see Aron Gurevich, *The Origins of European Individualism*, trans. Katharine Judelson (Oxford: Blackwell, 1995), and Timothy J. Reiss, *Mirages of the Selfe* (Stanford: Stanford University Press, 2003).

89. Greek *prosopon* and Latin *persona* both referred to stage masks. Traditionally, *persona* was thought to derive from *prosopon*, but that view is no longer widely held. See Stephen A. Hipp, *"Person" in Christian Tradition and the Conception of Albert the Great* (Münster: Aschendorff, 2001), 93.

90. In classical Roman law, *The Institutes of Gaius*, we read: "The main classification in the law of persons is this: all men are either free or slaves" (I, 9). In the most general sense of *persona*, then, slaves are persons. But in the technical meaning of a legal person (*persona legitima*), slaves are not persons: "It is perfectly true that slaves have no Legal Personality of their own and therefore take Legal Personality from their owners" [Citing *Institutes* 2.14.2, 3.17]. Roman lawyers did not develop a doctrine of corporate personality, but they recognized various corporate bodies as legal persons who could own property and sue in courts. P. W. Duff, *Personality in Roman Private Law* (New York: Augustus Kelley, 1938), 16 and 49. "Classical thinkers would see the term *persona* as signifying, above all, a social role that had been assigned by society to one or another of its members. This term was used in the world of the theatre or court procedure and was not linked with the field of psychology." Gurevich, *The Origins of European Individualism*, 90.

91. "Una substantia, tres personae."

92. Boethius: "Naturae rationalis individua substantia."

93. Aquinas, ST, part I, Q. 29, Art. 3.

94. By analogy because, as Aquinas says, nothing can be said univocally about God and his creatures. ST, I, 13.5.

95. The first *persona* we occupy, he says, is "the fact that we all have a share in reason"; every other *persona* we occupy, he says, "is derived from this." Cicero, *On Duties*, ed. M. T. Griffin and E. M. Atkins (Cambridge: Cambridge University Press, 1991), book I, 107–115.

96. A. M. Ferner describes this change from the classical conception of a person as a "phase sortal" to the Christian conception of a person as a "substance sortal" in *Organisms and Personal Identity* (London: Routledge, 2016), 124. "Our own notion of the human person is still basically the Christian one." Marcel Mauss, "A Category of the Human Mind: The Notion of Person; the Notion of Self," in *The Category of the Person*, ed. Michael Carrithers et al. (Cambridge: Cambridge University Press, 1985), 19.

97. "The various functions performed by our contemporary concept of person do not hang together: there is some overlap, but also some tension." Amélie O. Rorty, "Persons and Personae," 22.

98. As wholes, we are "incommunicable," meaning that we cannot be subsumed into a larger whole; as social beings, we realize our essence only by "self-communication" with others. "To be a person, then, is to be . . . at once present in itself, actively possessing itself by its self-consciousness (its substantial pole), and also actively oriented toward others, toward the loving self-communication to others (its relational pole)." W. Norris Clarke, "Person, Being, and St. Thomas," *Communio* 19 (Winter 1992): 601–618, at 610.

99. W. Norris Clarke, *Person and Being* (Milwaukee: Marquette University Press, 1993), 65–66.

100. See Clarke, *Person and Being*, 92–93, 77.

101. "The idea of person (I conclude) needs the idea of a being with a specific nature. It needs that idea as badly as the moral life of ordinary human beings needs the thoughts we now express most easily in terms of personhood." Wiggins, *Continuants*, 82.

102. When attempting to define or rather elucidate the notion of a person, David Wiggins rightly reminds us: "The thing we should notice here is the constant need for *aposiopesis*—the incompleteability that is registered by the dots. . . ." Wiggins, *Continuants*, 80.

103. See Frank R. Wilson, *The Hand: How Its Use Shapes the Brain, Language, and Human Culture* (New York: Random House, 1998).

104. The Latin *persona* literally means "to sound through" (a mask)—focusing our attention on the linguistic dimension of personhood.

105. See Wilkins, *Making Faces*.

106. See Ad Vingerhoets, *Why Only Humans Weep: Unravelling the Mysteries of Tears* (Oxford: Oxford University Press, 2013).

107. See Christina Starmans and Paul Bloom, "Windows to the Soul: Children and Adults See the Eyes as the Location of the Self," *Cognition* 123, no. 2 (May 2012): 313–318.

108. Philosophers who define human nature in terms of this intrinsic directedness include Patrick Lee, "The Basis for Being a Subject of Rights," in *Reason, Morality, and Law*, ed. John Keown and Robert P. George (Oxford: Oxford University Press, 2013), 236–247, at

244; and Rahul Kumar, "Permissible Killing and the Irrelevance of Being Human," *Journal of Ethics* 12 (2008): 57–80, at 72.

109. Every somatic cell in the human body possesses a complete genome, as do complete hydatidform moles, but none of these entities has an intrinsic directedness toward mature rationality. Lee, "The Basis for Being a Subject of Rights," 244.

110. Jeff McMahan, for example, permits the direct killing of human beings in cases where he prohibits the direct killing of human persons. McMahan, "Challenges to Human Equality," *Journal of Ethics* 12, no. 1 (2008): 81–104, at 82.

111. Jeff McMahan speaks for many philosophers in describing embryos as "unoccupied" organisms and expecting to die before "my organism does." *The Ethics of Killing*, 329 and 425.

112. A leading contemporary theorist of human rights, James Griffin, articulates the dominant view quite well: "In what should we say that human rights are grounded? Well, primarily in personhood." He asks, "What does *human* mean in *human* rights?" It means a rational and moral agent, he says, a person. "Human cannot there mean simply a member of the species *Homo sapiens*" because "infants, the severely mentally retarded, people in an irreversible coma, are all members of the species, but are not agents. . . . So by the word 'human' in the phrase 'human rights' we . . . should mean, roughly, a functioning human agent [i.e. a person]." See James Griffin, *On Human Rights* (Oxford: Oxford University Press, 2008), 33–35.

113. "By definition, persons possess a higher moral status (perhaps conferred by the enjoyment of rights) than that of non-persons. . . . An argument against the existence of human rights will almost certainly attempt to show that some human beings are not persons." Douglas Husak, "Why There Are No Human Rights," *Social Theory and Practice* 10, no. 2 (Summer 1984): 125–141, at 127.

114. "A human being in an irreversible coma is not a person; she does not have the properties and capacities that make for being a person. She once had them, but she no longer does and never will again. She remains a human being, however. So too, fetuses and newborn infants are not persons. If all goes well, they will shortly become persons; but they are not yet persons. But they too are human beings." Nicholas Wolterstorff, *Understanding Liberal Democracy: Essays in Political Philosophy*, ed. Terence Cuneo (Oxford: Oxford University Press, 2012), 201.

115. "To be a living person means one still has the active potential for further development and growth or at least survival as a being." Ford, *When Did I Begin?* 97.

116. "It is becoming increasingly obvious that potentiality or potency is an analogous notion, whose meaning may be somewhat elastic, referring to various degrees of real potency to actuality—from remote to proximate." Ford, *When Did I Begin?* 97. Marya Schechtman has usefully reminded me that the examples I offer of potentiality in artifacts (trees becoming bookcases) or in law (Charles becoming king) are very remote from the intrinsic dynamism of biological development. I cite these examples merely to illustrate how open–ended is the whole notion of potentiality.

117. For McMahan's argument that "there is no threshold that marks a sharp separation between cases of intrinsic potential and extrinsic potential," see "Challenges to Human Equality," 92.

118. As Eric Olson says: "Just as a human embryo has the second-order capacity to become rational and conscious in the ordinary course of development, a human vegetable has

the second-order capacity to become rational and conscious if the right surgical measures are taken." *The Human Animal*, 87.

119. On the future of regenerative medicine, see Lewis Wolpert, *Developmental Biology* (Oxford: Oxford University Press, 2011), 106–112.

120. On the relationship of total brain death to the death of a human being, see D. Alan Shewmon, "Recovery from 'Brain Death': A Neurologist's Apologia," *Linacre Quarterly* 64, no. 1 (1997): 30–96; and Patrick Lee and Germain Grisez, "Total Brain Death: A Reply to Alan Shewmon," *Bioethics* 26, no. 5 (2012): 275–284.

121. "Each stage in the trajectory is shadowed by a variety of ways in which things may go wrong, ways in which the organism, developed so far, may be harmed or disabled or fail to develop further. This is what we humans are like . . . this person, for all her or his disability, is *one of us*." Jeremy Waldron, *One Another's Equals* (Cambridge: Harvard University Press, 2017), 243–244.

122. Matthew Liao, among many others, begins his articles by asking two questions: "What are you essentially? What does it take for you to persist through time?" He then proceeds to discuss persistence conditions, as if they answer his first question. See S. Matthew Liao, "The Organism View Defended," *The Monist* 89, no. 3 (2006): 334–350, at 334; and "Twinning, Inorganic Replacement, and the Organism View," *Ratio*, n.s. 23, no. 1 (March 2010): 59–72, at 59.

123. Eric Olson rightly says: "We could know our persistence conditions and yet know little about our other properties of metaphysical interest." *What Are We?* 18.

124. Simple or ordinary numerical identity "is the identity relation as restricted to things that change." Wiggins, "Identity, Individuation and Substance," 5.

Chapter 8

1. See David Velleman, "Narrative Explanation," *Philosophical Review* 112, no. 1 (January 2003): 1–25, at 14.

2. By contrast, Gregory Currie claims that narratives must be communicated: "I said that a narrative *must* be an artefact." *Narrative and Narrators* (Oxford: Oxford University Press, 2010), 21.

3. "Even matters of chance seem most marvelous if there is an appearance of design as it were in them; as for instance the statue of Mitys at Argos killed the author of Mitys's death by falling down on him when he was looking at it; for incidents like that we think to be not without meaning." Aristotle, *Poetics* 1452a 6–10.

4. Barbara Hardy, quoted in Alasdair MacIntyre, *After Virtue* (Notre Dame: University of Notre Dame Press, 1984), 211.

5. "Man is in his actions and practices, as well as in his fictions, essentially a story-telling animal. He is not essentially, but became through his history, a teller of stories that aspire to truth." MacIntyre, *After Virtue*, 216 and 211.

6. Amy Kind distinguishes descriptive from prescriptive claims about narrative in *Persons and Personal Identity*, 126.

7. Galen Strawson argues that these two theses are logically independent (and both false) in "Against Narrativity," *Ratio* 17, no. 4 (December 2004): 428–451, at 428.

8. "Our tales are spun, but for the most part we don't spin them; they spin us. Our human consciousness, and our narrative selfhood, is their product, not their source." Daniel C. Dennett, *Consciousness Explained* (Boston: Little, Brown, 1991), 418.

9. Kierkegaard's *Journal*, quoted in Richard Wollheim, *The Thread of Life* (Cambridge: Harvard University Press, 1984), 162.

10. I owe this image of human life to a conversation with Alexander Wendt.

11. Wollheim agrees with Kierkegaard that "the attempt that a person makes to understand his life may interfere with his leading it." Wollheim, *The Thread of Life*, 162.

12. As Wollheim rightly concludes, "not only is understanding the life he leads intrinsic to leading it, but for much of the time leading his life is, or is mostly, understanding it." *The Thread of Life*, 283.

13. Aristotle, *Poetics* 1450b 26.

14. "The clock's *tick-tock* I take to be a model of what we call a plot, an organization that humanizes time by giving it form. . . . *Tick* is a humble genesis, *tock* a feeble apocalypse." Frank Kermode, *The Sense of an Ending* (Oxford: Oxford University Press, 2000), 45.

15. Aristotle, *Poetics* 1450a 16.

16. Philosopher Paul Ricoeur translates Aristotle's *muthos* as "emplotment": narrative is the organization of events. See Ricoeur, *Time and Narrative*, trans. Kathleen McLaughlin and David Pellauer (Chicago: University of Chicago Press, 1984), vol. 1, 33 and 37.

17. "For life is no uniform uninterrupted march or flow. It is a thing of histories, each with its own plot, its own inception and movement toward its close, each having its own particular rhythmic movement." John Dewey, *Art as Experience* (New York: Putnam's Sons, 1958), 35–36.

18. "Time ceases to be either the endless and uniform flow of the succession of instantaneous points which some philosophers have asserted it to be. It, too, is the organized and organizing medium of the rhythmic ebb and flow of expectant impulse, forward and retracted movement, resistance and suspense, with fulfillment and consummation. It is an ordering of growth and maturations." Dewey, *Art as Experience*, 23.

19. Velleman, "Narrative Explanation," 12–13, 19.

20. "We maintain, therefore, that the first essential, the life and soul, so to speak, of tragedy is the plot." Aristotle, *Poetics* 1450a 37.

21. Aristotle, *Poetics* 1450a 17.

22. Aristotle, *Poetics* 1450b 4.

23. Many contemporary philosophers share Aristotle's view that personal identity and character can be revealed or understood only as a narrative of events and actions: "Narrative is crucial for the understanding of the identity of persons because narrative (as distinct from chronicle or mere causal sequence) simply *is* the form in which self-conscious agents make themselves intelligible to themselves as agents persisting through time, and therefore through change." Anthony Rudd, "In Defense of Narrative," *European Journal of Philosophy* 17. no. 1 (2007): 60–75, at 63.

24. Aristotle, *Poetics* 1451a 16. Velleman agrees with Aristotle: "Even the shortest story must recount more than one event." Velleman, "Narrative Explanation," 5.

25. Aristotle, *Poetics* 1451b 27. "Every work of art follows the plan of, and the pattern of, a complete experience, rendering it more intensely and concentratedly felt." Dewey, *Art as Experience*, 52.

26. Aristotle, *Poetics* 1451b 5.

27. Ricoeur says that a narrator must comprehend his plot outside of time as a *totum simul*. See *Time and Narrative*, vol. 1, 159–160.

28. See Jean-Paul Sartre, *Nausea*, trans. Lloyd Alexander (New York: New Directions Books, 2007), 39–40.

29. Ricoeur emphasizes "the pre-narrative quality of human experience . . . we are justified in speaking of life as a story in a nascent state . . . life itself is an inchoate narrative." See Ricoeur, "Life in Quest of Narrative" and "Discussion: Ricoeur on Narrative," in *On Paul Ricoeur*, ed. David Wood (London: Routledge, 1991), 20–33 and 179–187, at 29 and 180.

30. Rudd, "In Defense of Narrative," 62. Other defenders of the narrative structure of human life include Frederick A. Olafson: "the account given of human affairs in a novel or a drama owes essential elements of its internal organization to the way in which our experience of the world is ordered for purposes of action." *The Dialectic of Action* (Chicago: University of Chicago Press, 1979), 52. Alasdair MacIntyre famously defends the narrative character of human life: "Stories are lived before they are told." *After Virtue*, 212. David Carr quotes Wilhelm Schnapp: "Die Geschichte steht für den Mann," in *Time, Narrative, and History* (Bloomington: Indiana University Press, 1986), 74. Charles Taylor adds: "as I project my life forward and endorse the existing direction or give it a new one, I project a future story." *Sources of the Self* (Cambridge: Harvard University Press, 1989), 48. A comprehensive survey of contemporary debates about narrative identity can be found in John J. Davenport, *Narrative Identity, Autonomy, and Mortality* (London: Routledge, 2012). Davenport strongly endorses Aristotelian realism about the narrative structure of human life. For a skeptical critique of MacIntyre's view of narrativity, see Bernard Williams's posthumously published "Life as Narrative," *European Journal of Philosophy* 17, no. 2 (2007): 305–314.

31. "Narrative, like drama, lyric, or dance, cannot be regarded simply as an aesthetic invention used by artists in order to control, manipulate, order and investigate the experiences of that life we tend to separate from art, but must be seen as a primary act of mind transferred to art from life." Barbara Hardy, *Tellers and Listeners* (London: Athlone Press, 1975), vii and 3–4.

32. Bernard Williams rejects the narrative conception of human life because of the disanalogies he sees between our own lives and the lives of characters in fictions: "The life of a fictional character is necessarily something that our lives are not, a given whole. . . . This peculiar unity of their lives cannot help us in trying to find coherence in our own." "Life as Narrative," 311. I shall discuss below the dangers of modeling one's life on a literary narrative.

33. Husserl opens his great treatise with this homage to Augustine: "For in these matters our modern age, so proud of its knowledge, has failed to surpass or even to match the splendid achievement of this great thinker who grappled so earnestly with the problem of time." *On the Phenomenology of the Consciousness of Internal Time*, trans. John Barnett Brough (Dordrecht: Kluwer Academic Publishing, 1991), 3.

34. Husserl, *On the Phenomenology of the Consciousness of Internal Time*, 31–33.

35. On the "comet tail" of experience, see David Carr's lucid discussion of Husserl, in *Time, Narrative, and History*, 21.

36. Psychologists have long proven that we perceive wholes before parts, which is why we are fooled by optical illusions.

37. I owe this helpful set of spatial analogies to Carr's discussion of Husserl in *Time, Narrative, and History*, 21–31.

38. Husserl, *On the Phenomenology of the Consciousness of Internal Time*, 31 and 54.

39. On the role of memory and anticipation in our sense of self, see Mark Rowlands, *Memory and the Self* (Oxford: Oxford University Press, 2017), 10.

40. "In field memory, one remembers 'from the inside,' the events as they took place. In observer memory, one remembers 'from the outside' so that one is oneself part of the content of what one remembers." Rowlands, *Memory and the Self*, 46.

41. "Stories based on personal experiences begin with what cognitive scientists call *episodic memory*.... Episodic memory provides the foundation for autobiography and identity—for our narrative sense of self in time." Dan P. McAdams, *The Redemptive Self* (Oxford: Oxford University Press, 2013), 58 and 60.

42. "If we could not travel back in time to recall particular scenes from our own lives, then we would probably be unable to think in a storied way." McAdams, *The Redemptive Self*, 58.

43. "An episode memory will include and exclude elements of the original experience or contain details that you fill in to make a coherent picture." Davenport, *Narrative Identity, Autonomy, and Mortality*, 57. As McAdams says, "much of what we remember relates to our current situation and future goals." *The Redemptive Self*, 66.

44. Wollheim calls episodic memory "event-memory." He strongly affirms its narrative structure: "Event memory too can be fruitfully described in terms of the work of an internal dramatist, an internal actor, and an internal audience." *The Thread of Life*, 102.

45. On Augustine's distinction here, see Rowlands, *Memory and the Self*, 12. The Roman poet Virgil gives classic expression to the narrative structure of memory in the experience of redemption: "A joy it will be one day, perhaps, to remember even this" (Robert Fagles's translation of *Aeneid*, book 1, line 203: *forsan et haec olim meminisse iuvabit*). Note how Virgil's evocation of redemptive memory unites past, present, and future.

46. "This [neurobiological] evidence strongly supports the claim that substantially similar chemical processes occur both when a memory is created in the first place and when it is later accessed . . . memory retrieval requires reconsolidation." Rowlands, *Memory and the Self*, 123.

47. "Thanks to free indirect style, we see things through the character's eyes and language but also through the author's eyes and language. . . . This is merely another definition of dramatic irony." James Wood, *How Fiction Works* (New York: Farrar, Straus and Giroux, 2008), 11.

48. Tolstoy, *Anna Karenina*, trans. Richard Pevear and Larissa Volokhonsky (New York: Penguin, 2000), part 3, chap. 20.

49. This example from Peter Goldie, *The Mess Inside* (Oxford: Oxford University Press, 2012), 39.

50. On dramatic irony and "free indirect style" in literature and in memory, see Goldie, *The Mess Inside*, 26, 34–39, 48, 66. I have adopted Goldie's examples.

51. "In every memory there is the possibility of this sort of distance between the 'you' who experienced and the 'you' who remembers: this distance is built into memory itself, as one of its essential structural features." Rowlands, *Memory and the Self*, 89.

52. "Previsagement is like event memory in that, when a person centrally previsages an event, it must be himself whom he centrally previsages. . . . By contrast, iconic imagination allows a person, within certain limits, to centrally imagine anyone he chooses." Wollheim, *The Thread of Life*, 263. Psychologist Dan McAdams also sees episodic memory as the basis for a previsaged future: "the uniquely human tendency to construe life in narrative terms is dependent on episodic memory. . . . Our brains are hard-wired to recall past events and connect them to imagined future scenarios." *The Redemptive Self*, 59.

53. "Given all the structural similarities and shared indeterminacies, it should come as no surprise how often it can be unclear whether one is remembering something or imagining it." Goldie, *The Mess Inside*, 80.

54. "All autobiographical writing is structured and conditioned by the 'distorting' conventions of art. . . . Autobiography is literature." Stephen A. Shapiro, "The Dark Continent of Literature: Autobiography," *Comparative Literature Studies* 5, no. 4 (December 1968): 421–454, at 424.

55. David Carr argues that almost all human actions fall into a small set of plots: departure and arrival, departure and return, means and ends, suspension and resolution, problem and solution. See *Time, Narrative, and History*, 49.

56. "Art is thus prefigured in the very processes of living." Dewey, *Art as Experience*, 24.

57. Russians during the Soviet period claimed that it is easy to know the future; it is the past that keeps changing.

58. According to the Rule of St. Benedict, the life of a monk comprises three very distinct activities: manual labor, public prayer, and private study. Benedictine monks over the centuries have come up with several creative narratives attempting to unify these activities. Thomas Merton and others argued that labor really is a form of prayer: "to work is to pray." Other monks say that their lives are unified by love: love of self in study, love of neighbor in labor, and love of God in worship. See James Bernard Murphy, "Opus Dei: Prayer or Labor?," in *The Charismatic Principle in Social Life*, ed. Luigino Bruni and Barbara Sena (London: Routledge, 2013), 94–111.

59. Bernard Williams argues that our "biological" or "animal" actions lack "interpretative depth." "Life as Narrative," 308.

60. See Hannah Arendt, *The Human Condition* (New York: Doubleday, 1959), chap. 11.

61. Similarly, when women formerly discussed the "curse" of menstruation, they were incorporating mute biological cycles into the story of the fall of Adam and the punishment of Eve.

62. "The mimesis between life so-called and narrative is a two-way affair. . . . Narrative imitates life, life imitates narrative." Jerome Bruner, "Life as Narrative," *Social Research* 71, no. 3 (Fall 2004): 691–710, at 692.

63. On the universality of these life scripts across cultures, see George Murdock, "Universals of Culture," in *Readings in Anthropology*, ed. E. Adamson Hoebel et al. (New York: McGraw-Hill, 1955), 4–5. "I propose that each culture's master narrative includes beliefs about what the sequence of life stages should be, what should happen within each life stage, and when people should make the transition from one life stage to the next." Arnett, "Life Stage Concepts Across History and Culture," 308.

64. According to Neugarten and Hagestad, individuals "internalize a social clock that tells them whether they are on time or off time." Bernice Neugarten and Gunhild Hagestad, "Age and the Life Course," in *Handbook of Aging and the Social Sciences*, ed. Robert Binstock and Ethel Shamas (New York: Van Nostrand Reinhold, 1976), 35–55, at 35.

65. For a comparison of the many similarities between life scripts in Denmark and in Turkey, see Ahu Erdoğan et al., "On the Persistence of Positive Events in Life Scripts," *Applied Cognitive Psychology* 22 (2008): 95–111, at 107. "In support of the idea that cultural life script data are generalizable, studies show a high degree of correspondence of the cultural life script in different countries and for males and females, underscoring the shared and de-personalized

nature of the cultural life script." Dorthe Kirkegaard Thomsen and Dorthe Berntsen, "The Cultural Life Script and Life Story Chapters Contribute to the Reminiscence Bump," *Memory* 16, no. 4 (2008): 420–435, at 433. (The "reminiscence bump" refers to the greater density of adult memories from the period of adolescence and young adulthood, when we reach several important milestones.)

66. "Neither children nor adults differed in their life scripts as a function of gender." See Annette Bohn and Dorthe Berntsen, "Life Story Development in Childhood," *Developmental Psychology* 44, no. 4 (2008): 1135–1147, at 1146. In the 1960s, subjects were asked to describe both a man's life and a woman's life; men and women fully agreed about the milestones of each other's lives, even though some of those milestones were gender specific.

67. "According to researchers on master narratives, children begin telling stories from an early age . . . and these stories often carry underlying meaning about how a human life should unfold. . . . However, it is not until early adolescence that there is the attainment of the ability to construct a full life narrative." Arnett, "Life Stage Concepts Across History and Cultures," 310. "Children seem to have established a relatively stable, but not adult-like, life script by age 12." Bohn and Berntsen, "Life Story Development in Childhood," 1145.

68. See Erdoğan et al., "On the Persistence of Positive Events in Life Scripts," 109.

69. "Life script events that happen 'on time' are usually considered positive . . . whereas events that conflict with the life script . . . often are seen as stressful and socially stigmatizing." Dorthe Berntsen and Annette Bohn, "Cultural Life Scripts and Individual Life Stories," in *Memory in Mind and Culture*, ed. Pascal Boyer and James V. Wertsch (Cambridge: Cambridge University Press, 2009), 62–82, at 65. "Depressed individuals tell life stories that focus on deviations from the expected life course pattern . . . whereas non-depressed people tend to describe their life stories as consistent with the expected life course pattern." David Rubin and Dorthe Berntsen, "Life Scripts Help to Maintain Autobiographical Memories of Highly Positive, but Not Highly Negative, Events," *Memory and Cognition* 31, no. 1 (2003): 1–14, at 12.

70. See Rubin and Berntsen, "Life Scripts Help to Maintain Autobiographical Memories of Highly Positive, but Not Highly Negative, Events," 2.

71. See Dorthe Berntsen and David C. Rubin, "Cultural Life Scripts Structure Recall from Autobiographical Memory," *Memory and Cognition* 32, no. 3 (2004): 427–442, at 440: "Life scripts provide a default structure for understanding and remembering personal life."

72. "Thus, cultural conceptions of the life span may be involved in both the recall of life story memories and the organization of memories into chapters." Thomsen and Berntsen, "The Cultural Life Script and Life Story Chapters Contribute to the Reminiscence Bump," 432.

73. Bohn and Berntsen, "Life Story Development in Childhood," 1145. "An important prerequisite for life story abilities is the internalization of a cultural life script." Berntsen and Bohn, "Cultural Life Scripts and Individual Life Stories," 79–80.

74. "Knowledge of the life script indeed predicts global coherence of life narratives." For evidence of cross-cultural similarities in life scripts, see Robyn Fivush et al., "The Making of Autobiographical Memory," *International Journal of Psychology* 46, no. 5 (2011): 321–345, at 332.

75. "Even if, with respect to life and narrative, we discover, as in Yeats's line, that we cannot tell the dancer from the dance, that may be good enough." Bruner, "Life as Narrative," 709.

76. "And can any of you by worrying add a single hour to your span of life?" (Matt. 6:27).

77. Two common narratives in meditation are the body scan (from toe to head) and the observation of our thoughts flowing like a river as we sit on the bank. These stories distract us from the longer-term stories we tell about our past and future.

78. Galen Strawson defends this ideal of a nonnarrative, "episodic" life in "Against Narrativity."

79. I owe this insight about the variety of dramatic "series" to Marya Schechtman.

80. Schechtman, *The Constitution of Selves*, 146–147.

81. According to Derek Parfit: "Persons are like nations, clubs, or political parties." Can anyone really believe this of himself? "Buddha claimed that, though it is very hard, it is possible. I find Buddha's claim to be true." Parfit, *Reasons and Persons* (Oxford: Clarendon Press, 1984), 277 and 280.

82. According to Galen Strawson: "I have absolutely no sense of my life as a narrative. . . . It's clear to me that events in my remoter past didn't happen to me." What about the glaring incoherence of "my past" not belonging to "me"? "They are certainly the experiences of the human being that I am. It does not, however, follow from this that I experience them as having happened to me, or indeed that they did happen to me." Strawson, "Against Narrativity," 433–434.

83. As Schechtman observes, "the renunciation of a narrative sense of self, in effect, dismantles the person." *The Constitution of Selves*, 101.

84. "It is possible—but it is not wise—to see one's life as that of a loser, a victim, or someone who is locked in a tragic relation with another." Goldie, *The Mess Inside*, 170.

85. Here I adumbrate three dangers listed in Goldie, *The Mess Inside*, 161–171.

86. Martha Nussbaum, "Living the Past Forward," in Martha C. Nussbaum and Saul Levmore, *Aging Thoughtfully* (Oxford: Oxford University Press, 2017), 125–143, at 142. Nussbaum makes it clear, however, that a life of practical wisdom necessarily involves narrative acts of memory and imagination.

87. In part 2 of *Don Quixote*, virtually the only character who has not read *Don Quixote* is Don Quixote. Perhaps *Madame Bovary* might have saved Madame Bovary and Anna Karenina might have been saved by *Anna Karenina*. Without any reference to these novels, MacIntyre comments on the virtues of multiplying literary models: "So it is that [we] are rescued from illusion by satire, parody, and caricature." Alasdair MacIntyre, *Ethics in the Conflicts of Modernity* (Cambridge: Cambridge University Press, 2016), 237.

88. Peter Goldie discusses grieving in terms of these two kinds of closure: "to satisfy the desire for emotional closure, it is not necessary to satisfy the desire for narrative closure." *The Mess Inside*, 167.

89. "Having sorted out its feelings toward events, the audience mistakenly feels that it has sorted out the events themselves: it mistakes emotional closure for intellectual closure. . . . Telling a story is often a means to being believed for no good reason." Velleman, "Narrative Explanation," 20, 22.

90. See Kahneman, *Thinking, Fast and Slow*, 384 and 409: "It does not make sense to evaluate an entire life by its last moments, or to give no weight to duration in deciding which life is more desirable" (409).

91. Kahneman, *Thinking, Fast and Slow*, 381.

92. For a discussion of the dangers of forensic DNA analysis, see Erin E. Murphy, *Inside the Cell: The Dark Side of Forensic DNA* (New York: Perseus Books, 2015). Murphy makes it clear that genetic profiling to establish individual identity over time is very reliable in a laboratory setting but much less so at a crime scene. Of course, knowing who committed a crime does not settle all questions of moral and legal responsibility. John Locke agrees that legal forensics rest on physical not psychological criteria of personal identity.

93. Mark Rowlands calls the embodied residue of our experiences "Rilkean memories," after the poet Rainer Maria Rilke. See Rowlands, *Memory and the Self*, 69–70.

94. "Behavioral and bodily dispositions are a part of a person's existential style in the same way that they can be a part of an athlete's style or an artist's style. Embodied Rilkean memories are identical with behavioral and/or bodily dispositions." Rowlands, *Memory and the Self*, 144.

95. "The style of a person holds the person together in the same sort of way that the style of any author can hold a book together. . . . It is Rilkean memories that provide one's life with the requisite style." Rowlands, *Memory and the Self*, 145 and 140.

96. Bruner discusses a neurological disorder called "dysnarrativia" which is associated with dementia. He quotes Kay Young and Jeffrey Saver with approval: "Individuals who have lost the ability to construct narratives have lost their selves." *Making Stories* (Cambridge: Harvard University Press, 2002), 86.

97. "Rilkean memories can help hold the autobiographical self together in the face of massive memory loss and endemic memory inaccuracy. . . . This is why you and I can survive catastrophic memory loss." Rowlands, *Memory and the Self*, 195 and 198.

98. From the objective point of view, we know that dementia does not remove personality, because "experienced clinicians report that no person with Alzheimer's disease is exactly like another." From a subjective point of view, "it is by no means obvious that Alzheimer's disease brings about a destruction of the first-person perspective." Dan Zahavi, "Self and Other: The Limits of Narrative Understanding," in *Narrative and Understanding Persons*, ed. Daniel Hutto (Cambridge: Cambridge University Press, 2007), 179–201, at 192.

99. The family of diseases called dementia usually involve physical and psychological degeneration far beyond mere memory loss.

100. "I develop a view according to which a person creates his identity by forming an autobiographical narrative—a story of his life." Schechtman, *The Constitution of Selves*, 93.

101. "The Narrative Self-Constitution View is explicitly committed to the fact that infants are not persons and that persons cannot survive severe dementia." Schechtman, *Staying Alive*, 103. This exclusion of some human beings from the world of self-narrating persons led Schechtman to revise her strictly autobiographical approach to identity.

102. Speaking of infancy, Augustine asks: "What do I now have to do with it, when I recall no traces of it?" *Confessions* 1.7.12, quoted in Sorabji, *Self*, 100.

103. As Vaillant points out, biographies, autobiographies, and memoirs all reflect the gaps, embellishments, and biases of retrospective memory. By contrast, the prospective Harvard Grant Study confronted eighty-year-old men with their twenty-year-old selves. "While butterflies recalling their youth tend to remember themselves as young butterflies, prospective studies capture the reality (hard to believe, and often avoided!) that butterflies and caterpillars are the same people." Vaillant, *Triumphs of Experience*, 3–4.

104. "Personhood . . . is an intrinsically social concept." Schechtman, *The Constitution of Selves*, 95. As noted above, the concept of "person" arose from ancient Christian debates

about the nature of a triune God. God is a person because He is three interrelated persons. The Christian God is an intrinsically social concept.

105. Marya Schechtman has revised her autobiographical approach to incorporate biography: "What I propose is that we think of identity-constituting narratives not just as the narratives we create for ourselves, but the narratives of our lives that are created in conjunction with other people. Infants and the demented cannot self-narrate, but other people can and do form narrative conceptions of them." *Staying Alive*, 104. Tellingly, her new emphasis on the biological and embodied nature of human persons has led her toward biography. Lockean persons are wholly autobiographical; human persons must also rely on biography.

106. Of course, third-person narratives can also distort our autobiographies by telling stories about us that damage our sense of self. See Hilde Lindemann Nelson, *Damaged Identities, Narrative Repair* (Ithaca, N.Y.: Cornell University Press, 2001).

107. As MacIntyre says: "we are never more (and sometimes less) than the co-authors of our own narratives." *After Virtue*, 213.

108. According to David Carr, a storyteller "has command, and embodies the voice of authority vis-à-vis his audience and the voice of irony vis-à-vis his characters, just as if he were the author. What counts in the complex interrelationship of storytelling, accordingly, is not authorship at all, but just narratorship." *Time, Narrative, and History*, 85.

109. "In what does the unity of an individual life consist? The answer is that its unity is the unity of a narrative embodied in a single life. . . . The unity of a human life is the unity of a narrative quest." MacIntyre, *After Virtue*, 218–219. I say "quest narrative" because MacIntyre's "narrative quest" could be interpreted to mean the quest for a narrative.

110. "No animal other than man, however, appears to have the capacity for reflective self-evaluation that is manifested in the formation of second-order desires." Frankfurt, "Freedom of Will and the Concept of a Person," 7.

111. "Orientation in moral space turns out again to be similar to orientation in physical space. We know where we are through a mixture of recognition of landmarks before us and a sense of how we have travelled to get here." Taylor, *Sources of the Self*, 48.

112. "Because we cannot but orient ourselves to the good, and thus determine our place relative to it, and hence determine the direction of our lives, we must inescapably understand our lives in narrative form, as a 'quest' . . . I can only know myself through the history of my maturations and regressions, overcomings and defeats. My self-understanding necessarily has temporal depth and incorporates narrative." Taylor, *Sources of the Self*, 51–52, 50. "To answer the question "'Who?' . . . is to tell the story of a life." Ricoeur, *Time and Narrative*, vol. 3, 246.

113. Dan McAdams argues that the people who give the most service to their communities almost always see their present generosity as a way to redeem their past suffering or failures. See McAdams, *The Redemptive Self*.

114. "If necessary, we want the future to 'redeem' the past, to make it part of a life story which has sense or purpose, to take it up in a meaningful unity. . . . To repudiate my childhood as unredeemable in this sense is to accept a kind of mutilation as a person; it is to fail to meet the full challenge involved in making sense of my life." Taylor, *Sources of the Self*, 50–51.

115. Aristotle's definition of time: "For time is just this—number of motion, in respect of 'before' and 'after.' Hence time is not movement, but only movement insofar as it admits of enumeration." *Physics* 219b 1. Quoted in Ricoeur, *Time and Narrative*, vol. 3, 16.

116. See Ricoeur, *Time and Narrative*, vol. 3, 99–128.

117. Here I extend Ricoeur's analysis to autobiography and memoir.

118. "Autobiography involves the social conditions of the confirmation of recollections." Rom Harré, *Personal Being* (Cambridge: Harvard University Press, 1984), 214.

119. "Here I adopt Royce's thought that a person may be regarded as a human life lived according to a plan." John Rawls, *A Theory of Justice* (Cambridge: Harvard University Press, 1999), par. 63, p. 358.

120. We find endorsements of life plans in the work of John Finnis, Robert Nozick, and Joseph Raz, among many others.

121. "For Royce an individual says who he is by describing his purposes and causes, what he intends to do in his life." Rawls, *A Theory of Justice*, par. 63, p. 358.

122. "We must not imagine that a rational plan is a detailed blueprint for action stretching over the whole course of life. It consists of a hierarchy of plans, the more specific subplans being filled in at the appropriate time." Rawls, *A Theory of Justice*, par. 63, p. 360.

123. "We try to organize our activities into a temporal sequence. . . . In this way a family of interrelated desires can be satisfied in an effective and harmonious manner." Rawls, *A Theory of Justice*, par. 63, p. 360.

124. "If his plan is a rational one, then I shall say that the person's conception of his good is likewise rational." Rawls, *A Theory of Justice*, par. 63, p. 358.

125. "A man is happy when he is more or less successful in the way of carrying out his plan." Rawls, *A Theory of Justice*, par. 15, p. 79; cf. par. 63, p. 359.

126. "Si jeunesse savait, si vieillesse pouvait." Michael Slote notes the Kierkegaardian irony of making a life plan while young in his *Goods and Virtues*, 52, as does Bernard Williams, "Moral Luck," in *Moral Luck* (Cambridge: Cambridge University Press, 1981), 20–39, at 35.

127. I owe this example to Schechtman, *The Constitution of Selves*, 160.

128. See Dan P. McAdams, "The Psychological Self as Actor, Agent, and Author," *Perspectives on Psychological Science* 8, no. 3 (2013): 272–295.

129. In my prior discussion of four-dimensionality, I argued that our whole life is always prior to its temporal parts, so we are literally "all there" at every stage of life.

130. In the words of Stephen A. Shapiro, "The Dark Continent of Literature: Autobiography," 445.

INDEX

action, as narrative, 158
actuality, 34–35, 37, 44–45, 137–38. *See also* self-actualization
Adam, 13, 51, 56, 59, 62, 68, 98, 200n38
Adeodatus, 60
adulthood: ancient conceptions of, 81–82; childhood measured against, 11–13, 25–26, 29, 40, 44, 99–102, 109–10, 188n16; as means of studying human nature, 8; rejuvenation in, 12, 81, 99–102, 110–11; responsibilities of, 101
ages of man. *See* stages of life
Ambrose, 60, 203n91
amour de soi (self-love), 68, 72
amour propre, 68. *See also* pride; vanity
Anacharsis, 44
analogy, vs. homology, 33
anamnesis, 48–49, 52
Anaxagoras, 50
animals: humans as, 122–23, 126; humans distinguished from, 1, 55, 117–20; humans likened to, 67–68, 118; infants/children likened to, 28, 33, 34–35, 38, 39–40; in ladder of nature, 34–41, 93. *See also* dogs; foxes; primates
anticipatory retrospection, 151–52, 173, 176, 184
Aquinas, Thomas, 88, 97, 132
Arendt, Hannah, 159
Ariès, Philippe, 103, 188n16
Aristotle, 2; biological basis of thought of, 2, 8; on childhood, 28, 35, 39–41, 58, 69, 94, 96–97, 195n42; developmental theories of, 3–4, 9, 17–18, 20, 28, 33–45, 63, 182–83, 193n12; on education, 43; epigenesis and, 38; on happiness, 29, 35, 39, 41, 42, 44–45, 94–96, 112, 149, 170; hierarchy of nature in, 28, 34, 36, 39, 192n1; homonymy principle of, 188n15; on human being, 117, 118; on human nature, 29, 35; on narrative, 147–49, 180; *Nicomachean Ethics*, 44; on play, 42–44; *Politics*, 44; preformationism and, 37–38; on prime of life, 28, 29, 35–36, 41, 45, 94–96; reason in the thought of, 39, 40, 50; on soul-body relation, 124; on substance, 15, 126–27; on time, 171; on virtue, 39–42, 45, 94–95, 109, 170–71
Arnett, Jeffrey Jensen, 187n5, 187n9, 191n44, 213n30, 238n63, 239n67
arrested development, 10, 40, 69, 76, 77, 80, 103, 105
attention, 121, 152–54, 166, 175, 178–79
Augustine, 2; on childhood, 54–58, 69–70, 87–89; *Confessions*, 46–54; conversion and other religious experiences of, 47, 58–61; developmental theory of, 28, 46–61, 97, 182–83; theory of preexistence, 51–53, 200n37; on human nature, 29–30, 56–57; on memory, 155; paradoxes in thought of, 46–47; and recapitulation, 202n72; Rousseau compared to, 29; on the soul, 51–52, 199n36, 201n49; on time, 53–54, 150, 152–53, 162, 165, 171
authenticity, 65, 131, 146, 181
autobiographical memory, 155–56, 160, 168
autobiography: Augustine's practice of, 48; authorial vs. editorial roles in, 146, 164, 169, 176, 179, 181–82; biography in relation to, 169–70, 175, 183–84; characteristics of, 48; human development and, 174; and identity formation, 175; limitations of, 168–69, 183; narrative essence of, 172; open-ended character of, 170;

246 Index

autobiography (*continued*)
    Rousseau and, 66, 98–99. *See also* life writing

Baer, Karl Ernst von, 23
Baltes, Paul B., 187n6, 216n1
Baudelaire, Charles, 26
Beckett, Samuel, 9
Belyaev, Dmitry, 79
Benedict, Saint, 238n58
Berntsen, Dorthe, 238nn65–66, 239n69, 239nn71–73
Bible, 47–49, 59, 62. *See also* Synoptic Gospels
biography, 169, 175, 178, 183–84
biology: essences in, 126–30; human being from perspective of, 36, 116, 118–25, 140, 177–78; narrative in relation to, 177. *See also* developmental biology
Bjorklund, David, 216n66
Blake, William, 109
Boas, George, 190n30, 215n54, 217n19
body: mind in relation to, 120–21, 178; personhood and, 135; soul in relation to, 51–52, 97, 106, 121, 124
Boethius, 132
Bohn, Annette, 239n66, 239n67, 239n69, 239n73
Bolk, Louis, 211n3, 211n6
Boyd, Richard, 230n81
brain death, 139
Brighouse, Harry, 222n74
Bruner, Jerome, 167, 187n2, 238n62, 239n75, 241n96
Buddhism, 162, 163

Calvin, John, 88, 214n53
Carr, David, 238n55, 242n108
change: development in relation to, 16, 18; Parmenides on, 49–50; time in relation to, 15
childhood: adulthood measured against, 11–13, 25–26, 29, 40, 44, 99–102, 109–10, 188n16; Ambrose on, 203n91; ancient conceptions of, 81–82; Aristotle on, 28, 35, 39–41, 58, 69, 94, 96–97, 195n42; Augustine on, 54–58, 69–70, 87–89; deficit view of, 96–97; early or "primitive" cultures compared to, 22; evil/wickedness associated with, 28, 40, 69–70; freedom for responsibility in, 101–2; goodness associated with, 29, 40, 69, 89–90; happiness of, 96; innocence associated with, 13, 29, 56, 69, 96, 109; intrinsic characteristics of, 13, 26, 82, 90, 97, 110, 221n73; Jesus and, 29, 57–58, 81–89, 99–100; learning in, 78, 216n66; as means of studying human nature, 7; narratives formulated in, 15; parables of missing, 13; preparation for adulthood in, 11–13; prolongation of, in human development, 77–81; Rousseau on, 66–70, 89–90; savage state compared to, 22, 62–63. *See also* rejuvenation
Chomsky, Noam, 20, 23
Christianity: conceptions of childhood in, 215n54; conceptions of personhood in, 132. *See also* Jesus
chronicle, 113–14, 162
Chrysippus, 198n24
Cicero, 132
citizenship, 42
civic education, 74
Clarke, W. Norris, 232n98
closure, intellectual vs. emotional, 164–65
creation of the world, Augustine on, 46, 48–51
Currie, Gregory, 234n2

Darwin, Charles, 2, 21
Davenport, John J., 236n30
Davis, Miles, 166
death: of brain activity, 139; human development in relation to, 17; life understood in relation to, 104, 152, 174, 184; narratives imagined from standpoint of, 151–52, 173–74, 184–85
decline, onset of, 9–10
Defoe, Daniel, *Robinson Crusoe*, 71
DeGrazia, David, 227n44
Dennett, Daniel C., 234n8
desire: Augustine on, 55–56; first- and second-order, 170; Rousseau on, 70, 72–73
development: Aristotle's theory of, 35; Augustine's theory of, 51; biological perspective on, 8, 16, 18–19; change in relation to, 16, 18; concept of, 2; direct vs. indirect, 21; embryonic, 9, 18–23, 27–28, 37–38, 116; goal-directed nature of, 2; meanings of, 17; narrative form of, 27;

stories (paradigms) of, 21–29, 93. *See also* human development
developmental biology: embryology as basis of, 18; evolutionary biology compared to, 2; goal-directed nature of, 2, 16–17; new, 17, 23; patterns of development in, 77. *See also* biology
Devitt, Michael, 230n77, 230n79
Dewey, John, 148
Dickens, Charles, *A Christmas Carol*, 174
diet, 68
dignity, 119–20, 125, 136–37, 140–41
Diogenes Laertius, 198n23
disability, 139
divine. *See* God/the divine
dogs, 79
domestication, 79
dramatic irony, 156–58

Ecclesiastes, book of, 161
education: Aristotle's theory of, 43; civic, 74; liberal-arts-based, 101; moral, 71, 73–74; Rousseau's conception of, 64, 71–74. *See also* learning
Einstein, Albert, 81, 214n40
elderhood: Aristotle on, 94; holistic view of life available in, 12, 15; Rousseau on, 99
Eliot, T. S., 175
embryonic development, 9, 18–23, 27–28, 37–38, 116
environment, organism in relation to, 19–20, 143
Epicureans, 187n1
epigenesis (individualization): analogy underlying, 27; Aristotle's theory compared to, 38; child-adult relationship in, 25–26; Erikson's theory of, 28, 102–5, 218n35; overview of, 23; preformationism compared to, 38
episodic memory, 154–57
Erikson, Erik, 9; developmental theory of, 28, 30, 102–5, 190n27, 218n35, 218n38; on prolonged childhood, 80, 81
essence, 126–30
eulogies, self-composed, 152, 173–74, 184–85
Eve, 13, 59, 62, 68, 98
evil/wickedness/vice: Aristotle on, 40; Augustine on, 28; childhood associated with, 28, 69–70; as human nature, 64; Rousseau on, 65, 68–70; society as cause of, 63, 65, 68, 70, 73–74
evolution: development compared to, 2; human development and, 76–79; human nature in perspective of, 140–41; modern society and, 70; neoteny and, 24, 99; and organism-environment relation, 19; recapitulation theory and, 21
expectation: narrative, 151–54, 160, 163, 165, 179; short-term vs. long-term, 154; temporal, 54, 152–54, 179

face, 135
Feibleman, James K., 188n12, 189n22, 220n55
Ferner, A. M., 232n96
Finnis, John, 243n120
Fischer, Kurt, 222n79
Fitzmyer, Joseph A., 87–88
Fivush, Robyn, 239n74
flashbulb memories, 154–55
flexibility, in personality and development, 24–25, 79, 100–101
flourishing. *See* happiness/flourishing
Fodor, Jerry, 190n32
Ford, Norman, 226n30, 226n34, 233n115, 233n116
four-dimensionalism, 113–14
foxes, 79
Frankfurt, Harry, 228n48, 242n110
free indirect style, 156
Freud, Sigmund, 9, 12, 22, 62, 102, 154, 155, 190n27, 190n28
friendship, 42

Gandhi, Mohandas, 158
Garrard, Graeme, 215n58
Garstang, Walter, 211n9
Gauthier, René, 194n32
Genesis, book of, 48, 49, 51, 62, 64, 132
genome: capacities determined by, 20; human, 130; identity based in, 3; preformationism and, 23, 46
Gewirth, Alan, 187n3, 191n42
Ghiselin, Michael T., 230n73
Gilson, Étienne, 200n37, 200n42
Godfrey-Smith, Peter, 231n84, 231n85
God/the divine: in Aristotle's theory, 34, 35, 44; in Augustine's thought, 46–61; human being in relation to, 118, 132; in Plato's

God/the divine (*continued*)
    theory, 43–44; reason associated with, 118, 132; triune, 132
Goldie, Peter, 156, 157, 238n53, 240n83, 240n88
goods and virtues, in life stages, 26, 35, 40–41, 94–96, 106–10. *See also* virtue
Gopnik, Alison, 102, 190n31
Gould, Stephen Jay, 24–25, 29, 38, 77, 193n12, 194n25, 211n7, 211n11, 212n13, 212n16, 213n34
Gramsci, Antonio, 210n93
great chain of being, 34
Griffin, James, 233n112
Gundry, Judith M., 85–86, 88, 214n43
Gundry, Robert, 82–88
Gurevich, Aron, 231n90
Gyges, 64–65

habit interference, 9, 100–101
habits, 4, 39
Hacker, Peter, 4, 117, 227n40, 228n51, 228n58, 228nn53–55, 229n68
Haeckel, Ernest, 22, 37
Hagestad, Gunhild, 238n64
Haldane, J. B. S., 79–80, 213n28, 214n42
Hall, Stanley, 9, 22, 62
Halliwell, Stephen, 196n69
Hammond, Carolyn, 203n90
happiness/flourishing: Aristotle's conception of, 29, 35, 39, 41, 42, 44–45, 94–96, 112, 149, 170; of childhood, 96; Norton's conception of, 106–7; Rousseau's conception of, 63, 66, 72
Hardy, Barbara, 145, 151, 236n31
Harré, Rom, 243n118
Harrison, Robert Pogue, 110–11, 214n41, 222n77
Hegel, G. W. F., 38, 62, 193n21
Heraclitus, 191n48, 196n68
heterochrony, 191n40, 211n8
Hilzheimer, Max, 218n29
Hobbes, Thomas, 64, 65, 67, 69–70
holistic view of human life: autobiography and, 48, 146, 168, 171; comparison of developmental stories from perspective of, 93–115; defined, 2; difficulty of attaining, 53; in Erikson's thought, 104; human capacity for, 11–12, 53; narrative shaping of, 113–15; Norton's theory and, 105–8;

personhood and, 123–24; role of development in, 9, 178; stages as facets in, 2–3, 9, 14–15, 31, 93–94, 113–14; time and, 153–54; whole-part relationship in, 2–3, 14–15, 113–15
Holloway, Richard, 224n6
homology, vs. analogy, 33
homunculus, 23, 46
Huizinga, Johan, 191n48
Hull, David, 230n73
human beings: biological vs. psychological perspectives on, 36, 116, 118–25, 140, 177–78; commonalities of, 1, 131; complex and puzzling nature of, 117–19; the divine in relation to, 118, 132; genetic profile of, 130; inner directedness characteristic of, 135–36, 138–39; language as characteristic of, 126; personhood in relation to, 118–26, 132, 134, 136–42; rationality essential to, 18, 126, 132, 178; species concept of, 127–31, 135–36; as substance, 15–16, 125–26; uniqueness of, 1, 134; unity and identity of, 15–16, 121–22, 140. *See also* human nature; personhood
human development: Aristotle's theory of, 34; arrested, 10, 40, 69, 76, 77, 80, 103, 105; biological perspective on, 21, 31, 116; complexity and variation in, 10, 25, 105; continuous and discontinuous, 9–11, 94, 105–6, 141; epigenetic theory of, 23; evolution and, 76–79; hierarchy of, 3, 4; holistic view of, 9, 178; lifelong, 8, 19, 20, 111; narrative conception of, 174; neotenic theory of, 24–25, 76–81, 99; preformation theory of, 22–23; prolonged childhood in, 77–80; psychological perspective on, 116; recapitulation theory of, 21–22; self-directedness of, 8; stadial theories of, 8–11; stories (paradigms) of, 21–29, 93. *See also* development; human life; maturation
human life: authorial vs. editorial roles in, 146, 164, 169, 176, 179, 181–82; evaluation of, 16–17, 111–15 (*see also* happiness/flourishing); narrative quality of, 143–76, 179–80; plans for, 172–74; reflective understanding of, 146–47; temporal character of, 54; unity of, 3, 172–73. *See also* holistic view of human life; human development; human nature; personhood; prime of life

human nature: Aristotle on, 29, 35;
   Augustine on, 29–30, 56–57; dignity of,
   140–41; evolutionary perspective on,
   140–41; flexibility characteristic of, 79;
   juvenility as peak of, 76; permanence characteristic of, 18; Rousseau on, 29, 64, 70;
   savage state indicative of, 29; study of, 7–8,
   29–30, 116–17. See also human being;
   human life; prime of life
human rights, 136–37
humility, 82–84, 86–88
Husak, Douglas, 233n113
Husserl, Edmund, 153–54, 162, 165
hypermorphosis, 213n36

identity: autobiographical formation of, 175;
   biological, 3, 31; change in relation to, 16;
   existential style as, 167; narrative, 3, 31,
   163, 166, 175, 179–80; personhood linked
   to, 121; psychological, 3, 31; temporal
   experience linked to, 154, 155; varieties of,
   1. See also self
imagination: in adulthood, 102; biological
   roots of, 178–79; in childhood, 11–12, 102;
   expectation, and 154; holistic view of life
   enabled by, 2, 13, 15; identity linked to, 3;
   memory compared to, 157; narrative and,
   152, 157–58, 179; practical reasoning and,
   146, 152; prospective, 156–57
individualization. See epigenesis
infancy. See childhood
Inman, Ross, 223n90, 224n97, 229n70
innocence: of Adam and Eve, 13, 56, 62; in
   adulthood, 109; Augustine on absence of,
   55–56; of childhood, 13, 29, 56, 69, 96,
   109; knowledge's destruction of, 64; loss
   of, in adulthood, 13, 64, 98; moral, 62, 82,
   96, 109; of primordial man, 29, 69;
   Rousseau on, 64, 69
intelligence: of childhood and adulthood,
   110–11; development and decline of,
   9–10; fluid vs. crystallized, 10
interpersonal connections, 124, 133–34, 169,
   175–76
irony. See dramatic irony

James, William, 222n78, 227n36
Jesus, 2; Augustine's understanding of,
   57–58, 62; childhood, and 29, 57–58,
   81–89, 99–100, 182–83; on living in the
   present, 161
Joachim of Fiore, 62
Joffe, Tracey, 212n15
Jolif, Jean Yves, 194n32
Jung, Carl, 9, 22, 62, 102, 220n56
juvenilization. See neoteny

Kahneman, Daniel, 112–13, 165, 240n90
Kant, Immanuel, 15, 119–20
Kaplan, Bernard, 189n23
Kelly, Christopher, 211n94, 212n95
Kennedy, John F., 154
Kenny, Anthony, 124, 216n11, 228n56,
   228n57
Kermode, Frank, 147–48
Kierkegaard, Søren, 146–47, 151, 173
Kind, Amy, 226n31, 226n33, 234n6
Konner, Melvin, 187n8, 212n14
Korzybski, Alfred, 145, 188n17

Lactantius, 98
ladder of nature, 21, 28, 34, 37–41, 44, 63,
   93, 192n1
language: as human characteristic, 7, 126;
   learning of, 20, 100–101; Rousseau's
   theory of, 67–68
learning: as anamnesis, 52; childhood as time
   for, 78, 216n66; Erikson's theory of
   human development based on concept of,
   103–5; habit interference in, 100–101;
   human capacity for, 24, 78; as means of
   maturation, 20; as perfectibility, 64. See
   also education
Lewontin, Richard, 190n35, 191n38, 191n39,
   191n46, 224n98
Liao, Matthew, 234n122
liberal arts, 101
life. See biography; human life
life plans, 109, 172–74
life scripts, 160–61, 163, 181–82
life writing, 180–85. See also autobiography
Locke, John, 64, 116, 118–22, 124, 126, 132,
   136, 140, 154, 159, 163, 224n13
Lorenz, Konrad, 79, 212n23

MacIntyre, Alasdair, 234n5, 236n30,
   242n107, 242n109
MacLean, Paul, 190n34
Maritain, Jacques, 133

Marx, Karl, 62
master narratives, 160, 181–82
Matthews, Gareth B., 97, 190n30
maturation: Erikson's theory of, 103–5; growth attributable to, 20; as inner-directed development, 20; variations in, 10, 17. *See also* human development; maturity
maturity: age in relation to, 12, 17; childhood in relation to, 12; descriptive vs. normative, 103; as gauge of something's nature or essence, 8; inner directedness toward, 135–36, 138–39; narrative conception of, 175–76; reproductive, 8, 16–18; spiritual, 25. *See also* maturation
Mauss, Marcel, 232n96
Mayr, Ernst, 129, 189n26, 230n73, 230n80
McAdams, Dan P., 237n52, 237nn41–43, 242n113
McKeough, Michael J., 199n31, 199n35
McKinney, Michael, 80, 191n41, 213n35, 213n36
McMahan, Jeff, 138–39, 227n37, 233n110, 233n111
McNamara, Kenneth J., 80, 191n41, 213n36
memoirs, 172
memory: Augustine on, 155; Augustine's theory of, 51–52; autobiographical, 155–56, 160, 168; biological roots of, 178–79; episodic, 154–57; holistic view of human life enabled by, 2, 15, 106; Husserl on, 153–54; imagination compared to, 157; narrative and, 152, 154–55, 157–58, 179; practical reasoning and, 146, 152; prospective function of, 156–57; semantic, 154–55, 160
Mencius, 191n49
metaphor, 149
midlife, 12
Miles, Margaret R., 202n69, 203n75
Mill, John Stuart, 12, 22
Miller, Richard B., 99
mind: body in relation to, 120–21, 178; defined, 124. *See also* soul
mindful meditation, 161
Minelli, Alessandro, 191n47
Mirandola, Pico de, 118
Montagu, Ashley, 29, 79, 80, 212n12, 212n22
moral education, 71, 73–74
moral innocence, 62, 82, 96, 109

morality: in Aristotle's theory, 40; personhood linked to, 119–20, 136–42; quest for ideals and, 170; Rousseau on, 70
Morey, Darcy, 212n25
Murphy, Erin E., 241n92
music, temporal experience of, 54, 165–66

Nagel, Ernest, 189n25
Napoleon Bonaparte, 1–2
narrative: absence of, 162–63; biological development in relation to, 177; children capable of, 15; chronicle vs., 113–14, 162; and closure, 164–65; dangers of, 164; defined, 144; development as, 27; emotions evoked by, 148; and episodes, 148, 162, 165; fictional vs. historical, 149, 171–72; of human development, 174; identity in relation to, 3, 31, 163, 166, 179–80; life characterized by, 143–76, 179–80; of maturity, 175–76; meaning created through, 144–45, 147, 171; and memory/imagination, 154–58, 179; as model for living our lives, 159–61, 164; personhood linked to, 163; pervasiveness of, 144, 145; plot and, 147–50; practical reasoning dependent on, 146, 152, 170, 174–75, 180; quasi-, 143, 144, 146, 148, 151, 154, 162, 178–80; quest narratives, 170; self in relation to, 145; time unified through, 14, 144–48, 150–54, 180; truth and, 147, 148, 150, 175; value of human life measured by, 111–15
natural kinds, 126–29
nature. *See* ladder of nature; savage state; state of nature theories
Needham, Joseph, 193n12, 193n21
neoteny (juvenilization): analogy underlying, 27; child-adult relationship in, 26, 76–77; evolution and, 24, 99; history of theory of, 29; human development and, 24–25, 76–81, 99; human nature as, 76; Jesus and, 29, 89, 214n42; obstacles in, 100–102; overview of, 24, 77–78, 213n36; recapitulation in relation to, 24–25; Rousseau and, 90; social vs. biological, 80; in Synoptic Gospels, 81–89
Neugarten, Bernice L., 188n10, 238n64
Newton, Isaac, 81, 214n40
Niebuhr, Reinhold, 224n3
Nietzsche, Friedrich, 106–7

Norton, David, 31, 105–8, 116
Nozick, Robert, 243n120
Nussbaum, Martha, 164, 240n86

obituaries, self-composed, 152, 184–85
O'Connell, Robert J., 197n12, 200n43, 201n49, 203n80
Oderberg, David S., 230n78, 231n82
O'Donnell, James J., 197n6, 197n8, 197n9, 197n12, 199n36, 202n72
Okasha, Samir, 230n75, 230n76
Olafson, Frederick A., 236n30
Olson, Eric, 223n97, 227nn42–45, 233n118, 234n123
ontogeny recapitulates phylogeny, 22, 37
organisms: Aristotle's developmental theories of, 33–38; biblical story of creation of, 50–51; developmental stories (paradigms) of, 21–29; environment in relation to, 19–20, 143; essence of, 126–30, 133; growth of, 16–18, 77; humans distinguished from other, 140; narrative structure of lives of, 143–44, 148; personhood in relation to, 119–22; potentiality and actuality of, 137–38; priority of, to their organs, 2, 115

paedomorphosis, 77, 79, 211n10, 213n36
pain and suffering, making sense of, 112–13, 155, 161, 164, 165, 171, 184, 242n113
Paradise, 98. *See also* Adam
Parfit, Derek, 240n81
Parmenides, 49–50
Paul, Saint, 100
Peck, A. L., 193n12
perfectibility, 64, 67
persistence conditions, 116–17, 119, 120, 140. *See also* natural kinds
personhood: and the body, 135; capacity for, 137–38; coherence of, 3, 31, 131–35; complexity of, 133; concepts of, 131–35, 231n89; dignity of, 120, 125, 136–37; genetic basis of, 130; in holistic perspective, 123–24; human being in relation to, 118–26, 132, 134, 136–42; identity linked to, 121; interpersonal character of, 133–35; morality in relation to, 119–20, 136–42; narrative linked to, 163; nonhuman, 122, 125, 131–32, 134; quest for ideals characteristic of, 170; reason associated with, 120–25; Roman concept of, 131–32, 231n90; self equated with, 119–20, 122; significance and value of, 1. *See also* human being
Philo, 217n17
Piaget, Jean, 9, 22, 62, 190n28
pity, 72
plan of life. *See* life plans
Plato: theory of preexistence, 48, 52–53; on human nature, 187n3; on identity and change, 16, 189n21; *Laws*, 43–44; on play, 43–44, 191n48, 196n68
Platonism, 59, 197n13
play, 42–44, 191n48, 196n68
plot, 147–50, 158
Plotinus, 49, 50, 52
Plutarch, 68
politics: origin and function of, 64–65; prime of life and, 36; Rousseau and, 64–65, 206n20
Pope, Alexander, 212n19
Porphyry, 49
Postman, Neil, 188n16
potentiality, 34, 37, 44–45, 137–38
practical reasoning, 146, 152, 170, 180
practical wisdom, 3, 36, 174–75
Pradeu, Thomas, 191n47
preformationism: analogy underlying, 27; in Augustine's thought, 28, 46–61, 97; child-adult relationship in, 25–26; epigenesis compared to, 38; in Erikson's thought, 104; overview of, 22–23
present, living in, 161–62
pride: Augustine on, 55–57, 59–60; Jesus on, 82; Rousseau on, 68, 74. *See also* vanity
primates: human development in relation to, 21–25, 76–78; humans compared to, 1–2, 24, 78–81
prime of life: in Aristotle's theory, 28, 29, 35–36, 41, 45, 94–96; human nature defined according to, 8, 107; mental vs. somatic, 36; Norton on, 107; political roles and, 36; reproductive capacity linked to, 35–36
primitive state. *See* savage state
protention, 154
prudence, 109
psychology: Aristotle's theory of, 36; human being from perspective of, 36, 116, 118–25, 177–78
puberty, 10, 16, 18, 20, 72–73, 94

quasi-narratives, 31, 143, 144, 146, 148, 151, 154, 162, 178–80
quest narratives, 170

Rahner, Karl, 188n11
Ramsauer, Gottfried, 194n32
rationality. *See* reason
Rawls, John, 172–73, 243n119, 243nn121–125
Raz, Joseph, 243n120
reason: in Aristotle's theory, 39, 40, 50; divinity associated with, 118, 132; essential to human being, 18, 126, 132, 178; guiding function of, 39; personhood associated with, 120–25; seminal reasons, 50
recapitulation: analogy underlying, 27; Aristotle's theory of, 28, 33–45, 193n12; Augustine and, 202n72; biological, 21, 28, 33–45; child-adult relationship in, 25–26; evolutionary theory and, 21; historical, 22, 29, 62–75, 202n72; neoteny in relation to, 24–25; overview of, 21–22; Rousseau's theory of, 29, 63–75
recollection: learning as, 52; long-term memory as, 154; of past lives, 49
redemption narratives, 184
rejuvenation, 12, 81, 99–102, 110–11
reproduction: divine immortality attained through species, 35; as goal of organism, 16–17, 35
reproductive maturity, 8, 16–18
Reynolds, Philip L., 202n73, 217n15
Ricoeur, Paul, 149–50, 171, 242n112
rigidity, in personality and development, 99–101
Rombs, Ronnie, 199n36, 201n49, 204n115
Rorty, Amélie, 188n13, 228n58, 231n87, 232n97
Rousseau, Jean-Jacques, 2; Augustine compared to, 29; on authenticity, 181; autobiographical writings of, 66, 98–99; on childhood, 66–70, 89–90; developmental theory of, 29, 63–75, 97–98; *Discourse on the Origins of Inequality (Second Discourse)*, 63, 74–75; on education, 64, 71–74; on elderhood, 99; *Emile*, 63, 64, 66, 68, 69, 71–75, 206n21; on goodness and vice, 29, 65–66, 69–70, 71, 73; on human nature, 29, 64, 70; on morality and moral education, 70, 73–74; on primordial man, 29, 63, 65–71, 208n59; *Social Contract*, 63; on society, 63–65, 67–74
Rowlands, Mark, 167, 237n40, 237n46, 237n51, 241n97, 241nn93–95
Rubin, David, 239n69, 239n71
Rudd, Anthony, 235n23

Salinger, J. D., *Catcher in the Rye*, 181
Sartre, Jean-Paul, *Nausea*, 150–51
savage state: childhood compared to, 22, 62–63; human nature defined according to, 29; innocence associated with, 29, 69; Rousseau on, 29, 63, 65–71
Saver, Jeffrey, 241n96
Schechtman, Marya, 227n47, 233n116, 240n83, 241n100, 241n101, 241n104, 242n105
Schleiermacher, Friedrich, 215n55
Schofield, Malcolm, 196n68
self: critique of inner, 124; critique of multiple, 163; interpersonal component of, 124, 169, 175–76; memory/imagination and, 155–57, 166–68; as narrative construction, 145, 163; personhood and, 119–20, 122, 124. *See also* autobiography; identity
self-actualization, 107, 133, 220n61
semantic memory, 154–55, 160
seminal reasons, 48–51
Setiya, Kieran, 188n14
sexuality: physical maturity in, 9, 24, 78; Rousseau on, 73
Shakespeare, William, 8–9, 118
Shapiro, Stephen A., 238n54
Shaw, George Bernard, 168, 183
Shelley, Mary, *Frankenstein*, 13
Shklar, Judith, 212n95
Shostak, Stanley, 213n31, 213n37
Sider, Theodore, 114, 223nn91–97
sin, 28, 56, 58, 59
Slote, Michael, 108–9, 111
Small, Helen, 216n2, 216n3, 216n5, 217n12
Smith, E. H., 200n37
Socrates, 52, 64, 118, 121
Solon, 95, 112
Sophocles: *Antigone*, 117; *Oedipus Rex*, 156
Sorabji, Richard, 197n13, 222n85

Index   253

soul: in Aristotle's theory, 36, 37; Augustine's conception of, 51–52, 199n36, 201n49; body in relation to, 51–52, 97, 106, 121, 124; Plato's theory of, 52; preexistence of, 51–52. *See also* mind
species, concepts of, 127–30
spiritual maturity, 25
stages of life: in Aristotle's thought, 94–96, 109–10; commensurability of, 105–8; developmental theories of, 8–11; Erikson's theory of, 28, 30, 102–5; as facets, not temporal phases, 2–3, 9, 14–15, 31, 93–94, 113–14; limitations of theories based on, 102; Norton's theory of, 31, 105–8; practical considerations for paradigm of, 10–11, 141–42; social paradigms of, 8–11
Starns, Colin, 202n68
state of nature theories, 64–68, 71–74
Stoicism, 50, 70–71, 75, 121, 187n1
Strawson, Galen, 165, 226n30, 226n35, 227n36, 227n39, 228nn48–50, 234n6, 240n82
style, existential, 167
subjective time, 171
substance, 15–16, 125–27, 130
suffering. *See* pain and suffering, making sense of
surprise: in human development, 105, 106; in life events, 163; as narrative element, 144, 153
Swift, Adam, 222n74
Synoptic Gospels, juvenilization in, 81–89

Taylor, Charles, 170, 236n30, 242n111, 242n112, 242n114
Tertullian, 132
Theseus, ship of, 16
Thomsen, Dorthe Kirkegaard, 238n65, 239n72
Thornton, Mark, 227n37
Thorsteinsson, Runar M., 214n43
time: Augustine's theory of, 53–54, 150, 152–53, 162, 165, 171; change in relation to, 15; cosmological, 171; as factor in evaluation of human life, 112–14; holistic nature of, 153–54; lived human experience in, 54; music and, 54, 165–66; narrative unification of, 14, 144–48, 150–54, 180; present-oriented, 161–62; subjective, 171

Tolstoy, Leo, *Anna Karenina*, 156
Tress, Daryl McGowan, 193n19
Trut, Lyudmila N., 212n26
truth, and narrative, 147, 148, 150, 168–69, 175
Twain, Mark, *The Adventures of Tom Sawyer*, 185

Vaillant, George E., 104–5, 190n27, 219n43, 219n46, 219n47, 219n49, 222n80, 241n103
Van Fleteren, Frederick, 197n11, 200n41
vanity, 46, 57–60, 68, 72, 73, 74. *See also* pride
vegetarianism, 68
Velleman, David, 111, 148, 164, 222nn82–84, 223n86, 235n24, 240n89
vice. *See* evil/wickedness/vice
Vico, Giambattista, 62
Virgil, 237n45
virtue: Aristotle's conception of, 39–42, 45, 94–95, 109, 170–71; ideal of, 110; narrative component of, 170–71; Rousseau's conception of, 63, 66, 69, 72–75
virtues. *See* goods and virtues
Voltaire, 79

Waldron, Jeremy, 139, 234n121
wholeness. *See* holistic view of human life
wickedness. *See* evil/wickedness/vice
Wiggins, David, 140, 227n46, 228–29nn59–62, 231n86, 232n101, 232n102, 234n124
Wilde, Oscar, 159, 180
Wilkins, Adam S., 212n20, 212n24, 213n27
Williams, Bernard, 226n32, 236n31, 238n59
Williams, Rowan, 197n2, 197n3, 197n5, 199n29, 202n59, 202n60, 202n61
Wilson, Robert A., 230n72, 231n82
Wittgenstein, Ludwig, 4, 131, 154
Wokler, Robert, 205n2, 205n7
Wollheim, Richard, 156–57, 235n11, 235n12, 237n44, 237n52
Wolterstorff, Nicholas, 137, 233n114
Wood, James, 237n47
Wordsworth, William, 29

Young, Kay, 241n96

Zahavi, Dan, 241n98

ACKNOWLEDGMENTS

I first learned about theories of human development back in college from my friend Eliott Mordkowitz, who championed Piaget's theory of stages of cognitive development. I learned about direct and indirect development from my brother, Timothy Murphy-Stevens, who is a biologist. In drafting the primary theoretical chapters, I wish to acknowledge the assistance of the following people. For human nature in a developmental perspective: Richard O. Brooks; for Aristotle: James R. Gordley, Margaret Graver, Chris Hauser, and Julie Rose; for Augustine: Margaret Atkins and Margaret Graver; for Rousseau: Roger D. Masters and Graeme Garrard; for the Bible: Matthew Kramer; for personhood and narrativity: Marya Schechtman. I am especially grateful to the participants in a Villanova University symposium about this book: Patrick Brennan, Marya Schechtman, James Gordley, Harry Brighouse, Shelley Burtt, and Phillip Reynolds; and to the participants in a faculty seminar about this book at Dartmouth College's Ethics Institute: Ronald Beiner and Bryan Garsten, as well as my Dartmouth colleagues Russell Muirhead, Luke Swaine, Michelle Clarke, and Sonu Bedi.

Throughout, I am indebted to the editorial expertise of Yevgenia Rem, Peter O'Leary, Joseph Torsella, Sarah Memon, Josie Pearce, and Katarina Nesic. I am especially grateful for the encouragement, patience, and editorial counsel of my wife, Kirsten Giebutowski.

Finally, I want to thank my University of Pennsylvania Press editor, Damon Linker, for believing in this book and skillfully shepherding it through the review and publication process.